M & E Handbooks are recommended reading for examination syllabuses all over the world. Because each Handbook covers its subject clearly and concisely books in the series form a vital part of many college, university, school and home study courses.

Handbooks contain detailed information stripped of unnecessary padding, making each title a comprehensive self-tuition course. They are amplified with numerous self-testing questions in the form of Progress Tests at the end of each chapter, each text-referenced for easy checking. Every Handbook closes with an appendix which advises on examination technique. For all these reasons, Handbooks are ideal for pre-examination revision.

The handy pocket-book size and competitive price made Handbooks the perfect choice for anyone who wants to grasp the essentials of a subject quickly and easily.

THE M & E HANDBOOK SERIES

Economics of Public Finance

Edmund Seddon
M.A.

Senior Lecturer in Economics,
Faculty of Business and Management Studies,
Liverpool Polytechnic

THIRD EDITION

MACDONALD AND EVANS

Macdonald and Evans Ltd.
Estover, Plymouth PL6 7PZ

First published 1968
Reprinted 1970
Second edition 1973
Reprinted 1975
Third edition 1977

ISBN 0 7121 0528 X

Printed in Great Britain by
Hazell Watson & Viney Ltd,
Aylesbury, Bucks

Preface to the First Edition

This HANDBOOK is intended primarily to cater for the needs of candidates for the Local Government Examinations Board's papers in the *Elements of Public Finance* and the *Economics of Public Finance*. To this end, attention is given not only to the theoretical and practical aspects of public finance but also to the general theory of price.

Part I outlines the growth of a mixed capitalist economy and defines the currently accepted scope of public finance.

Part II, in analysing the operation of the price mechanism in a free market economy, lays the foundations for the subsequent examination of tax theory.

Part III is concerned with the theory of who bears the burden of taxation and with what effects upon production and welfare.

Part IV looks at the effect of the whole structure of public finance upon the level of economic activity and at the way in which it is used by government as an instrument of economic control.

Part V describes the machinery of taxation and expenditure for both local and central government.

Since public finance is a major aspect of Applied Economics it is hoped that this book will also be of interest to students in this field, particularly those who are preparing for the G.C.E. in Economics at Advanced Level, the Applied Economics papers for the H.N.C. and H.N.D. in Business Studies and the economics papers of various professional bodies. It will also prove of some value as an introductory text for candidates in the Public Finance examination of the University of London B.Sc. (Econ.).

I am indebted to the following bodies for permission to reprint the examination questions which appear in Appendix III.

Joint Matriculation Board of the Universities of Manchester, Liverpool, Leeds, Sheffield and Birmingham (J.M.B.).

University of London.

Local Government Examinations Board (L.G.E.B.).

Liverpool City College of Commerce (L.C.C.C.).

June, 1968   E.S.

Note to the Third Edition

In line with the shift in academic thinking which has occurred in the 1970s, in this edition still more attention has been given to the monetary implications of the public finances. That part of public spending which is financed by borrowing from the banking system results in an accelerated growth of the money supply. Two new chapters have therefore been introduced to explain the role of money in the orthodox Keynesian system and the much more important position assigned to it by the monetarists.

Behind the Keynesian/monetarist debate lies the more fundamental discussion of the size of the public sector which is thought proper to a mixed economy. This issue has been brought out more fully in an introductory chapter devoted to alternative economic systems, supported later in the book by the introduction of a chapter on expenditure evaluation.

Elsewhere the text has been brought up to date to allow for the changes in economic practice which have occurred since the last edition.

September, 1977

E.S.

Contents

Preface to the First Edition   v
Note to the Third Edition   vi
List of Figures   xi
List of Tables   xiii

PART ONE: THE STATE AND THE NATIONAL ECONOMY

I   *Public Finance and the Changing Role of the State*   1
     The rise of *laissez-faire*; The development of the public sector

II   *Economic Systems*   12
     The nature of economics; The command economy; Market socialism; The market economy

III   *Functions of Public Finance*   27
     The allocation function; The distribution function; The stabilisation function; Budget functions in conflict

PART TWO: PRICE ANALYSIS

IV   *Demand, Supply and Price Relationships*   37
     Demand and supply determine price; The equilibrium price; Changes in the conditions of demand and supply; Elasticity

V   *Marginal Analysis*   55
     The foundations of demand; The foundations of supply in perfect competition; The foundations of supply in monopoly; The foundations of supply in imperfect competition

PART THREE: TAX AND EXPENDITURE ANALYSIS

VI   *The Evaluation of Public Expenditure*   73
     Allocative principles on a fixed budget; Deter-
     mination of the size of the budget; The measure-
     ment of costs and benefits; Discounting future
     costs and benefits; Other factors relevant to cost/
     benefit analysis

VII *Tax Incidence*   83
     Incidence of expenditure taxes; Incidence of in-
     come taxes; An equitable distribution of the tax
     burden

VIII *Tax Effects*   98
     Effects upon production; Effects of taxation upon
     distribution; Administrative effects

PART FOUR: MACROECONOMIC THEORY AND APPLICATION

IX   *The Business Cycle*   109
     The nature of the business cycle; Outline of busi-
     ness cycle theories; Keynesian employment theory

X   *Stabilisation Policies*   127
     The theory of fiscal remedies; The revenue ap-
     proach; The expenditure approach

XI   *The Problem of Growth*   140
     The basis for growth; Taxation, expenditure and
     the supply of labour; Taxation, expenditure and
     the supply of capital; Efficient utilisation of re-
     sources

XII *A Keynesian View of Money*   154
     Money and national income determination; A
     graphical presentation

XIII *The Monetarist Controversy*   162
     Money and prices in the Keynesian system; Money
     and prices in the monetarist system; Is there a
     trade-off between inflation and unemployment?

XIV *The National Debt*   175
     Composition of the UK National Debt; The bur-
     den of the Debt; Origin and growth of the Debt;
     Reducing the burden of the Debt; The National
     Loans Fund

XV   *The Management of the National Debt and Monetary
      Policy*   191
          Renewed confidence in monetary policy; The
          banks and the supply of money; The Bank of
          England and the mechanics of monetary policy

      PART FIVE: THE MACHINERY OF
      ADMINISTRATION

XVI   *Formulation and Control of Financial Policy*   209
          The public expenditure survey system; The finan-
          cial year; Public accountability; Accounting and
          Auditing

      APPENDIXES   226
          I The concept of the national income; II Biblio-
          graphy; III Examination technique; IV Examina-
          tion questions

      Index   245

List of Figures

1. Production possibility curve 13
2. Production possibility and level of employment 14
3. Problem of growth 15
4. Demand curve 40
5. Supply curve 41
6. Equilibrium price 42
7. A general increase or decrease in demand 43
8. A partial increase or decrease in demand 43
9. Changed conditions of demand 44
10. A general increase or decrease in supply 45
11. Changed conditions of supply 45
12. Interaction of the conditions of demand and supply 47
13. Perfectly elastic demand 49
14. Elastic demand 49
15. Perfectly inelastic demand 49
16. Inelastic demand 49
17. Varying elasticity of demand 49
18. Inelastic demand and taxation 51
19. Elastic demand and taxation 51
20. Perfectly elastic supply 52
21. Elastic supply 52
22. Perfectly inelastic supply 52
23. Inelastic supply 52
24. Margin of consumption 56
25. Average fixed cost curve 59
26. Average variable cost curve 59
27. Average total cost curve 60
28. Marginal cost in relation to average total cost 60
29. The firm in perfect competition 61
30. The industry in equilibrium 62
31. The industry in perfect equilibrium 63
32. Monopoly and inelastic demand 64
33. Monopoly and elastic demand 65
34. Output in monopoly, marginal cost increasing 66
35. Output in monopoly, marginal cost declining 66
36. Allocation of a given budget between two projects 74
37. Incidence of an expenditure tax, demand perfectly inelastic, supply elastic 85

xi

38. Incidence of an expenditure tax, supply perfectly elastic,
    demand inelastic   85
39. Incidence of an expenditure tax, supply perfectly inelastic,
    demand elastic   86
40. Incidence of an expenditure tax, demand perfectly elastic,
    supply inelastic   86
41. Incidence of an expenditure tax in perfect competition   87
42. Loss of consumer surplus   90
43. Loss of producer surplus   90
44. Incidence of an expenditure tax in monopoly   91
45. Loss of surpluses in monopoly   92
46. Demand for money, national income being given   158
47. Demand for money at a higher level of national income   159
48. The LM and IS curves in equilibrium   160
49. The Phillips curve   170
50. The fallacy in Phillips   171
51. The long-run effect of a Keynesian stimulus to aggregate
    demand   172
52. The national income   226

List of Tables

I	Production possibility schedule	13
II	Individual demand schedule	39
III	Composite supply schedule	41
IV	Declining marginal revenue	65
V	Ordering priorities on a fixed budget	75
VI	Allocation for more than one benefit in a defence budget	75
VII	Benefits and costs of a building programme	77
VIII	Classification of the National Debt, March 1976	175
IX	Maturity of funded debt, March 1976	176
X	Ownership of the National Debt, March 1976	177
XI	Debt holdings of other financial institutions, March 1976	178
XII	Debt holdings of overseas residents, March 1976	178
XIII	Other holders of National Debt, March 1976	179
XIV	Central government payments and receipts of interest, 1961–75	184
XV	Central government current surpluses and public sector borrowing requirements, 1961–71	186
XVI	Financing of central government borrowing requirement, 1961–8	187
XVII	The public sector borrowing requirement, 1970–8	188
XVIII	Reserve ratio, eligible liabilities and assets of banks in the UK, January 1977	200
XIX	Assets and borrowing of the London discount market, January 1977	201
XX	Supply services and Consolidated Fund standing services	218

PART ONE

THE STATE AND THE NATIONAL ECONOMY

CHAPTER I

Public Finance and the Changing Role of the State

THE RISE OF LAISSEZ-FAIRE

1. The Middle Ages. In medieval Europe there existed no strong sense of national identity. Frontiers were ill-defined and rarely was central authority sufficiently powerful to enforce its will over more than a limited geographical area. Moreover, the bonds of a Roman cultural heritage and of a Christian religion common to all exerted a unifying influence throughout Europe which tended to offset the divisive influence of national allegiances.

Nevertheless, the feudal structure of a society, in which all men owed allegiance to a lord and he to the monarch, guaranteed stability, good order and a way of life in which collective responsibility was accepted for each member of the community. However, discipline was exercised by *local institutions* rather than by *central government*. The routines of agriculture were collectively determined by the manorial courts. Industry was closely regulated by local associations of craftsmen, the craft gilds. Trade was supervised by similar associations of merchants, the merchant gilds.

2. The emergence of the nation state. From the fifteenth century onwards, this calm was gradually shattered by a rising tide of individualism. Increasingly prosperous merchants and craftsmen began to chafe against communal restraints. As markets at home and abroad grew wider, feudal restrictions seemed to bar the path of enterprise and progress. Local institutions disintegrated, leaving behind a void in which there grew a sense of insecurity, a fear

1

that there might no longer be justice in men's relationships.

In answer to the need for internal law and order and for protection from possible external aggression the *nation state* arose, forged by strong central government in the form of *absolute monarchy*. In Continental Europe the process of national unification was delayed, but in England it was accomplished under the Tudors.

3. The mercantilist view of public finance. Mercantilism was the political doctrine which aimed to promote strong central government and a powerful state. It had its economic aspects which impinged upon the practice of public finance.

(*a*) *Overseas trade*. To finance armies a nation required gold and silver. In the absence of mines within its territory it could earn these by ensuring a favourable balance of trade. To this end, mercantilists favoured subsidies for exports and a tariff which restricted imports.

(*b*) *The relief of poverty*. Expansion of the woollen industry in the fifteenth and sixteenth centuries brought a greater demand for raw wool and an extension of pasture farming at the expense of arable farming. The English peasantry was gradually separated from the land which had previously supported it and pauperism became a major problem for the first time. It was a problem inconsistent with the mercantilist conception of a powerful and healthy state and measures were enacted to remedy it. The great Elizabethan *Poor Law* of 1601 established a financial base for local public expenditure which has survived to the present time. The parish was made the administrative unit for poor relief which was to be financed by a rate levied upon householders.

4. Reaction to authoritarianism. In a wider context, mercantilism attempted to replace the disintegrating local controls of the Middle Ages with central government regulation of industry, trade and agriculture. In the short term these attempts were successful but they could not for long hold back the expanding force of individualistic free enterprise. By the seventeenth century, the view was increasingly accepted that the best interests of society would be promoted if every individual were allowed to pursue his own self-interest unhindered by the state. The struggle against the absolute power of the Crown in Britain continued for more than a century culminating in the Civil War of 1688–9 in which the unquestionable supremacy of Parliament was finally established. The political and social order which followed confirmed the new belief in *laissez-faire*. Based upon it there flourished an economic system rooted in private enterprise and which allowed little scope for collective action through the state.

5. Consequences to public expenditure. As long as the philosophy of *laissez-faire* dominated economic thinking, the only legitimate function of central government was thought to be the provision of defence and law and order. It was therefore only in time of war that state expenditure became significant and the raising of revenue a real problem. Locally, the function of government was confined to the administration of justice and the relief of pauperism and expenditure in this respect did not become an urgent problem until the end of the eighteenth century.

6. Consequences to the fiscal system. The Civil War of 1688 gave Parliament control of the national finances and public finance in the modern sense dates from this time. The monarch's personal expenses were separated from national expenditure and taxes were raised to meet specified requirements, i.e. the principle of *appropriation of supplies* was established, whereby it became illegal to use money for any purpose other than that for which it had been voted.

At the end of the seventeenth century, war with the French brought an increase in expenditure and a corresponding extension of the fiscal system. Customs and excise duties were the traditional source of revenue but these proved inadequate and in 1692 a *direct tax* on land was raised.

Public borrowing was also extended and took a new direction. In 1693, a group of businessmen made a loan of £1,200,000 to the government and were rewarded by a Charter to form the Bank of England. This was the beginning of the *funded debt*, i.e. no date was set for its repayment.

7. Expenditure and taxation in the eighteenth century. The eighteenth century was predominantly the age of *laissez-faire* and collective expenditure for all but defence purposes was minimal. Wars, however, caused a continuing increase in the burden of taxation and of the National Debt.

(*a*) *Direct taxes.* These were not favoured since their compulsory nature was viewed as an infringement of individual liberty. Walpole succeeded in reducing the level of the land tax but, by the end of the century, war expenditure was so heavy that Pitt, in an effort to balance the budget, introduced a series of direct taxes on items such as windows, carriages and servants. He followed these in 1799 with a temporary, emergency measure, an *income tax*.

(*b*) *Indirect taxes.* In principle, indirect taxation was more to the public taste since it gave the alternative of avoidance if purchases were not made. This seemed more compatible with English liberty. Customs and excise duties were extended to all items in general use. The effect upon trade was stifling and first Walpole and then Pitt adopted reforms which paved the way to nineteenth century free trade. Duties were simplified and reduced, so stimulating trade that the revenue was eventually increased.

(*c*) *National Debt.* It proved impossible to finance repeated wars from current taxation and despite the efforts of Walpole, then Pitt, to reduce the Debt by means of a *Sinking Fund*, there was a steady expansion from £54 million in 1713 to £819 million in 1815. Interest payments were a crippling burden upon the revenue.

THE DEVELOPMENT OF THE PUBLIC SECTOR

8. Social consequence of industrialisation. Industrialisation brought striking progress in Britain's ability to produce, but amidst wealth there was the direst poverty. In a society which had rejected all controls in favour of freedom of individual action, the bargaining strength of employer and workman were unevenly matched. Wages and conditions of work were correspondingly poor. The factory system brought the rapid and unplanned growth of towns which lacked the most elementary amenities and in which the death rate was rising. A market economy brought in its train a problem of involuntary unemployment, the causes of which were not understood. Education was still the prerogative of those who could afford it, while provision for old age was thought to be a matter of personal thrift.

9. Extension of laissez-faire. In the 1820s and '30s, the fortunes of the working class were at their lowest ebb. The remedy was thought not to lie in collective action and a return to the paternalistic society of an earlier age but rather in the more effective action of the principle of *laissez-faire*. If impediments to wage bargaining were removed, the working man's position would be that much stronger. In this belief, the Combination Laws were relaxed in 1825. (These laws of 1799 and 1800 had denied the workman the right to combine for the purpose of collective bargaining.)

Poor relief, which by the 1820s had become a crushing burden upon the ratepayer, was reformed by the Poor Law (Amendment) Act of 1834. A more stringent control of poor relief, it was thought, would make the working man more self-reliant and less disposed to raise a large family which he could not support. By limiting his numbers, he would thus increase his scarcity value.

Most important of all, a gradual abolition of all customs and excise duties would so stimulate trade that there would be prosperity for all.

10. "Laissez-passer." The great free trade movement gathered momentum in the 1820s with Huskisson at the Board of Trade. Perceiving that the existing tax system was strangling the foreign trade upon which Britain's industrial expansion depended, he abolished a wide range of duties. This work was continued by Peel and completed by Gladstone. By the 1860s, the transition to free trade had been accomplished and the nation's wealth grew apace. Both Tories and Liberals shared the view that the state had no part to play in economic affairs and that taxation and public borrowing should be kept to a minimum.

11. Utilitarianism and the "collateral aids". In parallel with the extension of *laissez-faire* philosophy, another distinct, yet complementary, line of thought was developing. Writers such as Jeremy Bentham and John Stuart Mill were advancing the view that the criterion for economic action should be "the greatest good of the greatest number". There was little that was revolutionary in this thinking since society was still regarded as a loose collection of individuals. It was not thought inconsistent with *laissez-faire*, however, that society should finance those "collateral aids" which it was unlikely that private enterprise would provide and which would create the kind of environment in which every individual had the opportunity fully to pursue his own enlightened self-interest.

(*a*) *Education*. Before 1833, education was exclusively the province of private enterprise. In that year, the state for the first time gave indirect support through grants to Church of England and Nonconformist organisations. Small at first, these grants were gradually enlarged. Finally, in the Education Act of

1870, the state acknowledged its responsibility to guarantee an education for all. School Boards were established throughout the country to build schools wherever the church organisations were inadequate.

At first it was argued that an educated working man would have a greater sense of responsibility and would be better able to meet his social obligation to support himself and his dependants. Later in the century it was appreciated that an educated population was essential to the prosperity of an industrial nation which was meeting growing competition from Germany and the USA.

(b) *Health.* In the 1830s, the pioneering efforts of Edwin Chadwick, the Secretary to the Poor Law Commissioners, led to a greater public understanding of the connection between poor water supplies, filth and bad ventilation, and disease and the high cost of poor relief. A *General Board of Health* was established in 1848 to supervise local boards. These local bodies were to be responsible for the provision of drainage, water supply and street cleaning. This early legislation was permissive but the Public Health Act 1875 compelled local authorities to maintain sewers, street paving, lighting and cleaning and fire services. It is to be noted, however, that nineteenth-century legislators were concerned only to provide an environment in which a man might expect to enjoy good health and therefore be capable of taking care of himself. The *personal* approach to the health problems of the individual was not to be achieved until the twentieth century.

12. Rationalisation of ad hoc authorities. The growth of public activity in the nineteenth century was accompanied by a similar growth of *local ad hoc bodies* since financial and administrative responsibility were not accepted by central government. Boards of Guardians representing groups of parishes administered poor relief. Highways Boards, Boards of Health and School Boards assumed responsibility in their own spheres. Rationalisation began with legislation between 1882 and 1894 which provided for elected multi-purpose local authorities covering the whole country: county councils, county borough councils, municipal borough and district councils.

These new authorities absorbed immediately the administrative work of J.P.s and the work of the Health and Highways Boards. In 1902 was added the work of the School Boards and in 1929 that of the Boards of Guardians.

13. The Liberal government, 1906. Under this reforming government, there occurred the next major development in the public sector. A Poor Law Commission recommended that more appropriate treatment than the poor law should be accorded to the sick, the elderly and the unemployed. These recommendations were implemented in the Old Age Pensions Act 1908 and in the great National Insurance Act of 1911 which catered for sickness and unemployment and whose funds were subscribed by employer, employee and state.

There was now emerging a *national* social policy no longer restricted by the limitations of local finance but able to draw upon the resources of the nation. In this part of the public sector, it only remained to absorb the work of the Guardians in 1929, to transfer it to a national agency in the Unemployment Act of 1934 and finally to weld the whole into an integrated system of social security in 1946.

14. Growth of central government departments. The 1834 Poor Law (Amendment) Act had established a central Board of Commissioners to co-ordinate the work of local Boards of Guardians. This was replaced in 1871 by a *Local Government Board* whose responsibilities expanded in step with the growth of local authority services. In 1919, it was replaced by the Ministry of Health.

The Board of Education was established in 1900, the first central government department with the responsibility of developing an integrated national social service. It was superseded in 1944 by a ministry with wider powers.

In line with the development of public services, there was therefore subsequent development of central government administrative organisations.

15. Changing character of taxation. As long as it was the accepted view that the only legitimate function of the state was the provision of security, taxation was seen as a necessary evil to be kept to a minimum. The transition to free trade had been accomplished without loss of revenue through the expedient of retaining an income tax as a purely temporary measure. Gladstone's obsession was with economy, even at the expense of the primary needs of defence and it was his intention ultimately to abolish income tax. With the growth of public activity in the 1880s, however, it was gradually being accepted as a necessary and permanent feature of the tax structure and the rate of tax was slowly rising. It was, however, based upon the principle of proportionality since it was the belief that an unavoidable tax should do nothing to disturb the *relative* incomes of individuals.

In the 1890s, this view receded as it was realised that a fixed percentage tax bore more heavily upon the poor than the wealthy. Sir William Harcourt s budget of 1894 marked a radical new departure with the introduction of the principle of progression, applied to a graduated estate duty. In a modified form, this principle was confirmed in Lloyd George's income tax of 1909.

Taxation was now being used as an instrument of social policy to reduce inequalities of wealth and income.

16. Municipal trading activities. As the social duties of the local authorities grew, they also began to acquire certain powers which marked the beginning of public interest in the economic side of the public sector.

(*a*) *Utilities.* By private Acts of Parliament and by some national legislation (e.g. the Electricity Acts), local authorities extended their activities to the provision of water, electricity, gas, tramways and other trading services.

(*b*) *Local authority housing.* While certain cities had shown interest in municipal housing before 1914, only in the 1920s did legislation introduce the general development of local housing departments.

Activity in these two fields indicated the acceptance of a new principle. Society might cater not only for collective needs but also for individual needs, applying commercial methods in the same way as private enterprise.

17. Central government trading activities. These can be classed as:

(*a*) *Postal services.* Initially, the Post Office was regarded as a necessary strategic service but it acquired more commercial characteristics after the purchase of telephone rights from the private sector. However, it is only recently with its re-constitution as a public corporation that it has come to be regarded wholly as an independent commercial service.

(*b*) *Marketing Boards.* Central government's trading activities were extended in the 1930s with the establishment of Agricultural Marketing Boards. They opened up a vast new public activity in commodity dealing and subsidisation which reached its height during the Second World War.

(*c*) *Nationalised industries.* The Labour government of 1945 added considerably to central government's trading activities.

The Bank of England, coal, transport and subsequently steel were taken from the private sector while gas and electricity were added from the local authorities.

During the 1960s, Clause IV of the Labour Party constitution, which calls for "the public ownership of the means of production, distribution and exchange", was considered something of an electoral embarassment. It was re-activated at the 1974 general election and the incoming government nationalised the shipbuilding and aircraft construction industries.

(d) *National Enterprise Board*. During the early 1970s Government repeatedly came to the rescue of "lame ducks" which were considered to be of such national significance that they could not be permitted to collapse. In this way the state acquired Rolls Royce, Herbert, the machine tool manufacturers and a number of smaller concerns.

The Industry Act 1975 established the National Enterprise Board which was to serve as a state holding company. In it were vested those assets already purchased. With a budget of £1,000 million it then bought the ailing British Leyland and in accordance with its terms of reference has begun to purchase interests in privately owned firms which it believes to have a strong future.

It may be noted that these state holdings are not viewed as "nationalised industries".

The growth of central government trading interests has given the public sector a predominant role in the national economy. Through its control of financial institutions on the one hand and, on the other, energy, transport and, since re-nationalisation, steel, the state is able directly to influence the whole of the nation's economic life.

18. A new application for fiscal policy. It has been shown that by the 1890s taxation was viewed not only as a means of raising revenue but also as an instrument of social policy. With the enormous growth of social expenditure in the twentieth century, of necessity the level of taxation has risen astronomically. These taxes have been raised in a way compatible with taxation's secondary function, in the sense that more steeply progressive taxes, coupled with appropriate tax-free allowances, have reduced inequalities of wealth and income.

Following the 1944 White Paper *Employment Policy* the public finances acquired a third function. The revolution in economic thinking initiated by John Maynard Keynes suggested that compensatory action through the public finances would offset the inherent instability of a free market economy. Henceforth, Government would assume responsibility for the management of *aggregate demand*, ironing out fluctuations and seeking to guarantee full employment, real growth and stable prices, Such an indirect approach would be consistent with social democracy and would avoid the illiberality and inefficiency of central planning in totalitarian socialist regimes.

The immediate results seemed favourable, but by the 1960s the economy was responding less readily to demand management techniques and inflationary pressures were gathering momentum. By the mid-1970s, with investment and output stagnant and unemployment and inflation rising it was evident that orthodox Keynesian techniques could no longer provide a solution. This failure led to progressive Government reliance upon more central planning, more detailed intervention in the economy through prices and incomes controls, further nationalisation, the public acquisition of parts of failing industries, subsidised investment and emphasis upon the merits of "the social wage" as opposed to "the private wage". This gradual and unintended change of economic strategy was nevertheless consistent with the development of political pressure for a transition to a fully planned socialist state.

Simultaneously, the course of events lent credence to those economists who had always been critical of the theoretical foundations of the Keynesian system. Its long-run failure was inevitable and its consequences were magnified by the associated growth of unwieldy bureaucracy. The crisis was one of socialist planning rather than of a market system which, since 1945, had operated under ever tighter constraints.

The theoretical background for this controversy will be considered in Chapter II and throughout Part Four.

PROGRESS TEST 1

1. Describe the nature of mercantilism. **(3)**

2. In what respects did the acceptance of *laissez-faire* reverse mercantilist views of public finance? **(3, 5, 6)**

3. What was the effect upon trade of eighteenth century indirect taxation? **(7(*b*))**

4. Why did the modern National Debt expand steadily throughout the eighteenth century? **(7(*c*))**

5. What remedies did early nineteenth century thinkers propose for the excesses of the Industrial Revolution? **(9)**

6. Define *laissez-passer*. How was it accomplished? **(10)**

7. What do you understand by the term "collateral aids"? Why were these not thought to be inconsistent with *laissez-faire*? **(11)**

8. Outline the way in which public activity increased in the nineteenth century. **(11, 12)**

9. What were the principal achievements of the 1906 Liberal government? **(13)**

10. Explain how the principle of "progression" came to be established in the British tax system. **(15)**

11. Describe the way in which the public sector was enlarged to include trading activities. **(16, 17)**

12. State briefly what has been the most recently accepted function of fiscal policy. **(18)**

CHAPTER II

Economic Systems

THE NATURE OF ECONOMICS

1. The economic problem. The previous chapter provides an account of the way in which the state in Britain has come to occupy an increasingly important position in the *mixed economy*. We should now examine more analytically the reasons for this change and subsequently make some assessment of how successful this mixture has been in solving *the economic problem*.

The root of the problem is to be found in the scarcity of goods and services relative to the demand for them, so that almost everyone is bound to leave unsatisfied certain of his wants. The basic reason for this is that there are insufficient of *the factors of production* (i.e. land, labour and capital) to provide enough to satisfy wholly everyone's wants. If we produce more of one class of goods or services then we must at any one time curtail our production of another. The fundamental decision to be made lies therefore in the *selection* of those goods and services which we will enjoy and in the determination of the quantity in which each will be produced.

2. The production possibility curve. The problem of choice may be illustrated by means of a simple diagram. It is worth emphasising here that economists frequently find it convenient to express ideas in this way both as a method of concise presentation and as a means of developing their thinking about economic problems.

The diagram is called a production possibility curve, and is derived from a number of simple assumptions made in Table I.

In this society which produces only food and coal we may select a variety of combinations ranging from a position where all resources are devoted to coal production leaving nothing for food to an exclusive concentration on food leaving no resources for coal production.

TABLE I.   PRODUCTION POSSIBILITY SCHEDULE

Food (in thousands of tonnes)	Coal (in thousands of tonnes)
0	525
100	515
200	495
300	465
400	420
500	360
600	295
700	205
800	95
850	0

These figures are expressed graphically in Fig. 1.

Basically the curve tells us nothing which is not shown in the Table but it does reveal something which is not so obvious in the figures. The curve is bowed out or concave to the origin and this is in fact fairly characteristic of all production possibility curves.

The significance is that it becomes progressively harder to increase output of one commodity in the sense that it becomes necessary to forgo ever greater amounts of the other commodity. In short opportunity cost rises.

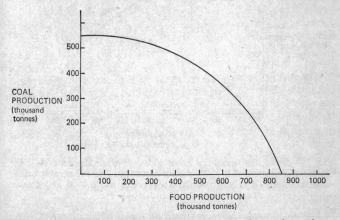

FIG. 1.—*Production possibility curve.* The curve indicates the various combinations of food and coal which may be produced when all resources are fully employed. It is concave to its origin.

The explanation lies in the empirical truth that factors of production are not homogeneous. In our example, as food production expands it is at first confined to fertile farmland with a relatively small loss of coal production. Ultimately, however, it becomes necessary to farm less fertile lands in the coalfields at the expense of losing rich coal seams.

So far we have concentrated upon the aspect of the problem which is concerned with choice. This is the area of the subject which economists describe as *microeconomics*. Since the 1930s an additional problem has received a great deal of attention. It has been treated by many economists as belonging to a distinct branch of the subject, namely *macroeconomics*.

3. Macroeconomics. Analysis here seeks to establish principles which govern the *level* of resource use. What considerations determine whether the labour force is fully employed, industrial, commercial and agricultural enterprises working to capacity, national income maximised?

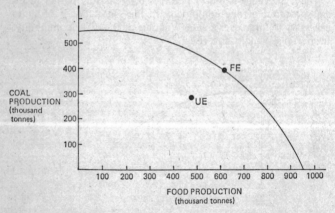

FIG. 2.—*Production possibility curve and level of employment.* At FE the curve is positioned to show the maximum possible full employment output. At UE it is still possible to produce more food and coal.

The position can be represented on our production possibility curve (Fig. 2) with FE showing full employment production and UE undercapacity production.

4. The problem of growth. In more recent years industrial societies have become more preoccupied with a further problem, that of sustaining long term growth. Some economists have seen this problem as one amenable to treatment by macroeconomic means. Others have viewed its solution as dependent upon structural change, upon the reallocation of resources and therefore belonging essentially to microeconomics. This problem is represented in Fig. 3.

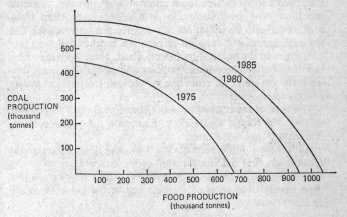

FIG. 3.—*The problem of growth.* Modern economies will attempt to secure a regular outward movement of the production possibility curve.

It may be thought that in, some measure this last problem has been solved by rapidly advancing technology. However, it will also be argued that this progress has been bought too cheaply with too little regard to the social costs of urbanisation, congestion, pollution, alienation of large sections of the population and an explosive use of the world's finite stock of natural resources.

Upon all these matters the economist will have something to say but the range of solutions he offers will ultimately be limited by their political acceptability to particular societies.

5. The relationship of politics and economics. The relationship between the two areas of study has always been close and in post-imperial Britain they appear frequently to overlap.

Before 1939, as a world power with wide ranging commitments, much political debate was outward looking. Shorn of empire and her nineteenth century world role assumed by the USA, a more introverted Britain has focused steadily upon her own economic problems. Frequently the solutions applied have been designed to deal with short term political difficulties rather than to provide a long term economic strategy. The problem is therefore to define the functions of the politician and the economist in relation to each other.

With the consent of the electorate, the politician establishes the framework within which the economist must provide, where he can, a range of possible solutions to an economic problem. However, it will also be within his terms of reference to indicate that the adoption of one solution rather than another may well lead to changes in the political framework itself. There is an inevitable interplay between economic policies and political policies, between the nature of an economic system and the political system which encompasses it.

The task of the economist is not therefore limited to problem solving. He should also seek to illuminate the socio-economic implications of his solutions.

With these considerations in mind we may now proceed to the proposition that the fundamental economic problem of choice and the derivative problems of macroeconomics may be resolved by a variety of systems each displaying certain advantages and disadvantages.

THE COMMAND ECONOMY

6. General characteristics. Central government makes basic decisions in respect of resource allocation, production targets, income distribution, growth rates *and does so in accordance with its collective preferences* rather than in response to the wishes of individual consumers. In practice, if every detail of economic life were so planned the complexities of the task would be beyond the capabilities of the most sophisticated group of central planners. Some decentralisation of decision making is therefore unavoidable, either to lower echelons of the government apparatus or to some approximation to a market mechanism. The central planners may simply concentrate upon main areas of the economy. Even with such limitations certain problems emerge.

7. The chain of command. A highly developed bureaucratic structure is necessary so that decisions may be speedily handed down from the centre to the shop floor. Equally, there must be a rapid and unrestricted flow of information back to the centre in order that decisions may be well informed. In practice, this is difficult to achieve and at best the economy must support a heavy burden of administrators.

8. Effective use of resources. Where there exists no genuine pricing system or profit motive to test how efficiently resources have been deployed in one use rather than another an obvious difficulty arises. What principles will be used to determine whether a particular line of production warrants the scarce resources which it absorbs? This is a problem to which we shall return (*see* VI, **8–13**).

9. Co-ordination of inputs and outputs. Given an effective chain of command it is still not possible to establish targets for a variety of industries independently of each other. The prospect of industry A achieving its target may depend upon it receiving a vital input from industry B. In turn, industry B's ability to supply this output may depend upon it receiving a vital input from industry A. Across the economy a complex network of interdependencies will emerge, the co-ordination of which will prove extremely difficult for the central planner.

10. Incentives for producers. In practice, this has proved a very real problem for many command economies. A dynamic labour force and enterprising management cannot be established by invocation or command. It is a problem which has only been resolved by moving away from extreme egalitarianism towards some degree of differential rewards.

11 Basic economic objectives. Invariably these will be determined by the political and military goals of the leadership. In general, this will mean that fewer resources are devoted to the satisfaction of consumer preferences than would have been the case in a market economy while more are devoted to the expansion of the industrial infrastructure and to the development of military potential.

In liberal western societies such centralisation of economic and political decision-making has been unacceptable. Indeed, even in some communist command economies there has been a reaction, with experiments to restore a limited market order.

MARKET SOCIALISM

12. Oskar Lange. Oskar Lange, a Polish economist, attempted a synthesis of the best features of the command and market economies in an essay *On the Economic Theory of Socialism*, 1936. He could see the advantages of Adam Smith's "invisible hand" which spontaneously produced harmony and equilibrium but was concerned with the inequalities of income distribution, the tendency to monopoly and the unemployment which were features of the market order.

13. The principles. The state will own land and capital but there will be a free market in labour. However, market wages will be subsidised as necessary to secure a more equitable income distribution and supply and demand for labour will be so equated as to avoid mass unemployment. The state will determine the basic allocation of resources between consumption and investment but in consumer markets firms will be obliged to behave as they would in perfect competition, pricing the product at marginal cost of production. (V, **15**)

14. Pricing of land and capital. As owner of these factors, the state will supply them to businesses at certain prices. These are simply *accounting prices* since there need not be an income flow from state owned business to state owned factors. However, factor costs will be taken into account by business managers in the same way as in a market economy.

15. Criticisms. While offering a coherent compromise there are evident weaknesses. Will subsidised wages and the absence of opportunity to create private wealth affect the incentives of labour and management? Will the state allocate resources to consumption in any way which corresponds to the wishes of consumers? Will an artificially induced full employment equilibrium be at the expense of production for which there is no consumer demand?

16. Market socialism in Yugoslavia. From 1947–51, Yugoslavia had a highly centralised economy on the Soviet model. She subsequently embarked upon her own experiment in a brand of market socialism which, while distinctive, has similarities to Lange's model.

There is public ownership of the major enterprises, and some central planning. However, the market mechanism is used to relate individual enterprises to the economy as a whole. These enterprises compete with each other and plan their outputs in accordance with anticipated sales. The degree of central price control has varied from time to time.

Incentives and co-operation are established in two ways. Enterprises are managed by workers councils which elect an executive managing body and wages and salaries are determined by the level of profits. The councils also have a part in determining the ploughback of profits into further investment.

Agriculture is almost entirely in private hands and there is also some private ownership of smaller-scale trading activities.

17. **Evaluation.** The evidence suggests that decentralised decision making has reduced bureaucratic waste and improved economic efficiency and work incentives. On the other hand it has tended to lead to a heavy concentration of economic power in the hands of successful enterprises and to some imbalance in regional development. Market forces naturally attract fresh investment funds to those areas which have already proved profitable.

On balance however, the interest in this experiment shown by other East European countries and even by the USSR would indicate some measure of improvement upon the extreme models of the command economy.

THE MARKET ECONOMY

18. **Adam Smith.** It has been observed (I, 4) that the eighteenth century opened upon a society which, in England, had accepted the principles of *laissez-faire*. The seal of approval for this new philosophy was given by Adam Smith in the *Wealth of Nations* (1776). Smith argues that only the individual knows where his own self-interest lies and that if he is permitted to pursue this in an enlightened fashion, individual and social interest are brought into harmony. It follows that legal restraints imposed by the State should be the minimum consistent with the preservation of society. In economic matters the state has no part to play. The best results are achieved by the working of a free economy.

19. **The market and the price mechanism.** In a free economy it is the *price mechanism* which determines how the factors of production will be allocated and which simultaneously governs the distribution of the end product. An increase in the consumer's preference for one commodity rather than another will be ex-

pressed in his willingness to pay a higher price for the same quantity. The rise in price will induce suppliers to produce more, i.e. land, labour and capital will be attracted into this use from less profitable ventures.

If supply is now extended beyond the quantity which the market will absorb at the prevailing price then price will tend to fall and factors of production will be diverted into other channels.

On the side of distribution, the individual is free to make his own personal selection of goods and services and he may enjoy these in the quantity for which he is able to pay.

It may therefore be seen that at any one time, for each line of production, there is an *equilibrium price* which will bring into harmony demand and supply. It may also be thought at first that such a system of production would provide the ideal solution to the economic problem since the equilibrium price would ensure an allocation of resources which reflected exactly the requirements of the individual and, by extension, the sum total of the requirements of society.

The first objection to this view lies in its dependence upon the concept of *perfect competition*.

20. Perfect Competition. The output policy of the firm and the subsequent relationship between supply and price will vary with the degree of competition which prevails in that particular market. The theory of price is worked out initially upon the assumption of perfectly competitive conditions (*see* V, **12–17**) and it was implicit in nineteenth century faith in a free market economy that these conditions existed. With the growth of a more analytical approach to economics in the twentieth century, economists attempted to define precisely what the conditions of wholly perfect competition would be and it was soon appreciated that in practice they certainly did not exist, at least in the short period of time. In their attempts therefore to produce a more realistic working model of a competitive market, economists have tended to prescribe conditions which are less than perfect while they continue to use the term perfect competition.

NOTE: To avoid confusion, it would have been useful to adopt the recommendation of Chamberlain and more recently of Stigler and distinguish between conditions which are perfectly competitive in every respect and those which fall short of perfection. Stigler suggests the use of the terms *industrial competition* and *market competition* and reference will be made to this distinction later (*see* V, **16, 17**). However, the term "perfect competition" has remained in general use to describe both degrees of competition and to distinguish them from *imperfect competition* and *monopoly*.

21. Characteristics of a competitive market. Whatever the shade of "perfect competition," however, *the* distinguishing characteristic of a competitive market is:

(*a*) *A large number of buyers and sellers.* No individual buyer or seller is in a position to influence price by boycotting the market. In other words, each buyer or seller has control of such an insignificant fraction of total demand or supply that price will be unaffected by his withdrawal from the market.

Additionally, both "industrial" and "market competition" require:

(*b*) *A perfect market* The characteristic of a perfect market is that there can be only one ruling price. This will be achieved where there is:

(*i*) *A homogeneous commodity.* All units of a perfect market are identical in every respect.

(*ii*) *A portable commodity.* It must be possible to move the product freely to all corners of the market.

(*iii*) *Perfect knowledge.* All buyers and sellers must be in close contact and fully aware of all offers made.

(*iv*) *Rational choice.* All bargains must be concluded with reference to price alone and must never be influenced by emotional considerations, e.g. prejudice, habit, patriotism.

(*v*) *No social impediments* to the free movement of the factors of production into or out of the market in response to demand, e.g. legislation, licences.

If conditions (*a*) and (*b*) (*i*)–(*v*) are fulfilled, there is *market* competition and in practice some markets may approximate to this situation, even in the short period of time, e.g. organised commodity markets, the Stock Market. The two further conditions of *industrial* competition will not be achieved in the short period, although it is conceivable that they are produced in the long period. These are:

(*vi*) *Perfect mobility of the factors of production.* This implies that land, labour and capital may move freely and without economic friction between industries and into the use where the price bid is highest, e.g. labour would move easily both geographically and between jobs requiring different skills.

(*vii*) *Infinite divisibility of the factors of production.* Not only must the factors be perfectly mobile but they must be able to move in large or infinitely small units in response to demand.

NOTE: (*i*) The concept of a perfect market is not to be confused with perfect competition, for which it is only *one* of the *two* necessary conditions.

(*ii*) Possibly as a result of confusing the two concepts, it is sometimes claimed that a perfect market requires a large number of buyers and sellers. In fact it is conceivable that a market may be more perfect where there is monopoly or only a few buyers and sellers, since there is greater likelihood of perfect knowledge and therefore a single ruling price.

22. Monopoly and imperfect competition. It was widely assumed in the nineteenth century that there existed a degree of competition which through the operation of the price mechanism would guarantee the maximum use and optimum allocation of resources. In the 1930s, realisation of the shortcomings of competition led economists to construct fresh working models of markets where there existed monopoly or imperfect competition.

23. Monopoly. Monopoly implies the absence of all competition. Monopoly was seen to be frequently exercised by sellers although seldom by buyers. The supplier derives his power from his total control of a commodity for which it is difficult to find a substitute. By deliberately restricting output, he is able to influence price.

24. Imperfect competition. Imperfect competition exists where, either separately or together, the following conditions are found:

(*a*) *Oligopoly* (a few suppliers only). Each producer has control over a sufficient fraction of total supply to enable him to influence price by restricting output in the same way as the monopolist.

(*b*) *An imperfect market.* For any of the following reasons a market will be imperfect and hence competition will be imperfect.

(*i*) *Poor communications and lack of knowledge* may impede a unified market and give rise to a number of relatively insulated markets in the same product.

(*ii*) *State intervention,* either directly (e.g. licences) or indirectly (e.g. taxation and subsidies), distorts the free interplay of demand and supply and the free movement of the factors of production in response to changes in price.

(*iii*) *Differentiation between units of the commodity*. The modern practice of branding aims to prove not that Brand X is better than Brand Y but that it is a totally different product.

(*iv*) *Irrational decisions*. Human choice is not always rational and we may be prepared to pay a higher price because of prejudice, habit or other emotional considerations.

25. Conclusions. It can be seen that:

(*a*) Where there is an imperfect market, there is unlikely to be a single market price. If there is, it is likely to be the result of collusion between suppliers.

(*b*) Where there is monopoly or imperfect competition, price may be artificially high as a result of the deliberate restriction of output. In this situation, price ceases to mirror the true state of demand and supply and is therefore impeded in its function of channelling scarce resources into those uses in which demand is greatest.

26. The inadequacies of the price mechanism. From the foregoing discussion we are led to conclude that in the real world the action of competition is strictly limited and that consequently a market which is left wholly free and unregulated will not automatically solve the problem of securing the optimum allocation of resources. Moreover, by the 1930s as was indicated earlier (*see* **2, 3**) a further shortcoming was having a powerful impact upon society. The inter-war period was characterised by mass unemployment for which the free market model of the economy could provide no explanation.

27. Unemployment and the price mechanism. The classical, *laissez-faire* model of the economy provided only an explanation of economic equilibrium at full employment. Fundamental to this equilibrium was the complete flexibility of price in every market. It followed that unemployment of resources could not persist since there would always be some price at which the market would be cleared.

However, the development of trade union power enabled monopoly influence to be exerted in the labour markets with some corresponding resistance to downward pressure on wages. Success in this respect was paralleled by a greater number of unemployed than would otherwise have been the case.

Furthermore, economists were now pàying a good deal more attention to a phenomenon which had long been observed, *the trade cycle*. It seemed that the free market economy was inherently unstable, given to alternating periods of high and low productive activity. In terms of our earlier analysis, there were protracted depressions during which the production possibility curve lay far to the left. The price mechanism was failing to secure the maximum use of resources.

28. Economic justification of the mixed economy. Recognition of these weaknesses in the functioning of the price mechanism (at least as they manifested themselves in the 1930s) provided the economic justification for the extension of the supervisory role of the State, particularly after 1945 (I, **18**).

Not only has Government steadily enlarged the sphere in which it directly influences the allocation of resources to selected productive processes (e.g. the nationalised industries, the National Enterprise Board), but it has, through the public finances, achieved a substantial redistribution of real income from taxpayer to welfare beneficiary, from "*the private wage*" to "*the social wage*".

Additionally, the regulatory function of the price mechanism has been greatly modified by macroeconomic policies aimed at controlling aggregate demand in a way which would eliminate the trade cycle. Taxation and public expenditure have been the principal instruments.

Some indication of the balance of the mixed economy in 1977 lies in the figure of 62% of the national income which is absorbed by the public sector. Put another way, 62% of resources are allocated by political decision rather than in response to the play of market forces.

29. "The Expences of the Sovereign or Commonwealth". While these supervisory roles would have been contested in the eighteenth and nineteenth centuries, it was universally agreed that the price mechanism and the free market were unsuited to the satisfaction of wants which were collective in character. This position was acknowledged by Adam Smith who writes of "The Expences of the Sovereign or Commonwealth" which he says fall into three categories:

(*a*) "defending the society from the violence and injustice of other independent societies".

(*b*) "securing internal justice between citizens".

(*c*) "erecting and maintaining those public institutions . . . and works which though they be in the highest degree advantageous to a great society, could never repay the expense to any individual".

The traditional scope of public finance stems from the acceptance that there are such collective wants which could never properly be satisfied through the mechanism of the free market.

30. Aspects of modern public finance. From the preceding discussion we may now establish certain basic functions for a system of public finance. We will refer to these as:

(*a*) *The allocation function.* The principles upon which total resources are divided between the production of *private* goods and *social* goods.

(*b*) *The distribution function.* The principles upon which adjustment is made to the distribution of income and wealth, established by the market.

(*c*) *The stabilisation function.* The principles upon which a system of public finance is structured to achieve high employment and growth coupled with stable prices and balance of payments equilibrium.

In Chapter III we shall pursue these themes in greater depth.

PROGRESS TEST 2

1. Define "the economic problem". **(1)**
2. Explain the nature of a production possibility curve. **(2)**
3. What is the relationship of the economist to the politician? **(5)**
4. Specify some of the features of a command economy. **(6)**
5. List some of the weaknesses of a command economy. **(7–10)**
6. Describe the nature of "Lange socialism". **(12–14)**
7. How are resources allocated in a free market economy? **(19)**
8. What are the principal characteristics of a perfect market? **(21(*b*))**
9. Explain the power of the monopolist. **(23)**
10. What is oligopoly? **(24(*a*))**
11. What is "the trade cycle"? **(27)**

12. What do you understand by "the mixed economy"? **(28)**

13. What was Smith's view of "the expences of the Sovereign"? **(29)**

14. Specify three basic functions for a modern system of public finance. **(30)**

CHAPTER III

Functions of Public Finance

THE ALLOCATION FUNCTION

1. Private and social goods. In agreement with Smith we make the proposition that certain goods which are *social* in character cannot be adequately catered for by the market system.

To understand this proposition fully calls for a clearcut distinction between social goods and private goods. The distinction does not depend upon the need for social goods being felt collectively since only individuals have wants. Just as individuals may prefer a motor car to a bicycle so they may prefer a motorway to a cycle track. The difference in the latter case is that the benefits of motorways and cycle tracks are not limited to any one individual while the benefits of a motor cycle or bicycle are restricted to the purchaser.

The consumption of social goods may therefore be said to be *externalised* in the sense that their enjoyment by one consumer does not limit their enjoyment by another. In contrast the consumption of private goods *internalises* the benefit to a particular consumer, excluding consumption by others.

2. The inability of the market to exclude. The functioning of the market mechanism is dependent upon private property, upon the ability to exclude others from particular benefits in order that exchange may subsequently take place. In the case of social goods such exclusion is impossible and would in any case be inappropriate when consumption by one individual does not *rival* that of another, e.g. the individual cannot readily be excluded from the benefits of national defence. Moreover, in such a situation the consumer will not be prepared voluntarily to offer payment for the services he receives since he enjoys them only in common with others. The market link between demand and supply has broken down.

3. The "political market". In the absence of a market the problem remains to determine the quantity of social goods to be produced and the way in which their cost is to be apportioned between consumers. The "benefit principle" will clearly not work since Government will never be in a position to assess the benefit of say a pollution-free environment to one individual as against another.

It is at this point that a vote by ballot substitutes for a vote cast by spending a pound. Depending upon the effectiveness of the political process it will be assumed that the decision of the majority is broadly in line with the wishes of all. It may also of course be argued that if the "political market" is imperfect or unresponsive to the electorate then this is not necessarily the case.

4. Social goods and public enterprise. In considering the allocative function of public finance we should be careful to distinguish between social goods for which collective provision is made and which may be supplied by privately or publicly owned enterprises and private goods which are offered on the market by publicly owned industries. In short, we must define the public sector.

5. The public sector. Certain characteristics distinguish the public sector from the private.

(a) In the public sector there is no relationship between the size of payment made (i.e. taxation) and the service received.

(b) There exists no direct link between any *particular* form of taxation and any *particular* expenditure in the public sector.

(c) Profitability governs the decision to produce in the private sector but not in the public sector.

6. The character of public enterprise. Into this clearcut separation of sectors must be fitted public enterprise. In the twentieth century the state has extended its economic interests, sometimes in competition with private enterprise, e.g. the BBC and the London Passenger Transport Board in the 1920s and, since the Second World War, the nationalised industries.

At this point the distinction between the sectors becomes blurred since public, like private enterprise caters for the wants of individual consumers as they are reflected through the price mechanism. It differs, at least in Britain, in that public corporations are enjoined only to cover their costs and not required to make trading profits. In the event that losses are incurred they may be met from taxation.

We may therefore conclude that public enterprise will be *excluded* from the scope of public finance in so far as pricing and output policy are determined on purely economic grounds in response to market forces. It will be *included* to the extent that social or political considerations over-ride the economic, making collective provision necessary, regardless of cost. This hazing of the frontiers of public finance is exemplified by the modern problem of railway adminstration. It is desired to support an adequate public service (if necessary from taxation) yet one which, if possible, pays its own way.

7. Exhaustive and transfer expenditure. Within the public sector, the state *directly* employs a vast number of people, e.g. teachers, doctors, soldiers, civil servants, policemen. *Indirectly*, as many again are employed in the private sector in the production of goods and services which will be purchased by the public sector for the satisfaction of collective wants, e.g. educational and hospital equipment and buildings, military supplies. Such expenditure may be termed "real" or "exhaustive" in the sense that resources are diverted from their free market use to that use determined by the state.

Distinct from this, "transfer expenditure" (e.g. pensions, family allowances) involves only the transfer of income from the taxpayer to the recipient who is then free to dispose of it in response to free market forces.

THE DISTRIBUTION FUNCTION

8. Determination of the distribution of income and wealth. Economic efficiency requires that in all economic systems the price of a factor of production should equate with the value of its marginal product (*see* V, **15**). This is to say that in the case of labour, for example, the wage paid should be governed by the value added to output by the last man employed.

In socialist societies factor pricing in this way may be solely for accounting purposes as a means of planning the most productive deployment of resources. *Actual* wages may differ (*see* II, **13**). Moreover, the return to capital and land will be retained by the state.

In market economies, depending upon the degree of perfect competition the actual return to the factors will be regulated by their marginal net productivity. Labour is heterogeneous. The return in different occupations will therefore reflect differences in education, training and skill.

These variations in wage and salary incomes will now be augmented by the distribution of capital income. In turn this is governed by the existing ownership of property including that acquired by inheritance.

The net result is likely to be that in unregulated market economies we will find substantial inequalities in income distribution. Society may wish to make adjustments.

9. Criteria for optimising distribution. Having decided that public policy should achieve some measure of redistribution, the question remains how much? Modern welfare economics sheds no light. It proceeds on the assumption that economic efficiency is improved if A is better off without B being worse off. While this approach is useful in evaluating the functioning of the market it is clearly of no assistance in establishing criteria for an optimal distribution.

We are therefore forced to the conclusion that the ideal distribution will reflect current social values and political pressures which themselves will have been conditioned by the existing state of income distribution.

However, it should be recognised that socially determined distributional objectives may have undesired economic results. In recent years in Britain there has been concern not only to improve the position of the lower income groups but to establish what are virtually income ceilings. Subsequently there has been further concern that in avoiding socially offensive inequalities, incentives to work, save and invest have been impaired.

10. Fiscal methods for reducing income inequalities. This may be achieved in two ways. A negative income tax will be progressive both positively and negatively. Income is transferred from those above a stated minimum to those below that level without disturbing the provision for social goods. Alternatively, progressive taxation may be used to finance an increased level of social goods whose benefits are enjoyed by all.

Secondly, general tax revenues may be used to finance social benefits in kind, e.g. free school meals, which are concentrated upon low income earners.

In addition to devices designed to reduce inequalities of existing income the attempt may be made to influence income earning potential through education, training and housing programmes, which aim to improve labour's quality and mobility.

THE STABILISATION FUNCTION

11. Is there a need for a stabilisation function? The conventional answer of the past thirty years has been that the state has a major responsibility in ironing out the fluctuations which lead to unemployment and stagnation on the one hand or inflation and balance of payments disequilibrium on the other. It would immediately be agreed that poorly conducted public policy will itself be a destabilising agent. What is currently more controversial is the view held by an increasing number of economists that the theoretical basis of stabilisation policies is invalid and that even were it not so the practical difficulties of short-term economic management are insuperable. We shall return to a detailed discussion of this controversy in Chapter XIII.

12. The problem defined. The levels of employment and prices are dependent upon the level of aggregate demand relative to productive capacity. The level of demand is a function of the spending decisions of millions of consumers and business investors. These decisions are in turn affected by present income and wealth, the availability of credit and business expectations. At any one time demand may be deficient to or in excess of full capacity output. When it is deficient, *in the absence of downward flexibility of wages and prices* unemployment will result. (It should however be noted that not all unemployment is caused in this way.) When it is excessive, inflation results.

The problem is complicated by international trade payments and capital flows. Without a wholly free exchange rate system there exists no mechanism for ensuring external balance. Any attempt at domestic stabilisation policy must therefore be coordinated with the need to achieve foreign balance.

In the 1960s stabilisation policy in Britain had to encompass a further objective, more rapid economic growth. Not only was demand to rise in line with expanding output, it was to be manipulated in order to accelerate that expansion.

13. The fiscal instruments of stabilisation. It will be appreciated that even if positive stabilisation policies were not to be pursued it would still be necessary to consider the effect upon demand of a neutral or balanced budget. It may however be the intention to use variations in the budget deliberately to offset variations in private sector demand.

Government expenditure on goods and services adds to final demand. When this expenditure is financed by taxation, although some existing private spending will be displaced, the net effect will be expansionary. The incidence of at least part of taxation will have been upon savings. Much more expansionary will be expenditure financed through borrowing, i.e. a budget deficit.

14. The monetary instruments of stabilisation. Fiscal policy operates directly upon aggregate demand either by varying the level of disposable private income or by varying public expenditure. It may therefore be thought to have a more immediate and precise effect than monetary policy, whose relationship to aggregate demand depends upon the cost and availability of credit.

For many years therefore, attempts at short-run demand management have emphasised the former rather than the latter. The principal role of monetary policy was conceived to be a structure of interest rates which influenced international capital flows in a way which would secure foreign balance.

The "monetarist controversy" of the 1960s and 1970s has redirected discussion to a more positive role for monetary policy as a stabilisation instrument. Briefly the case is that no attempt at "fine tuning" of aggregate demand should be made by either fiscal or monetary means. Since there exists a systematic but ill-understood link between the rate of monetary expansion and aggregate demand, for *long run* stability a reasonable but arbitrary rate of monetary growth should be declared. Market forces would then oblige the economy to adjust to this rate which would be sufficient to allow for real economic growth.

In practice however, there continues to be a high dependence upon fiscal policy for stabilisation purposes.

It may be guessed that in attempting to design a budget which simultaneously carries out the functions of allocation, distribution and stabilisation conflicts will arise.

BUDGET FUNCTIONS IN CONFLICT

15. Co-ordination of functions in theory. In theory, there is no obstacle to producing a compromise between conflicting objectives within a single budget.

On the assumption that distribution and stabilisation objectives will be achieved, an allocation budget will be designed which reflects consumer evaluation of social goods and the taxes which finance them. Secondly, a distribution budget which assumes that allocation and stabilisation aims are met utilises a system of progressive taxation and transfer payments to achieve the desired redistribution. By their nature, each of these budgets balances.

The stabilisation budget assumes that the other two goals have been achieved and then adjusts aggregate demand through taxes or payments. By its nature this budget will be in imbalance. Its taxes or transfers will be proportional to the taxes or transfers of the distribution budget so that the pattern of the latter is unaffected.

The three budgets are then cleared against each other, only the net taxes and transfers being implemented in a final combined budget.

While feasible in theory, in practice political considerations dictate that if one goal is achieved another is likely to be sacrificed.

16. Allocation and stabilisation functions in conflict. Keynesians have viewed variations in the level of public expenditure as the most direct means of controlling aggregate demand and hence recessions and periods of inflation. This course of action will obviously affect allocation, the supply of social goods. There will be an unwarranted shortfall in periods of rising price when spending is cut back. There will be a wasteful excess in attempting to spend one's way out of a recession.

In Britain the criticism has been made that recovery from recession has repeatedly resulted in more resources being directed to the public sector. Some recovery having been initiated, it was unsustainable since sufficient resources were now unavailable. In short, such policies have progressively brought about a fundamental structural imbalance in the economy, too few resources being devoted to industrial production in the private sector and too many to labour intensive service activities in the public sector.

It will be seen that this problem arises because of the use of methods which confuse the stabilisation and allocation functions.

17. Distribution and stabilisation functions in conflict. A similar situation arises. The propensity to spend of the lower income groups being greater than that of the higher income groups, tax reductions aimed at stimulating demand will be aimed at them. Conversely, in periods of inflation they will bear the brunt of tax increases designed to cut demand.

In this case the stabilisation and distribution functions are confused.

18. Allocation and distribution functions in conflict. Although attained in some measure through taxation and transfer payments the main thrust of redistribution comes through the provision of social goods financed by progressive taxation, i.e. the better off carrying the greater burden. When such provision was small-scale there existed a powerful redistributive effect and the allocation and distribution functions were harmonised.

In Britain, in 1977, this is certainly no longer the case. The huge extension of social provision not only for welfare goods, but in the subsidisation of transport, car manufacture, shipbuilding, etc., has been accompanied by much heavier taxation of even the very low income groups. The redistributional effect has therefore been reversed.

19. Conclusion. In *Part One* we have examined the changing economic role of the state, the contrasting types of system by which we might seek to solve the economic problem and the compromise in Britain of a mixed economy established largely through an extension of the scope and functions of public finance.

In *Part Two* we shall analyse the operation of a free market economy drawing conclusions on the effectiveness with which the price mechanism allocates resources and achieves a desirable pattern of distribution.

In the light of this analysis *Part Three* will consider taxation and expenditure as means of improving both allocation and distribution.

In *Part Four* we shall deal with the stabilisation function of public finance adopting the conventional theory of the past thirty years. We shall then subject that theory to the criticisms which have developed particularly strongly in the 1970s.

PROGRESS TEST 3

1. Distinguish between private and social goods. **(1)**
2. What do you understand by "the political market"? **(3)**
3. Give a precise definition of the public sector. **(5)**
4. Explain the difficulty of characterising public enterprise. **(6)**
5. Why are there likely to be substantial inequalities of income distribution in unregulated market economies? **(8)**
6. What basic fiscal methods may be used to reduce income inequalities? **(10)**

7. Is there a need for a stabilisation function? **(11)**

8. What are the three basic objectives of the stabilisation function? **(12)**

9. Explain in general terms the nature of the fiscal and monetary instruments of stabilisation. **(13, 14)**

10. Give examples of how the various budget functions may conflict with each other. **(15–18)**

PART TWO

PRICE ANALYSIS

CHAPTER IV

Demand, Supply and Price Relationships

DEMAND AND SUPPLY DETERMINE PRICE

1. The problem of value. A problem of value was apparent to the economists of the nineteenth century, but the theories which they devised were concerned with long-run tendencies towards a natural or inherent value as distinct from day-to-day fluctuations. They saw two aspects to the problem:

(*a*) *The paradox of value.* Frequently those things which are most useful have least value in exchange, and vice-versa, e.g. water and diamonds.

(*b*) *A stable measure of value* which would remain constant through time. Clearly this was not money, since money's own value varied.

2. The labour theory of value. Adam Smith sought to solve these problems first distinguishing between value in use and value in exchange, i.e. price. He thought this distinction necessary to account for the "paradox of value" since value in exchange would be determined by principles different from those governing value in use.

Differences of value in exchange were to be explained by the differing amounts of labour necessary to their production. It was natural that an article requiring two day's labour should therefore be twice the price of one requiring only a day's labour. Diamonds involved considerable labour in their production and were therefore costlier than water.

This explanation also seemed to solve the problem of stable, long-term value, since a day's labour was the same, irrespective of when it was performed.

The theory was happily accepted by Marx and the "scientific socialists" to prove that the entire fruits of production were due to labour which was the sole creator of value.

3. Criticisms of this theory. Unfortunately, it is not so simple.

(a) An article which fulfils no need will have no value in exchange, irrespective of how much labour has been involved, i.e. the theory takes no account of demand.

(b) Even from the side of supply, the theory gives only a partial explanation. Labour is certainly in limited supply and it is true that value is often related to it, since in many cases the goods which are scarcest require most labour to produce. However, the key factor is scarcity and the other factors of production, land and capital, are equally in scarce supply.

4. The cost of production theory. The "labour theory" was refined by John Stuart Mill into a "cost of production theory", which is more complete in that it takes account not only of labour costs but also of the costs of land and capital and a profit return to the entrepreneur. Once again, however, price is approached from the side of supply alone and the theory is incomplete. The following criticisms are made:

(a) There is no single cost of production for any product. It varies with output. Output, however, varies with demand and therefore cost of production and price must in some way be related to demand.

(b) Where there is monopoly, there is no necessary close relationship with cost of production but demand must be considered.

(c) The theory can only explain incompletely the influence of supply, since if a firm is producing several commodities, how are overhead costs to be assigned between them?

5. The influence of demand. We may conclude that no theory of value can be complete unless it takes account both of supply and of demand.

(a) *In the short period*, demand will be the dominant influence since once an article has been offered for sale in a competitive market, the supply is fixed and cost of production will have no bearing upon price.

(b) *In the long period*, however, sales cannot continue to be made below cost of production and supply will react accordingly to become the dominant influence.

6. Definitions. We should now attempt to clarify the terms which we have used.

(*a*) *Demand* is the quantity of a commodity which a consumer is prepared and able to buy *at a given price*.

(*b*) *Supply* is the quantity of a commodity which a producer is prepared to offer for sale *at a given price*.

(*c*) *At a given price*. This phrase is vitally important. It is impossible to speak of demand or supply without presupposing a given price since demand and supply will react to price changes. We should therefore be careful to remember that:

(*i*) Demand and supply determine price and a change in one or the other will produce a change in price.

(*ii*) Demand and supply are conditioned *by* price. A change in price will affect them both.

The first part of this problem will be dealt with next.

THE EQUILIBRIUM PRICE

7. Demand schedules and curves. Demand may be illustrated statistically or graphically.

(*a*) *Individual demand schedules*. If the necessary statistical information was available, we could draw schedules for each prospective buyer in a particular market in order to illustrate his *present* attitude to a product. In the normal way, we should expect that the lower the price, the more he would be willing to purchase, e.g. Table II.

TABLE II.   INDIVIDUAL DEMAND SCHEDULE

Price per unit	Demand per week
£5	1
£4	2
£3	3
£2	4
£1	5

(*b*) *Composite demand schedules*. Theoretically, we could combine all the information derived from individual demand schedules to give us a composite demand schedule to cover all the prospective buyers in a particular market.

(*c*) *Demand curves*. The same information may be represented graphically as in Fig. 4. With price per unit on the vertical scale

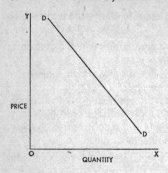

Fig. 4.—*Demand curve.* A demand curve DD of even slope which illustrates a regular and continuous increase in the quantity bought in response to a regular and continuous fall in price. In practice it is unlikely that the curve will slope evenly throughout its length since the sensitivity of demand will vary at different price levels.

and quantity bought on the horizontal scale, the declining demand curve illustrates how there will be an even and continuous increase in the quantity bought in response to an even and continuous fall in price.

NOTE: The conventional symbols are used in the diagram.

(*d*) *Exceptional demand.* In exceptional circumstances, the demand curve may slope upwards over part of its length, i.e. within certain price ranges, the higher the price, the greater the quantity which will be bought. This may occur for the following reasons:

(*i*) *Snob appeal.* Certain things such as jewellery may derive attraction from their high price since they distinguish the purchaser from other people.

(*ii*) *An anticipated further price rise.* If the price of a commodity appears to be rising continuously more may be bought now in anticipation of a further rise.

(*iii*) *Staple purchases of low income groups.* Where there occurs a rise in the price of any staple purchases of low income groups, their capacity to buy luxuries is diminished. They may then substitute a greater volume of the relatively cheaper goods.

8. Supply schedules and curves. Supply, as we have defined it, means the quantity of a commodity which will be drawn on to the market at a given price. We should expect that the higher the price available, the greater will be the quantity suppliers will offer for sale. To illustrate this, we may draw supply schedules for individual firms and then combine the results to give a composite supply schedule, as in Table III.

TABLE III.   COMPOSITE SUPPLY SCHEDULE

Price per unit	Quantity offered for sale per week
£1	100
£2	200
£3	300
£4	400
£5	500

Once again the same information may be presented graphically in the form of a supply curve (Fig. 5). We see that an even and continuous rise in price produces an even and continuous increase in the quantity offered for sale.

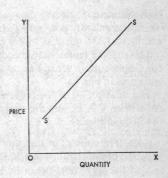

FIG. 5.—*Supply curve*. A supply curve SS of even slope which illustrates a regular and continuous increase in the quantity offered for sale in response to a regular and continuous rise in price. In practice it is unlikely that the curve will slope evenly throughout its length since like demand, the sensitivity of supply will vary at different price levels.

9. Exceptional supply curves. There are certain exceptional conditions of supply. These are:

(*a*) *Fixed supply*. Normally, the supply curve may be expected to slope upwards from left to right but in certain circumstances it may be vertical, indicating that whatever the price available, supply remains unchanged. This will be so, for example, when the item is unique, e.g. a painting. It will also commonly be the case for most things *in the short period*, i.e. there will be a delay before supply can respond fully to a higher price.

(*b*) *Regressive supply*. Within certain price ranges the supply curve may even slope backwards, telling us that a higher price will call forth a smaller supply, e.g. the labour market where a higher wage may cause the number of hours worked to diminish.

10. The equation of demand and supply. Demand and supply are

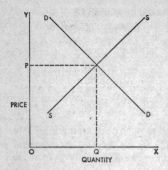

FIG. 6.—*Equilibrium price*. The intersection of the demand curve DD and the supply curve SS is the point at which price OP establishes equilibrium in the market. At that price buyers are prepared to purchase and sellers to supply a quantity OQ. At no other price are the interests of buyers and sellers harmonised.

brought into harmony by the *equilibrium price*. This is the price at which the quantity consumers are prepared to purchase equates exactly with the quantity sellers are prepared to offer for sale.

This may be represented by combining composite demand and composite supply schedules or by utilising demand and supply curves, as in Fig. 6.

The intersection of the two curves is the point of equilibrium. At a price OP, buyers are prepared to purchase and suppliers to sell quantity OQ.

NOTE: The concept of the equilibrium price suggests a sufficient period of time to allow market forces to produce harmony.

In the very short period, a price may be struck which does not represent the long-term position of demand and supply since there has been insufficient time for full adjustment.

CHANGES IN THE CONDITIONS OF DEMAND AND SUPPLY

11. Changes in the conditions of demand. It is necessary to distinguish between a change in demand which results *from* a change in price and a change which occurs in consequence of changing external conditions and which will have an effect *upon* price, e.g. the consumer may be prepared to buy more or fewer eggs because of a price change or because of a change in his valuation of eggs.

To avoid confusion, it is better to employ the terms "*an extension or a contraction of demand*" for the first case in which there is implied a movement along the *same* demand curve (*see* **21**). For the second case, the terms *"an increase or a decrease in demand"* will be used and here the construction of a new demand curve is made necessary.

EXAMPLE 1. *A general increase or decrease in demand*

Curve DD in Fig. 7 represents the original state of demand. A change in the consumer's valuation of the commodity produces an increase in demand and this necessitates the construction of a new curve to the *right* at D_1D_1. This tells us that at *any* given price, the consumer is prepared to buy more than previously, e.g. at price OP, originally quantity OQ would be bought, but now the quantity will be OQ_1.

A decrease in demand will produce a new demand curve to the *left* at D_2D_2. At price OP, a smaller quantity OQ_2 will now be bought.

EXAMPLE 2. *A partial increase or decrease in demand*

A change in the conditions of demand will not of necessity affect the whole length of the demand curve. In Fig. 8, in the higher price range demand has been unaffected by changed conditions.

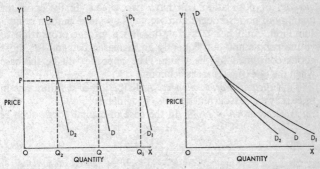

FIG. 7.—*A general increase or decrease in demand*

FIG. 8.—*A partial increase or decrease in demand*

12. The causes of changing conditions of demand. The consumer may be caused to re-value a commodity for a number of reasons.

(*a*) *Changing tastes.* Public taste is difficult to explain but in an age of high pressure selling, advertising is a major formative influence. Similarly, widespread publicity of an adverse character will affect public taste. The phrase "educating public taste" is sometimes heard and there is no doubt that education does exercise a long-term influence. Fashions, however, may run an entirely unpredictable course, some capturing the imagination and causing an increase in demand while others are never wholly accepted.

(*b*) *Changes in purchasing power.* A change in money wages, the availability of credit or the general level of prices will affect the consumer's purchasing power and this is likely to influence him to purchase more or less of certain goods. If his real purchasing power is increased, he will probably buy more luxuries and vice-versa.

(*c*) *Taxation.* Taxes may serve to:

(*i*) *Re-distribute incomes* in such a way that the capacity of the rich to save is reduced while the capacity of the poor to spend is increased *or* vice-versa.

(*ii*) *Restrict consumption,* e.g. a 10% surcharge designed to decrease demand for imports.

(*d*) *Obsolescence.* Economic progress necessitates change and new goods are constantly replacing old, e.g. the demand for coal decreases while the demand for electricity increases.

(*e*) *Changes in size and structure of population.* A rising *rate of increase* of population will have two effects, firstly upon the quantity of goods bought and secondly upon the pattern of consumption. A higher birth rate implies a greater proportion of young people and consequently an increased demand for those goods consumed by the young. The opposite will be the case when the rate of increase is declining.

(*f*) *Anticipated price changes.* Anticipation of a future rise in price may cause a current increase in demand.

(*g*) *Expectation of profit.* In the case of capital goods such as

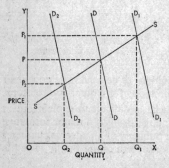

FIG. 9. —*Changed conditions of demand.* When the conditions of supply remain unchanged but demand is increased, the demand curve DD will move to D_1D_1 to establish a fresh market equilibrium at the higher price OP_1. Conversely if demand is decreased the curve moves to the left to D_2D_2 and equilibrium is reached at the lower price OP_2.

machinery, the businessman's demand will be governed by his expectation of profit from further investment.

13. The effects of changed conditions of demand.

The effects of fluctuating conditions of demand can be shown graphically, as in Fig. 9.

The original equilibrium lies at the intersection of the demand curve, DD, and the supply curve, SS, quantity OQ being bought at the price OP. The conditions of supply remaining unchanged, an increase in demand will cause the demand curve to move to the *right*. A fresh equilibrium is reached at the intersection of D_1D_1 and SS. A greater quantity, OQ_1, is now bought at the higher price, OP_1.

Conversely, a decrease in demand will cause the demand curve to move to the *left* to D_2D_2. A new equilibrium is reached at the point where this curve intersects SS. In this position, a smaller quantity, OQ_2, is sold at a lower price, OP_2.

14. Changes in the conditions of supply.

As with demand, it is necessary to distinguish between a change which *results from* a change in price and one which occurs because of a change in external conditions and which *brings about* a change in price. As before, it is preferable to employ the terms "an extension or a contraction of supply" to denote a movement along the *same* supply curve in response to a price change, and to reserve the terms " an increase or a decrease in supply" to mean a change in the quantity which will be offered for sale *at any given price*, as is shown in the example given in Fig. 10 below.

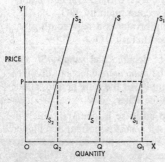

FIG. 10.—*A general increase or decrease in supply*

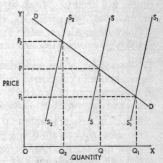

FIG. 11.—*Changed conditions of supply*

An *increase* in supply will cause a movement from SS to the *right* to S_1S_1. Now, at price OP, for example, whereas OQ was previously supplied, the quantity is now OQ_1.

A *decrease* in supply will produce a fresh curve to the *left* at S_2S_2. At price OP, the smaller quantity OQ_2 will now be supplied.

15. The causes of changed conditions of supply. Changes in the quantity which a producer is prepared to supply at a given price will be governed by:

(*a*) *Changes in the cost of production.* This may result either from a change in the price the businessman pays for land, labour or capital or from a change in the productivity of these factors; e.g. a wage increase will raise costs and decrease supply; conversely a more economical use of labour or the introduction of a more advanced machine may lower costs and increase supply.

(*b*) *Taxation.* Where the tax is borne wholly by the producer and cannot be passed on, it is equivalent to a cost of production. A higher tax will therefore decrease supply and vice-versa.

(*c*) *Natural causes.* With certain primary products, supply is governed largely by unpredictable natural factors, e.g. a good harvest resulting from a spell of good weather.

16. The effects of changed conditions of supply. Figure. 11 shows how the market equilibrium is affected by changes in supply.

The original equilibrium lies at the intersection of the demand curve DD, and the supply curve, SS. Assuming in this case that the conditions of demand remain unchanged, an increase in supply will produce a fresh supply curve, S_1S_1, and a new equilibrium at the lower price, OP_1, and greater quantity, OQ_1.

Conversely, a decrease in supply produces a new equilibrium at the higher price, OP_2, and smaller quantity, OQ_2.

17. Interaction of the conditions of demand and supply. So far, there have been considered only the *immediate* effects of changes in the conditions of demand or supply. In the long period, changes in one may produce changes in the other.

EXAMPLE. It is probable that an increase in demand which in the short period results in a greater quantity bought at a higher price may in the long period enable a firm to reduce costs through the economies of large-scale production. This may then result in a still greater quantity being bought at a much lower price.

FIG. 12.—*Interaction of the con-*
ditions of demand and supply.
When quantity OQ is sold,
demand and supply are harmonised at a price OP. A *general*
increase in demand moves the
demand curve DD to the right
to D_1D_1 to establish a fresh
short-term equilibrium at price
OP_1 and quantity OQ_1. In the
longer period the lower costs of
production which are now possible move the supply curve to
the right to S_1S_1 where equilibrium is ultimately established
at price OP_2 and quantity OQ_2.

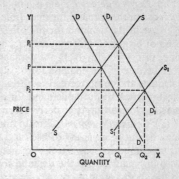

In Fig. 12, at the original equilibrium OQ is bought at a price
OP. An increase in demand produces, in the short period, a
new equilibrium in which OQ_1 is bought at a price of OP_1. In
the long period, economies of large-scale production facilitate
lower costs and an equilibrium is ultimately reached in which
OQ_2 is bought at a price OP_2.

**18. Interaction of the conditions of demand for different commodi-
ties.** We have seen that a change in the conditions of demand may
produce a change in the conditions of supply and vice-versa. In a
similar way, it is not uncommonly the case that a change in the
conditions of demand or supply for *one* product will affect the
conditions of demands or supply for *another* product. The
commonest relationships may be analysed as follows:

(*a*) *Joint demand.* Certain commodities are complementary to
each other and an increase or decrease in the demand for one is
likely to be accompanied by a corresponding change in the demand for the other, e.g. knives and forks; needles and thread.
The change in demand is *likely*, but not necessarily, to be of the
same proportion in each case.

The effects upon price will now depend upon the conditions
of supply for each commodity, i.e. whether the supply curve
slopes steeply or gradually.

(*b*) *Competing demand.* Two commodities may compete with
each other in such a way that an *increase* in the demand for one
will lead to a decrease in the demand for the other, e.g. electricity
and coal. The more easily one substitutes for the other, the more
powerful will be the effect.

(*c*) *Derived demand.* This is similar to joint demand in that an *increase* in the demand for one commodity is accompanied by an *increase* in the demand for the other. It differs in that the goods are not produced independently of one another. The demand for one springs directly from the demand for the other. It will therefore be true of the demand for most raw materials, semi-finished products and components, e.g. the demand for raw wool and wool cloth derives from the demand for clothing and furnishings; the demand for carburettors derives from the demand for motor cars.

(*d*) *Composite demand.* Certain things, especially raw materials, may be put to a variety of uses and the demand for them is said to be composite, e.g. sheet steel may be used for motor cars or washing machines. If the demand for motor cars increases, then in the short period there may be a rise in the price of sheet steel which washing machine manufacturers will also have to pay.

19. Interaction of the conditions of supply for different commodities. This may be considered under two heads:

(*a*) *Joint supply.* It may be impossible to increase the supply of one commodity without simultaneously increasing the supply of others, e.g. an increase in the supply of petrol implies an increase in the supply of fuel oil and vice-versa. The increase will not of necessity be of the same proportion in each case. The independence with which each supply responds will often be a question of technology.

(*b*) *Competitive supply.* In the broadest sense, it may be said that all things are in competitive supply with each other. If the nation builds more ships, then it leaves itself with fewer resources to build more aeroplanes. In certain cases, however, the competition is particularly marked, e.g. the supply of dwelling houses is in competition with the supply of commercial buildings since the country's available building resources, especially land, are strictly limited.

ELASTICITY

20. Definition. Having examined the way in which demand and supply interact to determine price, it is necessary to turn to the second aspect of this relationship in order to see how price influences demand and supply (*see* **11**). This aspect is referred to as the *elasticity of demand or supply* and may be defined as the responsiveness of demand or supply to a change in price.

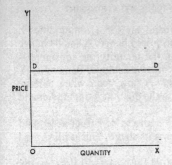

FIG. 13.—*Perfectly elastic demand*. At a given price an infinite quantity will be bought.

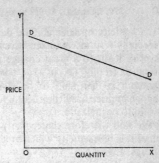

FIG. 14.—*Elastic demand*. A curve of moderate and uniform elasticity.

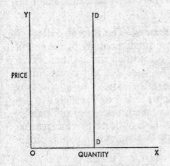

FIG. 15.—*Perfectly inelastic demand*. The other limiting case where the same quantity is bought irrespective of price.

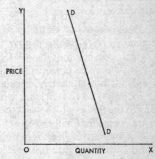

FIG. 16.—*Inelastic demand*. A curve of moderate and uniform inelasticity.

FIG. 17.—*Varying elasticity of demand*. In practice it is more likely that the slope of the curve will vary at different price levels.

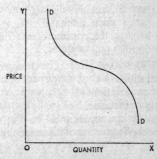

21. Elasticity of demand. The demand for some commodities is especially responsive or sensitive to price change. A small change in price leads to a great change in the quantity the consumer is prepared to buy, i.e. an *extension* or *contraction* of demand (**11**). Demand is then said to be elastic. Conversely, when a large change in price has little effect upon the quantity bought, demand is said to be inelastic.

We find therefore that when we come to construct a demand curve it is its elasticity which governs its shape. This is illustrated in Figs. 13 to 17.

In practice, it is highly unlikely that the curve will slope evenly throughout its length. Elasticity is likely to vary within different price ranges.

In Fig. 17, the curve illustrates a demand which is inelastic at high prices, elastic within the middle price range and again inelastic at very low prices.

22. Determinants of elasticity of demand. The responsiveness of demand to price change is governed fundamentally by the extent to which one commodity will be substituted for another. For a variety of reasons considered below, substitution may be simple or difficult but ultimately, because of the limitations imposed by our incomes, *all* those things which we do not consume are options to the things which we do consume. If price rises sufficiently, we are *compelled* finally to exercise these options. For this reason, the demand curve which is perfectly inelastic throughout is purely hypothetical (*see* Fig. 15).

(*a*) *Presence of similar commodities.* Substitution will be greatly facilitated by the presence of similar commodities and demand will be correspondingly elastic (e.g. carrots and peas). On the other hand, if there is no feasible alternative, then demand will be inelastic (e.g. petrol).

NOTE: Demand will only remain inelastic within a certain price range since ultimately, if petrol prices reach astronomical heights, the consumer sells his car and for petrol substitutes another pair of shoes.

(*b*) *Income group.* The man with a large income is unlikely to substitute one commodity for another as a result of a price change. Price variations are relatively unimportant to him and his demand will be inelastic. Not so the man with a low income whose demand will be elastic. He must be that much more careful to make the most effective use of his limited resources.

(c) *Necessity.* Certain things not only have no close substitute but also are essential to our wellbeing (e.g. salt). It is likely therefore that our purchases will be governed by our basic needs, price exercising little influence, i.e. demand will be inelastic. In general, it is easier to substitute or forgo goods in the luxury class. We shall therefore expect demand to be more elastic.

(d) *Habit and prejudice.* There exists a certain rigidity in the pattern of consumer expenditure, the product of habit and prejudice. To the extent therefore that irrationally we are *unwilling* to substitute, demand will be inelastic. We may observe that this will quite commonly be the case in the short period of time before the consumer has fully adjusted his purchases to the new price.

(e) *Age group.* Generally, demand becomes more inelastic with advancing age since both the capacity and the willingness to substitute diminish. Many things which for the young are luxuries may be necessities to the elderly (e.g. electric blankets). Habit, too, is likely to be more deeply ingrained.

23. Relevance of elasticity of demand to taxation.

Whether a tax which is borne wholly by the consumer serves principally to yield revenue or to restrict consumption depends upon the elasticity of demand. This is shown in the following examples, illustrated in Figs. 18 and 19.

EXAMPLE 1. *Inelastic demand*
Before tax, a quantity OQ is sold at a price OP. A tax, PP_1, is imposed. Consumption contracts only slightly to OQ_1, but a considerable revenue, shown by the shaded area, is produced.

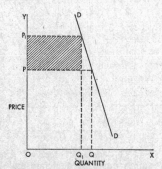

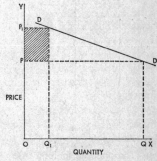

FIG. 18.—*Inelastic demand and taxation*   FIG. 19.—*Elastic demand and taxation*

EXAMPLE 2. *Elastic demand*

The result for a commodity in elastic demand is quite different. The imposition of a tax, PP_1, results in a considerable contraction of demand from OQ to OQ_1, while the revenue yield is very small.

24. Elasticity of supply. The sensitivity of supply to price change appears in the shape of the supply curve. With some goods, a

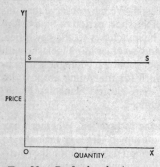

FIG. 20.—*Perfectly elastic supply*. The limiting case where at a particular price an infinite quantity is offered for sale.

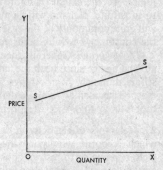

FIG. 21.—*Elastic supply*. A supply curve of moderate and uniform elasticity

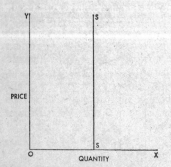

FIG. 22.—*Perfectly inelastic supply*. The opposite limiting case where supply will not respond to any increase in price.

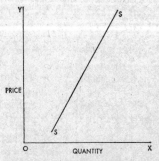

FIG. 23.—*Inelastic supply*. A supply curve of moderate and uniform inelasticity.

small rise in price may call forth a considerable extension of supply which is then said to be elastic. In other cases, a big increase in price may have little effect upon supply which is described as inelastic.

Figures 20 to 23 shows how supply curves of varying elasticity respond to increases in price.

Where supply is elastic, an increase in demand will cause only a small increase in price but a big extension of supply. Where supply is inelastic, an increase in demand will cause a big rise in price but only a small extension of supply.

NOTE: As with the demand curve, a supply curve in practice is unlikely to have an even slope. It may be elastic within certain price ranges and inelastic within others.

25. Determinants of elasticity of supply.

The ease with which supply can respond to price change depends upon a number of considerations, but in general it may be said that in the short period, the supply of all things tends to be inelastic. There will be a time lag before supply is able to readjust to the new price. The longer the period, the more elastic supply will be.

(a) *Natural factors.* Certain primary products, in particular rare minerals, are in fixed supply and it is impossible to increase their output more than marginally. Others, notably those of agriculture, are in large measure dependent upon the hazards of the weather and a higher price will not inevitably produce an extension of supply. In any case, there is likely to be a considerable time lag before additional crops can be produced.

(b) *Flexibility of industry.* In general, the supply of manufacturing industry will be more elastic but there will be considerable variations. Where an industry makes use of a high proportion of fixed capital (machinery, etc.), readjustment will be difficult, whether to a higher or lower level of output. In the long period, however, a rise in price will draw new firms into the industry while existing firms extend their output. A fall in price will have the opposite effect, driving some firms out and causing the remainder to contract.

PROGRESS TEST 4

1. What do you understand by the "paradox of value"?   (**1** (*a*))
2. For what reasons does a labour theory of value give only a partial explanation of price?   (**2–4**)

3. Explain the influence of demand upon price.   (5)

4. Give precise definitions of demand and supply.   (6)

5. Draw and explain an "exceptional demand curve".   (7 (d))

6. Draw and explain a "regressive supply curve".   (9 (b))

7. Illustrate the concept of the equilibrium price.   (10)

8. Distinguish between an increase in demand and an extension of demand.   (11)

9. Illustrate a partial decrease in demand.   (11)

10. Account for an increase in demand.   (12)

11. Illustrate the effect upon price of an increase in demand (13)

12. Illustrate a decrease in supply.   (14)

13. Account for a decrease in supply.   (15)

14. Illustrate the effect upon price of a decrease in supply.   (16)

15. Illustrate the effect upon price of a decrease in demand and a decrease in supply.   (17)

16. Distinguish between joint demand, competing demand, derived demand and composite demand.   (18)

17. Distinguish between joint and competitive supply.   (19)

18. Define the term "elasticity of demand".   (20)

19. Illustrate a perfectly inelastic demand curve.   (21)

20. What is the fundamental determinant of elasticity of demand?   (22)

21. Illustrate a situation in which a Chancellor of the Exchequer may accurately predict a tax yield.   (23)

22. What factors govern the elasticity of supply?   (25)

CHAPTER V

Marginal Analysis

1. Introduction. The preceding chapter dealt with the interaction of demand and supply and their determination of price. Price itself was also seen to play an important part in determining the nature of demand and supply, but clearly it is not the only factor. The demand curves sloped downwards from left to right and it was accepted that the consumer would buy more but only if the price was lower. The consumer's reaction has now to be explained. On the other hand, the supply curves sloped upwards from left to right indicating that at a higher price the supplier would be induced to extend his output. This reaction, too, requires further explanation.

2. The margin. An analytical tool, *the margin*, was developed by the mathematical school of economists of the late nineteenth century and subsequently has had many applications. Its use here is necessary to explain the base upon which demand and supply rest.

THE FOUNDATIONS OF DEMAND

3. The theory of demand. This rests upon three premises which are explained in subsequent paragraphs:

   (*a*) The Law of Diminishing Utility.

   (*b*) The concept of the margin of consumption.

   (*c*) A distinction drawn between total utility and marginal utility.

4. The Law of Diminishing Utility. Before explaining this law, it is first necessary to define the "utility" of the economist.

   (*a*) *Utility.* The word "utility" when used in a specifically economic context means the power of a unit of a commodity to satisfy a human want at a given point in time. It is therefore not to be confused with the word's everyday meaning of "usefulness". To have utility, a commodity may or may not be useful, but it must *yield satisfaction*. This interpretation leads to three observations:

(*i*) Utility is a purely subjective concept and no commodity will yield precisely the same utility to two different individuals.

(*ii*) Even to the same individual, the utility yielded by a unit of the commodity will not be the same at different points in time.

(*iii*) In assessing utility, no moral judgement is made. A thing may be considered socially undesirable yet have high utility if it has a great power to satisfy a human want.

(*b*) *Utility diminishes with the quantity already possessed.* It is a psychological generalisation that the more we have of a commodity, the less highly we prize additional units of it. To a man dying of thirst, a glass of water will have a very high utility. A second glass will yield rather less utility and a third still less.

The Law of Diminishing Utility therefore asserts that *additional units of consumption yield utility at a diminishing rate.*

5. The margin of consumption. Utility is a quality and like happiness cannot be measured. If it is supposed for a moment that measurement *is* possible, then a curve could be constructed to illustrate the operation of the Law of Diminishing Utility, as in Fig. 24.

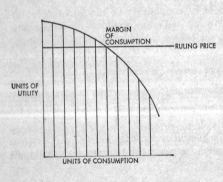

Fig. 24.—*Margin of consumption.* Additional units of consumption yield progressively less utility. This is illustrated by a declining utility curve. If a ruling price is assumed and is illustrated by a horizontal straight line, at its intersection with the utility curve will lie the margin of consumption.

The curve is *likely* to be concave since with every additional unit consumed, the utility yielded diminishes more than proportionately. If a ruling market price is assumed, then there will be a point at which the consumer hesitates to make one more purchase. The margin of consumption is therefore the line which separates those purchases which are considered worth while from those which are not, *at a given price*, i.e. it is not a fixed margin but one which moves inwards as price rises and outwards as price falls.

It may also be seen as the *margin of transference* since it is the point at which, by transferring expenditure to other commodities, a higher yield of utility may be enjoyed from the whole range of purchases.

6. Distinction between total utility and marginal utility. It will be observed from Fig. 24 that while the utility yielded by additional units diminishes, that yielded by the whole supply (total utility) increases with further consumption. Total utility is shown by the whole area below the curve. However, it is not total utility which exerts pressure upon price but the utility yielded by the unit at the margin of consumption, viz, *marginal utility*. In other words, from the side of demand, price is determined by the value we set upon the least significant unit of consumption.

The "paradox of value" which puzzled the classical economists (*see* IV, **1** (*a*)) is now explained. Water is consumed in very large quantities and while its total utility is very high, its marginal utility and hence its price is low. Diamonds are available in only small quantities and yield a low total utility but a high marginal utility. Their price is correspondingly high.

7. The relationship of demand schedules and diminishing utility. It is now possible to see the psychological basis for demand schedules and the reason why demand curves slope from left to right. As the margin of consumption is pushed outwards, so the utility yielded by additional units diminishes. The price we are willing to pay falls accordingly, since we will not pay more than our assessment of the money value of marginal utility.

8. Consumer's surplus. Price is determined at the margin of consumption by the value we set upon the least significant unit. However, since all units are interchangeable, this is the price paid not solely for the marginal unit but for the whole supply. If for any reason supply had been restricted, a higher price would have been paid since a higher value is set upon infra-marginal units. Since a lower price is in fact paid, a surplus utility is enjoyed. This is described as a *consumer's surplus*. It is shown in Fig. 24 by the area below the curve and above the ruling price.

9. Equi-marginal utility. Every consumer will instinctively attempt to allocate his expenditure between different purchases in such a way that his total satisfaction is maximised. He will not spend £3 on another shirt if for £3 he can enjoy greater utility from the consumption of a pair of shoes. In short, he will aim for a position in which the marginal utilities derived from each line of expenditure are equal. This is a position of *equi-marginal utility*.

10. Some weaknesses of the marginal utility theory. Certain criticisms have been levelled against this theory; these are discussed below and in the next paragraph.

(*a*) *Irrational expenditure.* The economist works upon the assumption that men always behave rationally and will therefore carefully consider the diminishing marginal utility yielded by successive units of consumption. This view makes no allowance for the purchase made through habit or impulse.

(*b*) *Divisible commodities.* The theory also assumes that we can add to our satisfactions by purchasing quantities of the commodity. In fact, many consumer durables, to mention but one category of goods, are not at all divisible, e.g. a house.

(*c*) *Increasing marginal utility.* There are occasions on which marginal utility in fact *increases*. This will be so in cases of addiction or where a collection is being made. It must therefore be remembered that while the Law of Diminishing Utility is generally true, there are many exceptional circumstances.

11. The problem of measuring qualities. The principal criticism of the marginal utility theory must be levelled against the terms in which the theory is conceived. Implicit in the concept of equating marginal utility with price is the idea that utility, a quality, is capable of objective measurement (e.g. that an article purchased for £1 yields £1 of utility). In fact, the only way of estimating the satisfaction yielded by one form of consumption is by comparing it with that yielded by another. Alfred Marshall made this plain when he claimed that "value is relative and expresses the relation between two things at a particular place and time". In the process of consumption, we make a choice between alternatives and, in so doing, exercise our personal scale of preferences. (In our previous terminology, this is a scale of marginal utilities.) The prices we are prepared to pay for two commodities establishes an exchange relationship between them which reflects our scale of preferences.

This last criticism has led to a re-statement of the theory of demand in terms of the *marginal rate of substitution*, i.e. the rate at which, at the margin of consumption, we are prepared to substitute units of one commodity for units of another. (For an account of this theory, the student is referred to J. L. Hanson's *A Textbook of Economics*, pp. 219–20.)

THE FOUNDATIONS OF SUPPLY IN PERFECT COMPETITION

12. Marginal cost. In order to determine the relationship between supply and price, the principles which govern the output policy of the individual firm must be established. It has been seen that from the side of demand it is *marginal* utility and not *total* utility which governs price. Similarly, from the side of supply, it is not *total* cost but *marginal* cost which determines how much will be offered for sale at any given price.

13. Cost curves. There is no single cost of production. Average cost per unit of output will decline while economies are made through increasing the scale of production. They will increase once these economies have been exhausted. Moreover, the various elements which enter into average total cost will react in differing degrees to changes in output.

(*a*) *Average fixed cost.* Fixed costs include investment in premises and plant, administration and various other "overheads"

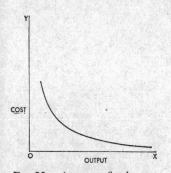

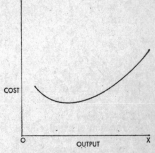

FIG. 25.—*Average fixed cost curve.* Fixed cost when borne by one unit of output alone will cause the curve to start at a high level. When averaged over an increasing output it will fall steeply at first and then more gradually.

FIG. 26.—*Average variable cost curve.* Successive units of output will at first cause the curve to fall owing to the economies which result from a larger scale of production. When these economies are exhausted the curve rises.

which remain unchanged in total amount irrespective of output. When averaged over an increasing output, the curve will fall steeply at first and then decline more gradually to infinity, as in Fig. 25.

(b) *Average variable cost.* By definition, these are costs which vary with output and include wages, raw materials and power. Extension of output will at first produce economies of scale but ultimately, average variable cost per unit will begin progressively to rise (*see* Fig. 26).

(c) *Average total cost.* Average total cost per unit will decline more steeply and rise less steeply than average variable costs, under the influence of fixed costs being averaged over a greater output. This is illustrated in Fig. 27.

(d) *Marginal cost in relation to average total cost.* Marginal cost is the addition to total cost of one more unit of output. As long as marginal cost remains below average total cost per unit for that output, it will pull down the average. When it rises above the average, it will pull up the average, i.e. the two curves intersect at the point of minimal average total cost (*see* Fig. 28).

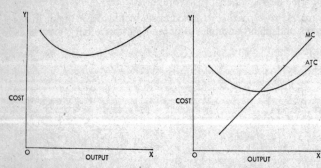

Fig. 27.—*Average total cost curve*. The sum of average fixed and average variable cost gives average total cost.

Fig. 28.—*Marginal cost in relation to average total cost*. MC intersects ATC at the latter's lowest point.

14. Degree of competition. When examining the influence of demand upon price, highly competitive market conditions were considered axiomatic since it is rarely the case that buyers are able deliberately to influence price by boycotting the market. Amongst producers, however, the degree of competition varies very considerably and it is necessary to allow for the differing behaviour of supply curves in conditions of perfect competition, monopoly and imperfect competition (*see* II, **20–25**). To begin with, a model is constructed of firms producing in conditions of perfect competition.

15. The firm in perfect competition. The individual firm is faced with a demand curve which is perfectly elastic, i.e. the firm controls such an insignificant fraction of total supply that if it increases or decreases output, price will be unaffected. It must therefore accept the ruling market price and at this price it will be able to sell whatever output it produces. The only means it has of increasing profit in these circumstances is to extend output to the point where *marginal cost equals marginal revenue*. Marginal revenue is the addition to total revenue from one more unit of output which in conditions of perfect competition is the price at which every unit of output can be sold, i.e. price and marginal revenue curves are identical. This is illustrated in Fig. 29.

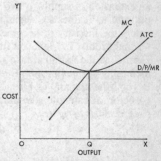

Fig. 29.—*The firm in perfect competition.* In perfect competition the demand curve for the firm's product is perfectly elastic since the consumer will not be prepared to pay a higher price for any single unit of the firm's output. By definition therefore, the same curve also illustrates both the price at which any output will be sold (P) and the marginal revenue which results from any extension of output (MR), i.e. each extra unit of output adds to total revenue its own selling price. The output which will in fact be produced must be OQ, since only at this point do marginal cost and marginal revenue equate, i.e. the marginal unit adds to cost exactly what it adds to revenue. Only in this position is profit maximised.

To maximise profit, the firm must produce output OQ. A shortfall leaves marginal cost below marginal revenue with further profits still to be made. A greater output sets marginal cost above marginal revenue. In a position where there is no incentive to expand or contract output, the firm is said to be in equilibrium.

In the case of the marginal or least efficient firm in the industry (*see* Fig. 29) this will also be the point at which average total costs are at a minimum. For the marginal firm, therefore, there is an additional reason why output can only be OQ since with either a smaller or greater output, average total cost exceeds price. At output OQ, the marginal firm makes only *normal profits*, a concept which is built into the cost curves and which implies the minimum profit without which production would not take place.

16. The industry in equilibrium. Not all firms make only normal profits since some are low cost firms while others are high cost firms. These differences in efficiency spring essentially from the lack of mobility of the factors of production which has been seen to be a characteristic of *market competition*. The result is that some firms, at least in the short period, are able to secure the exclusive use of higher-quality resources, e.g. a particularly favourable site, more modern machinery or more skilful labour and management.

EXAMPLE. When price is £1, it is only possible for Firm A to enter the industry and to supply a quantity consistent with minimal average total cost. At this point it is the marginal firm and it makes only normal profits. A rise in price to £2 will cause an extension of supply in two ways. Firm A will increase output and as it does so begins to make *surplus profits*. Firm B enters the industry to become the marginal firm making only normal profits. In Fig. 30, a further price rise to £3 introduces Firm C as the marginal firm while A and B extend output, A increasing surplus profits, B enjoying them for the first time. Beyond the margin lies Firm D which awaits a rise in price to £4 before it can enter the industry. *The supply curve therefore rises from left to right.*

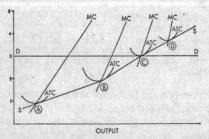

OUTPUT

FIG. 30.—*The industry in equilibrium.* In "market competition" differences in efficiency cause the average total cost curves of competing firms to lie at different levels. Infra-marginal firms like A make surplus profits. Only the marginal firm C makes normal profits.

The industry is said to be *in equilibrium* when there is no tendency for new firms to enter the industry or for old firms to leave it. This is an *imperfect equilibrium* when, owing to the imperfect mobility of the factors of production, there is some impediment to the entry of a new firm or the departure of an old one. In this situation, it is possible for the marginal firm to make profits which are greater or less than normal.

17. The industry in perfect equilibrium. In the long period, the mobility of the factors of production between industries is improved and there is a much stronger tendency towards the conditions of *industrial competition* (*see* II, **21**). The incentive for this

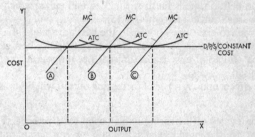

Fig. 31.—*The industry in perfect equilibrium.* In "industrial competition" all firms make normal profits and all may be considered marginal. They are identical units of production with identical cost curves, each contributing the same amount to total supply, i.e. the supply and cost curves of the industry as a whole are identical.

movement lies in the desire of the owners of the factors of production to equate the marginal net return of the factors in their various uses.

The long period effect of *wholly* perfect or industrial competition is therefore to reduce differences in the cost structures of competing firms. For the industry in perfect equilibrium, all firms make only normal profits; the output of the industry is at constant cost and the supply curve is perfectly elastic. This is shown in Fig. 31.

THE FOUNDATIONS OF SUPPLY IN MONOPOLY

18. Monopoly power. *Absolute* monopoly power is purely hypothetical since it would require:

(a) the producer to have total control of supply;

(b) the impossibility of substitution.

In practice, the first condition may be found but the second is never completely fulfilled for reasons which have been considered previously (*see* IV, **22**).

Nevertheless, to the extent that the producer controls the supply of a product for which substitution is *difficult*, he is in a positition to exercise monopoly power. This power is expressed in his ability to vary supply at will. He has not, however, any power to control demand and must accept that if he restricts output, he may enjoy a high price, but that if he wishes to increase his sales, he will receive a lower price. In contrast to the producer in perfect competition, he is faced with a demand curve which slopes downwards from left to right (*see* **15**).

In order to exploit his power to the best advantage, the monopolist will choose an output at which the difference between total revenue and total cost is maximised, i.e. monopoly profits are maximised.

The effects upon *revenue* of increasing output will be considered first.

19. The effects of increasing output upon total revenue. The advantage to the monopolist's revenue of *restricting* output is determined by the elasticity of demand for the product.

(a) *Inelastic demand*. Where demand is inelastic, an extension of supply will reduce total revenue. For example in Fig. 32, at a price of £5, 10 are sold to yield a revenue of £50. To sell 20, price must fall to £1, total revenue declining to £20. It will therefore be in the monopolist's interest to restrict output severely.

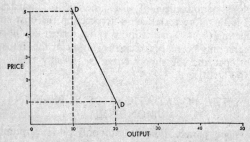

FIG. 32.—*Monopoly and inelastic demand*

(b) *Elastic demand.* When demand is elastic, total revenue will be increased by an extension of supply. Figure 33 shows that at a price of £5, 10 are sold to yield a revenue of £50. An output of 50 can be sold at a price of £3, increasing total revenue to £150. The monopolist in this case will not curtail output so severely.

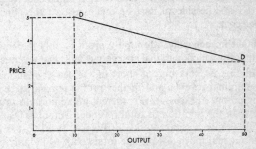

FIG. 33.—*Monopoly and elastic demand*

20. The effects of increasing output upon marginal revenue. In perfect competition, it has been noted that marginal revenue and average revenue or price are one and the same (*see* **15**). Each unit of the whole supply sells at the same price and therefore adds this amount to total revenue.

In monopoly, successive units of output add less to total revenue than the price at which they sell, whether demand is elastic or inelastic, i.e. the marginal revenue curve declines more steeply than the average revenue or price curve. This may be explained in tabular form as follows:

TABLE IV. DECLINING MARGINAL REVENUE

Output	Average Revenue or price	Total Revenue	Marginal Revenue
1	£6	£6	£6
2	£5	£10	£4
3	£4	£12	£2

An output of 1 sells at a price of £6 to give a total revenue and a marginal revenue of £6. To sell 2, price must fall to £5, *not only for unit* 2 *but also for unit* 1. In other words, the supplier sacrifices the monopoly advantage which he would have enjoyed if he had restricted output to 1. Total revenue is £10 and marginal revenue

£4. The net advantage to the supplier of a second sale is not therefore the £5 for which it sells, but the £4 which it adds to total revenue.

On the revenue side, it is the concept of *marginal* revenue which the monopolist employs in his search for an output which maximises the difference between total revenue and total cost. Similarly, on the side of cost he makes use of the concept of *marginal* cost.

21. Output in monopoly. Monopoly profit is only maximised at the output for which marginal cost equals marginal revenue.

(*a*) In Fig. 34, any output short of OT leaves marginal cost below marginal revenue and further profits remain to be made. For any output in excess of OT, there is an addition to total cost greater than the addition to total revenue. Output OT sells at a price OP to give a total revenue of PQTO. Total cost is SRTO (i.e. output multiplied by average total cost). Monopoly profits, PQRS, are now maximised.

(*b*) In the foregoing analysis, it was assumed that marginal

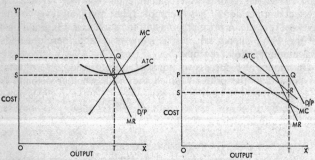

FIG. 34.—*Output in monopoly, marginal cost increasing.* In monopoly the demand curve slopes downward from left to right since the producer can only increase sales by lowering price. In these circumstances marginal revenue declines more steeply than price. Output, however, will always be determined at the intersection of the marginal cost and marginal revenue curves.

FIG. 35.—*Output in monopoly, marginal cost declining.* Even when the marginal cost curve, MC, is declining, output will be limited to OT, in accordance with the need to equate marginal cost and marginal revenue. Any extension of output can only result in less being added to total revenue than to total cost. Any smaller output means that monopoly profits have not yet been maximised.

costs were rising. To this it may be objected that, especially in manufacturing industry, long-run marginal costs are likely to be fairly constant or even to fall. Long-run price must cover average total cost including a profit return to the entrepreneur but if additional units are adding to cost less than, or at worst the same as, the average, then they would seem to be adding to total profit. Why in these circumstances does the monopolist restrict his output? The analysis still holds good. Although marginal costs may be declining, ultimately the curve will intersect the marginal revenue curve. Only at this output is profit maximised. Further units will add more to cost than they add to revenue. This is shown in Fig. 35

22. Discriminating monopoly. On occasion, the monopolist may be in a position to divide his market, keeping one part insulated from the other. Provided that the elasticity of demand for his product differs in each market, he may increase surplus profits by selling monopoly output in the first (i.e. the output at which marginal cost equals marginal revenue) and an additional output in the second at *any* price which covers *marginal* cost. It is not necessary for price to cover average total cost for the reason that it is no longer essential for the additional output to contribute to *fixed* cost. "Dumping" is an example of this situation. The producer monopolises his home market with the aid of a protective tariff. With this springboard for his operations, he may extend output (possibly in search of economies of scale) and sell the surplus abroad at lower prices, sometimes below average total cost.

However, the monopolist's total profit will be maximised only when in each market marginal cost equals marginal revenue, since otherwise his position would be improved by the transfer of a portion of his output from one market to the other.

The ability to practice price discrimination therefore strengthens monopoly power. Monopoly profits will be increased because if output had been extended in the first market alone, the price of the *whole* supply would have been lowered. The additional output can be sold in the second market without affecting the price charged in the first. Other examples of this practice include the discriminatory tariffs charged by the gas, electricity, telephone and railway undertakings.

THE FOUNDATIONS OF SUPPLY IN IMPERFECT COMPETITION

23. Imperfect competition. It has been shown that absolute monopoly does not exist, but that on the other hand there is not infrequently a single supplier who is able to exercise a high degree of monopoly power (*see* II, **23**). Equally, the wholly perfect state of industrial competition does not exist, at least in the short period, although production *may* take place in the lesser state of market competition (*see* II, **21**(*b*)).

In the twentieth century, however, it has become increasingly the case that most goods and services are provided in conditions of *imperfect competition* (*see* II, **24**). This state arises because of the concentration of supply in the hands of a few producers or because of the absence of a *perfect market* (*see* II, **21**(*b*)). Consequently the characteristics of imperfect competition will be found in either:

(*a*) the ability of the individual producer to influence price by restricting output (i.e. to exercise a degree of monopoly power); *or*

(*b*) different selling prices in contrast to the single selling price of the perfect market.

Corresponding to these two deficiencies are two clearly defined types of imperfect competition, *oligopoly* (*see* **24**) and *monopolistic competition* (*see* **28**).

NOTE: Imperfection may arise in other forms but these do not lend themselves so easily to clear analysis.

24. Oligopoly. In oligopoly, supply is in the hands of a few producers. While in perfect competition the individual firm is faced with a perfectly elastic demand curve and must accept the ruling market price, in oligopoly it is confronted with a sloping demand curve, which is indicative of its ability to influence price by restricting output. In general, price will therefore be above marginal cost to the extent that the marginal revenue curve declines more steeply than the average revenue or price curve (*see* Figs. **34** and **35**).

Oligopoly will be *perfect* when the market is perfect and there is in consequence a single price. It will be *imperfect* when the market is imperfect and prices vary.

25. Price in perfect oligopoly. The producer who anticipates an increased revenue from a larger output at a lower price, in assessing the elasticity of demand for his product must take account of the reactions of his competitors. Since the market is perfect, only the cheaper product will be bought and therefore all competitors must immediately cut price to the same level. Frequently it will be the case that the dominant firm assumes the price leadership of the industry. To the extent that less efficient firms must follow the price established by the leader, so the gap between their marginal costs and price will be closed. Their surplus or monopoly profits will be correspondingly diminished.

26. Price in imperfect oligopoly. Oligopoly will become imperfect when an imperfection exists in the market. The most likely cause will be some differentiation in the product. Within limits, the producer is then free to pursue an independent policy similar to that of the monopolist, supplying an output which maximises his surplus profits and at a price which may differ from that of other producers.

(*a*) *Brand competition.* It has been previously observed that the practice of branding together with a large element of advertising is concerned to foster the idea that a particular brand is unique. The success of this policy will be reflected in a more inelastic demand curve for the product, a correspondingly greater difference between marginal cost and price and greater surplus or monopoly profits.

(*b*) *Price-cutting.* However, if in order to improve his position the producer seeks to expand his sales by lowering price at the expense of his competitors, he will expect retaliation and a price-cutting war may follow. Prices will be forced closer to the marginal costs of the competing firms but it is difficult to predict precisely where they will settle. When they do, the share of the market enjoyed by each firm is likely to remain unchanged unless marginal firms have been forced out of business. Price differences may still remain. The initial advantage will, however, lie with the firm which cuts price first (e.g. the "petrol war" of 1976–7).

27. Advertising and service competition. Rather than run the risk of spoiling the market through *price* competition, firms producing in conditions of imperfect oligopoly may seek to expand sales by *increasing* rather than *extending* demand. The intention is to move the demand curve to the right (*see* IV, **11**).

This aim is accomplished by advertising campaigns, competitions, after-sales service, gift schemes, improved quality, credit facilities and other sales promotion devices. Price competition is therefore replaced by what is termed "service" competition. Frequently, this is economically wasteful. The consumer may have preferred a lower price at unchanged costs but it is in fact price which remains unchanged while costs rise. He has *no choice* but to accept a better quality, an after-sales service or "gifts" which he may not require. The price mechanism therefore ceases to direct resources accurately into those uses for which there is most demand.

28. Monopolistic competition. Monopolistic competition is similar to imperfect oligopoly in that it arises from imperfection of the market. There will be an absence of one or all of the features of the perfect market with some consequent variation in the prices charged by different producers. It differs from both forms of oligopoly in that there are *many producers*.

The most striking example is to be found in the distributive trades, particularly in retailing. Although two retailers may be dealing in homogeneous goods the *services* which they sell differ. They are distinguished by:

(*a*) Proximity to a particular group of clients.

(*b*) Personal relationships which engender goodwill.

(*c*) Surroundings and an atmosphere which the customers find agreeable.

In some degree, each retailer is able to exercise monopoly power, Prices may differ between the two shops yet the higher-priced shop still retains its patrons. Within fairly narrow limits, these differences may remain a permanent feature of the price structure.

29. The effects of monopolistic competition in retail distribution. The consequence of monopolistic competition in the retail trade is to encourage excess capacity rather than large surplus profits. Entry to small-scale retailing is relatively simple, involving little capital outlay and, where it is a family business, low wage bills. High cost firms which at lower prices would be driven out are enabled to stay in business.

In recent years, however, retailing has experienced a considerable increase in the element of competition. The advent of supermarket trading, discount warehouses, direct selling and the growth of chain store and mail order business has produced a sufficient difference in price levels to reduce the monopoly power exercised by the high cost retailer. Some have been forced out of business while others have been impelled to greater efficiency in association with other retailers or with wholesalers in order to enjoy the advantages of bulk buying and other forms of co-operation.

PROGRESS TEST 5

1. What are the three bases of the theory of demand? **(3)**

2. Define the Law of Diminishing Utility. **(4)**

3. What do you understand by the "margin of consumption"? **(5)**

4. What is the relationship between utility and price? **(6)**

5. Illustrate the concept of a consumer's surplus. **(8)**

6. Criticise marginal utility theory as an explanation of demand **(10)**

7. Explain the composition of an average total cost curve. **(13)**

8. Why is the demand curve in perfect competition perfectly elastic? **(15)**

9. Illustrate the way in which output is determined in perfect competition. **(15)**

10. Explain why in "market competition" the supply curve rises from left to right. **(16)**

11. Explain why in "industrial competition" the supply curve is horizontal. **(17)**

12. Explain why in conditions of monopoly the demand curve slopes from left to right. **(18)**

13. Illustrate the effect upon a monopolist's revenue of a small rise in price when demand is elastic. **(19** (*b*)**)**

14. Why does the marginal revenue curve in monopoly decline more steeply than the demand/price curve? **(20)**

15. Examine the determinants of output in monopoly. **(21)**

16. What do you understand by the term "discriminating monopoly"? **(22)**

17. Outline the circumstances in which imperfect competition may arise. **(23)**

18. How will price be determined in "imperfect oligopoly"? **(26)**

19. In what respect may service competition be considered wasteful? **(27)**

20. What circumstances engender monopolistic competition? **(28)**

PART THREE

TAX AND EXPENDITURE ANALYSIS

CHAPTER VI

The Evaluation of Public Expenditure

ALLOCATIVE PRINCIPLES ON A FIXED BUDGET

1. A more precise approach to expenditure evaluation. In Chapter III (*see* III. 3) we mentioned the way in which through the *dolitical market* a vote might register the preferences of consumers for *broad categories* of social goods. *Detailed* expenditure decisions are consequently delegated to representatives and public servants. If these are to be wise decisions then they need to be made systematically. The problem of establishing appropriate principles has necessarily received a good deal of attention since the 1950s, an era which has witnessed a vast and continuing growth of public spending.

There are two distinct aspects to the problem.

(*a*) *Assuming costs and benefits to be known.* We must here determine

(*i*) how we will allocate resources on a budget of a given size and

(*ii*) how we will determine the size of that budget.

(*b*) *The principles by which costs and benefits are measured.*

2. Allocation of a given budget between two finely adjustable projects. We assume that costs and benefits are known and that the problem is to allocate a fixed expenditure between two projects X and Y in a way which maximises the difference between benefits B and costs C (*see* Fig. 36). Since total costs are prescribed by the size of the budget, it remains to maximise benefits. This is achieved where $MB_x/MB_y = MC_x/MC_y$, when MB is *marginal benefit* and MC is *marginal cost*. In other words each line of expenditure will be pursued to the point where an additional £1 spent on X will yield the same extra benefit as an additional £1 spent on Y.

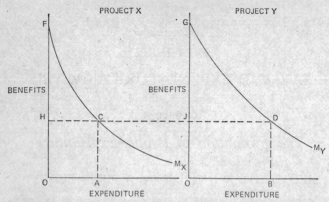

Fig. 36.—*Allocation of a given budget between two projects.* Total expenditure OA + OB is prescribed by the budget. The M_x and M_y curves show the marginal benefit (the additional to total benefit) of successive units of expenditure on X and Y. Each expenditure will be pursued to the point where the marginal benefit of X (AC) is equal to the marginal benefit of Y (BD). Since the marginal benefit of consuming X declines more rapidly than that of consuming Y the smaller amount OA will be allocated to Project X. Only on this allocation will total benefits represented by OACF + OBDG be maximised.

3. Establishing priorities between lump sum projects.

The principles enunciated so far will serve well enough when marginal expenditures can be freely adjusted in a way which equates marginal benefits. However, in many cases marginal adjustments are not possible. If undertaken at all the project will involve a large fixed amount. For example, in a desired motorway construction programme to link a number of towns each motorway will require a large and unadjustable outlay. If the limited budget precludes all being built which will receive priority?

Table V shows seven motorway projects each costed at different amounts and each yielding differently valued benefits. In ordering our priorities it would be unreliable to give first place to Project C, since although it yields the highest *absolute* benefit it is also one of the two most costly. Nor should we accord first place to Project B even though it reveals the greatest *absolute* difference between costs and benefits. In order to maximise the benefits from the programme as a whole we should consider benefit/cost ratios (B/C) of each project separately and establish our priorities accordingly. A similar result will be achieved if we

TABLE V.   ORDERING PRIORITIES ON A FIXED BUDGET

Motorway	Cost (C)	Benefit (B)	Benefit minus Cost	Benefit/Cost Ratio		Priority
	(in £ millions)			$\dfrac{B}{C}$	$\dfrac{B-C}{C}$	
A	20	24	4	1·2	0·2	5
B	40	80	40	2·0	1·0	2
C	60	90	30	1·5	0·5	3
D	60	54	−6	0·9	0·1	7
E	30	39	9	1·3	0·3	4
F	10	25	15	2·5	1·5	1
G	25	25	0	1·0	0	6

use net benefit/cost ratios $(B-C)/C$. The latter approach is closer to the method of measuring returns in the private sector.

In our example, if the fixed budget amounts to £140 million then the selection of Projects F, B, C and E will maximise total benefits.

4. Projects with more than one distinguishable benefit. On many occasions it will be possible to distinguish a number of benefits which result from one project. In this situation it may be desirable to design expenditure in a way which gives emphasis to one aspect rather than another. For example, let us suppose a defence budget of £6,000 million is to be divided between the Army and the RAF. Let us further suppose that each £1,000 million spent on the Army contributes twice as much to *defensive* capability as the same amount spent on the RAF. Conversely, that each £1,000 million spent on the RAF contributes three times as much to *offensive* capability as the same expenditure on the Army.

It will not of course follow that Plan IV will automatically be chosen simply because the total unit gains are maximised. The

TABLE VI.   ALLOCATION FOR MORE THAN ONE BENEFIT IN A DEFENCE BUDGET

Plan	Expenditure on		Units gained in	
	Army	RAF	Defensive Capability	Offensive Capability
I	6	0	12	6
II	4	2	10	10
III	2	4	8	14
IV	0	6	6	18

plan selected will depend upon the valuation placed upon defensive units in terms of offensive units, i.e. the measurement of their respective benefits (*see* 7–18).

DETERMINATION OF THE SIZE OF THE BUDGET

5. Budgets are variable not fixed. We have so far proceeded on the assumption of a *fixed* budget to be allocated between different projects. On that assumption the opportunity cost of one project in the public sector will be the benefit lost by forgoing another public project. When in practice Government determines the size of the total budget it must consider the opportunity cost of public projects in terms of the benefits lost from projects forgone in the private sector.

6. Public and private projects which are finely adjustable at the margin. The analysis parallels the one made previously (*see* 2). The objective is to maximise the difference between total benefits and total costs *in both public and private sectors*. This will be achieved when the last £ spent in each sector equates the marginal benefits of public and private projects.

In Fig. 36, if Project X represents the public project and Project Y the private project, then total benefits are maximised when OA is spent on X and OB upon Y.

7. Unadjustable lump sum projects. As before it is necessary to recognise that certain projects involve a large fixed outlay. If Project X in Fig. 36 is indivisible and requires an outlay of £1 million then the total benefit derived will be OACF (i.e. the *whole* area beneath the marginal benefit curve). The benefits lost to the private sector are usually measured in terms of the resource cost, i.e. the £1 million of productive resources which the private sector forgoes.

This procedure may be criticised for inconsistency. Since total benefit gained by the public sector is measured by the whole area beneath the marginal benefit curve it would seem more appropriate to calculate the total benefit lost to the private sector in the same way, i.e. OBDG in Fig. 36. As it is, no account is taken of the loss of *consumer surplus* JDG (*see* V, 8).

It follows therefore that the common practice is to treat the benefit/cost ratio in the private sector on a 1/1 basis. When in the public sector that ratio is greater than 1/1 the public project will be undertaken in preference.

With an open-ended budget therefore in Table V all projects would be undertaken with the exception of D.

THE MEASUREMENT OF COSTS AND BENEFITS

8. Which benefits and which costs? The immediate problem is to determine the costs and the benefits to be included in our analysis. It is possible to distinguish a number of broad categories.

    (*a*) *Monetary benefits and costs.*
    (*b*) *Real benefits and costs* which may be
        (*i*) Direct or indirect.
        (*ii*) Tangible or intangible.
        (*iii*) Final or intermediate.

TABLE VII.   BENEFITS AND COSTS OF A BUILDING PROGRAMME

	Benefits	*Costs*
Monetary	Relative increase in building wages and land values	
Real		
Direct tangible	Fewer homeless	Building costs
intangible	Improved quality of life for the newly housed	Loss of open spaces
Indirect tangible	Reduced costs of emergency welfare services	
intangible	A more contented and better motivated workforce	

9. Monetary benefits and costs. The *real* cost of social goods is the loss of resources to other uses to be balanced against the *real* benefit of the additions to the welfare of society as a whole. It is with these aspects that cost/benefit analysis concerns itself.

Quite distinct are the monetary costs and the monetary benefits which accrue not to the whole community but to particular individuals. This occurs in consequence of a change in the structure of prices subsequent to a shift of resources from one use to another. For example, a general increase in the level of public spending will tend to bid up the price of labour, goods and services in the public sector relative to the private sector where demand will be relatively depressed due to the necessary increase in taxation. This has been characteristic of Britain in the 1970s where the position of many categories of public sector employees has improved in comparison to their private sector counterparts.

Since purely monetary gains will be made by some but only at the expense of others there can be no net gain to society as a whole. They will therefore be irrelevant to benefit evaluation *unless* we are concerned with the implied *redistribution of real benefits* between particular individuals. If such redistribution is viewed as a cost and a benefit to the whole of society then we may attach weights to particular cost and benefit flows.

10. Direct and indirect real benefits and costs. Public projects will be aimed at some specific objective to which there will be *directly*, attached real benefits and costs. Frequently there will also be side effects which give rise to *indirect* benefits and costs.

A building programme may be aimed primarily at housing the homeless but it will also have the indirect effect of reducing pressure on the welfare services. In evaluating the benefit of the programme we should clearly include both primary and secondary results.

11. Tangible and intangible benefits and costs. Tangible benefits and costs can be valued on the market. Intangible cannot.

(*a*) *The measurement of tangibles.* On the assumption of a competitive market (*see* II, **21**) the tangible benefit from a social good will be determined by the price it would fetch in the market. The cost of resources devoted to the project will be priced in the same way. If however, there is a state of imperfect competition then the market price is distorted. It ceases to reflect the true social cost and the true social valuation of the benefit.

For example, sales taxes raise prices and distort the true opportunity cost of that production. Equally, monopoly influences distort relative prices in a way which disguises the true cost of using resources in one way rather than another. If, say, the monopoly power of a trade union produces a wage bill of £1 million when in perfect competition it would have been £800,000 then the true opportunity cost is the lower figure and this is the one which will be used.

Similarly, if sterling is 20% overvalued then the true cost of £1 million raw materials imports for a particular use should be valued at £1,200,000. This process is known as *shadow pricing* and is intended to produce an allocation of resources which more accurately represents true costs.

(b) *The measurement of intangibles.* While a building programme will provide tangible benefits in the form of more houses and therefore fewer homeless and at the tangible costs of building inputs there are also intangible benefits and costs. The living standards of the newly housed are improved and one may expect that better conditions could be associated with a more contented and more motivated labour force. On the other hand there is the *intangible* cost of the loss of amenity of open spaces (*see* Table VII).

We now confront head on the fundamental problem of placing a valuation on social goods. It has to be admitted immediately that this can only be resolved through the "political market" (*see* III, 3).

Paradoxically, cost benefit analysis is more easily applied to those projects where the benefits are tangible and there is least need for public intervention in the first place. The technique can only be of real assistance in *choosing between projects once a value has been ascribed to the benefit of each.*

However, analysis can assist this valuation in two ways. Firstly, it can indicate *all* of the benefits and costs, direct and indirect, tangible and intangible which would not at first sight be apparent. Secondly, it can show how to maximise the various benefits from a given outlay thus providing a sounder basis for the valuation of the project as a whole.

12. Uncertainty of future benefits and costs. A further complication should now be mentioned. As in the private sector forward planning in the public sector is subject to the risk of certain predictions being unfulfilled. For example, the benefits of a housing programme will be measured on the basis of a predicted number of homeless. If that figure proves an over-estimate then the benefits will have been over-estimated.

One way of rectifying this shortcoming is to add a premium for risk in calculating the *cost* of the project.

13. Valuation of final and intermediate benefits. If the final good is tangible, say a postal service, then the principle enunciated in **11**(*a*) will apply. If it is an intangible, say a public park, then the difficulties of **11**(*b*) are encountered.

However, the benefits of *intermediate goods* lend themselves more readily to valuation when the final goods are sold at a price determined by the market. For example, the benefit of a new commercial consulate abroad may be computed as the increased value of British exports less any specific exporting costs.

DISCOUNTING FUTURE COSTS AND BENEFITS

14. The problem of measurement of future costs and benefits. Our analysis has so far proceeded on the assumption that benefits and costs both accrue immediately. In some cases this will be so. Operating a hospital casualty department incurs immediate running costs for the health service and immediate benefits for society. However, investment in the hospital building itself will yield a continuing flow of benefits over a good many years. Since future benefits will be less highly valued than present benefits they must be discounted in order to measure their present value, e.g. to enjoy the right to a benefit worth £100 in twelve months we may be prepared to pay £95 today. We have discounted that benefit at 5% p.a.

The approach is similar on the side of costs. A present cost will be calculated in terms of present consumption forgone. A future cost will be calculated in terms of the loss of future consumption (as investment has been switched from private to public sectors) and discounted to present values.

15. The importance of the discount rate to the selection of projects. Firstly, since discounting future benefit reduces their present valuation it will follow that some projects which were previously considered viable may no longer be so. If in Table V, for simplicity, it is assumed that the flow of benefits continues for one year only and that the discount rate of the benefit of each project is 5% p.a. then on an open ended budget all will be undertaken with the exception of D and G. Previously, without discounting, G would have been included (*see* 7). Now its benefit/cost ratio is reduced below 1 to 0.95. The higher the discount rate the lower will be the present valuation of the investment and more projects are likely to be discarded.

Secondly, the period of time over which benefits continue to flow will affect present valuations of one project relative to another. In principle lower discount rates will raise present valuations more when benefits accrue over a longer period of time. Conversely, higher discount rates improve the relative position of shorter term investments.

It therefore follows that in ordering the priorities of different projects (*see* 3) we should pay careful attention to the rate of discount and the term of the investment.

16. Selection of discount rate. The next problem is to determine the most appropriate rate of discount for our calculations. There are a number of possibilities. One is to use, for the purpose of discounting benefit flows, the cost of the Government's own borrowing. Rates on long rather than short term loans will be used on the view that they give a better prediction of *future* yields.

OTHER FACTORS RELEVANT TO COST/BENEFIT ANALYSIS

17. Level of employment. Our analysis to this point has rested upon the assumption of full employment and of the use of resources for one project involving an opportunity cost in their loss to other projects. These other uses would be in the public sector in the case of a fixed budget or in the private sector when the budget is open ended. A different situation arises if there are unemployed resources since their use has an opportunity cost of zero. This seems to imply that *any* public project will automatically produce a net benefit when unemployment exists and should therefore be undertaken. This view holds *provided that* no other employment policies can be found.

However, it is clear that it would still be preferable to be guided by cost/benefit principles in selecting the best project and it would then be appropriate to include the benefit of employment in the analysis. For example, Project A may initially be considered superior to Project B but if the effect on employment is taken into account and its benefit exceeds the difference between the two then Project B will be undertaken.

18. Distributional consideration. A parallel case arises when we consider the effects of different projects upon income distribution. Project A may tend to favour those whose incomes are already high while a similar but inferior Project B favours the lower income groups. Preferably the distributional problem would be treated separately by other policies such as tax-transfers, the choice of project being made on merit. If that option is not open then redistribution will be treated as a benefit in its own right and consequently considered in the cost/benefit calculation.

19. A cautionary note. It will be seen that cost/benefit analysis seeks to place market values upon benefits and costs in areas where no market exists. It can therefore only be a pale reflection of the true state of demand and supply.

The task is simpler in the case of tangible and intermediate goods and, as we have determined, the technique is useful in making a choice between projects. However, in the wide area of direct and intangible benefits attributable to most categories of social goods, a true valuation depends upon the effectiveness of the "political market" in appraising the preferences of the electorate.

PROGRESS TEST 6

1. What are the two principal aspects of the problem of expenditure evaluation? **(1)**

2. What principle will be adopted in allocating a given budget between two projects? **(2)**

3. Explain the nature of the particular problem of establishing priorities between "lump sum projects". **(3)**

4. How may the concept of opportunity cost be applied to the determination of the appropriate size of a budget? **(5)**

5. What criticism may be levelled at the standard procedures for assessing benefits in the public sector and in the private sector? **(7)**

6. Which costs and which benefits should be included in a cost/benefit analysis? **(8)**

7. In what circumstances should monetary costs and benefits be excluded from cost benefit analysis? **(9)**

8. Give an example of "an indirect benefit". **(10)**

9. What is meant by "shadow pricing"? **(11)**

10. Give an example of "an intangible cost". **(11(b))**

11. How may the uncertainty of predicting future benefits be offset when planning public expenditure? **(12)**

12. Distinguish between benefits which accrue immediately and those which do not. **(14)**

13. How will the application of the principle of discounting affect the selection of budget projects? **(15)**

14. Which is likely to be the most appropriate type of discount rate? **(16)**

15. How may the level of employment affect the conclusions of cost/benefit analysis? **(17)**

CHAPTER VII

Tax Incidence

INCIDENCE OF EXPENDITURE TAXES

1. Definition of tax incidence. All taxation imposes a burden which may manifest itself in several different ways.

(a) *Direct money burden.* Having determined who in fact pays the money we have solved the problem of tax incidence. Some economists have questioned whether there is any value in examining this problem outside of the wider *effects* of a tax. Moreover it frequently proves extremely difficult to analyse incidence without taking account of effects. However, while it would be a mistake to assume that a study of incidence is central to tax analysis, it is clearly of practical importance to know something of the distribution of the direct money burden. It is with this aspect of the tax burden that incidence is concerned.

(b) *Indirect money burden.* A tax may be levied upon the goods in which a wholesaler deals. Ultimately he will recoup the tax in the price which he charges to the retailer, but he has meanwhile lost the use of his money. This represents an indirect money burden.

(c) *Direct real burden.* Every tax payment represents an immediate loss of economic welfare to the taxpayer. The lower his income, the greater his sacrifice will become. This represents the direct real burden.

(d) *Indirect real burden.* A tax-induced price increase may cause decreased consumption of a commodity, owing to the limitations of our income. This constitutes the indirect real burden of the tax.

NOTE: THE student should bear in mind that in determining the *incidence* of taxation we are concerned to discover who bears the *direct money* burden.

2. Nature of expenditure taxes. Historically, taxes upon expenditure have proved popular since they are easier to collect than an income tax, particularly when there exists no complex revenue machinery. Moreover they have an immediate yield, a factor of particular importance in recent years on the occasions when taxes have been imposed to counter inflation. They are less desirable when viewed from the standpoint of equity since they are essentially regressive, i.e. all consumers pay the same tax without regard to their taxable capacity. A study of their incidence is therefore of special importance and must be made carefully in order to take account of different market conditions and costs of production.

Expenditure taxes may take a number of different forms. They may be imposed upon:

(a) Goods which are used up in a single process of production or consumption.

(b) Production and consumption services.

(c) Producer and consumer durables. Taxes in this category may be levied in two ways:

(i) They may be imposed upon total capital value or its annual value in use.

(ii) There may be an annual licence of fixed amount.

(d) A single commodity, e.g. tobacco.

(e) A group of commodities, e.g. wines and spirits.

(f) A wide range of commodities, e.g. purchase tax.

3. Assessment of expenditure taxes. Looked at from the standpoint of assessment, expenditure taxes are of two types.

(a) *Specific taxes.* These are based upon quantity in terms of numbers or weight and in the past have been the traditional British method of assessment.

(b) *Ad valorem taxes.* The basis is the value of the goods inclusive of insurance and freight to the UK, of which a percentage is charged as duty. This method is favoured for protective duties since the yield varies with import values.

4. Elasticity and the incidence of expenditure taxes. Two propositions can be established. These are outlined and illustrated below.

(a) *The less elastic the demand for a commodity, the greater will be the incidence of taxation upon the consumer.* Factors already considered will govern elasticity of demand, but in general the most useful principle will be that the demand for luxuries is less elastic than the demand for necessities. Thus a Chancellor whose primary aim is to raise a given revenue may well look for a commodity in inelastic demand, e.g. petrol, tobacco.

(b) *The less elastic the supply of a commodity, the greater will be the incidence of taxation upon the producer.* It has been observed earlier (IV, **25**) that while in the short run most commodities are in inelastic supply, once conditions of production have had time to adjust, the supply of many goods will be elastic. It therefore follows that while in the short run the incidence of a new tax will be upon the seller, it is likely to be shifted in the long run to the buyer.

It follows from these two propositions that the incidence of a new tax is shared between buyers and sellers in accordance with the strength of their respective bargaining positions. In the case where elasticity of demand equates with elasticity of supply the money burden is shared equally.

EXAMPLE 1. *A tax where demand is perfectly inelastic and supply elastic.* Fig. 37 represents one limiting case in which demand is completely inelastic. Originally there is equilibrium at price OP_1. The incidence of a new tax P_1P_2 will be wholly upon the consumer, price increasing by the full extent of the tax to OP_2.

EXAMPLE 2. *A tax where supply is perfectly elasitc and demand inelastic.* In Fig 38 supply is completely elastic and demand

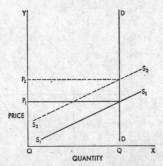

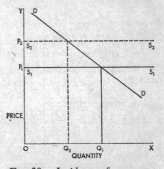

FIG. 37.—*Incidence of an expenditure tax, demand perfectly inelastic, supply elastic.* Demand is perfectly inelastic and therefore quantity OQ will be purchased irrespective of price. The supply curve rises to S_2S_2 to allow for the increased cost resulting from tax P_1P_2 which is passed on wholly to the consumer.

FIG. 38.—*Incidence of an expenditure tax, supply perfectly elastic, demand inelastic.* Rather than accept any price lower than OP_1 output will be discontinued. The supply curve therefore rises to S_2S_2 to allow for the increased cost resulting from the tax P_1P_2 which is passed on wholly to the consumer.

relatively inelastic. Once more the incidence of a tax P_1P_2 will be wholly upon the consumer. Price will rise by the full amount of the tax to OP_2 although a smaller quantity OQ_2 will be purchased at that price.

EXAMPLE 3. *A tax where supply is perfectly inelastic and demand elastic.* Fig. 39 represents one of the two opposite limiting cases. Supply is completely inelastic and demand *relatively* elastic. The incidence of a new tax PT will now be wholly upon the supplier. The same quantity OQ is sold and price inclusive of tax remains unchanged at OP.

EXAMPLE 4. *A tax where demand is perfectly elastic and supply inelastic.* The remaining limiting case is represented in Fig. 40. Demand is completely elastic and supply relatively inelastic. The incidence of a tax PT is wholly upon the supplier. The original price OP remains unchanged but is now inclusive of tax. However, in these conditions a smaller quantity OQ_2 is now offered for sale.

The preceding examples illustrate the limiting cases. The more probable sequence of events is outlined in **7** below and illustrated in Fig. 41.

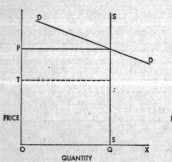

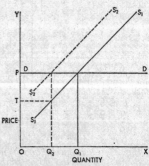

FIG. 39.—*Incidence of an expenditure tax, supply perfectly inelastic, demand elastic.* The only possible output is OQ since supply is inelastic. For this quantity the buyer will only pay OP. The whole tax PT must therefore be borne by the supplier.

FIG. 40.—*Incidence of an expenditure tax, demand perfectly elastic, supply inelastic.* Since demand is perfectly elastic, at no price higher than OP will any purchases be made. The supply curve shifts to the left and the tax is borne wholly by the supplier.

5. Interrelated demand and supply curves. The analysis so far is based upon the assumption that the conditions of demand and supply for associated commodities remain unchanged. This is unlikely to be the case, with the result that in part the incidence of a new tax will be shifted to both the buyers and the sellers of these goods, e.g. an increased purchase tax upon washing machines may compel producers to hold down or cut selling prices and at the same time exact lower prices from the suppliers of components.

6. Elasticity and the incidence of import and export duties. The theory which has just been applied to expenditure taxes on internal trade. may be applied equally to duties on international trade The analysis can be simplified by thinking in terms of goods rather than money and the elasticity of the trade in these goods between two countries.

EXAMPLE: If British demand for Argentinian meat is inelastic but its supply is elastic, then either an Argentinian export duty or a British import duty would be borne primarily by the British. The opposite would be the case where Argentinian demand for British manufactures is inelastic relative to their supply. In short, the incidence of import and export duties is determined by the relative bargaining strength of each country, e.g. before the Second World War the supply of raw materials

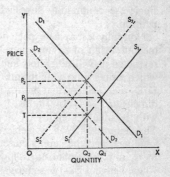

FIG. 41.—*Incidence of an expenditure tax in perfect competition.* When a tax P_2T is imposed, a new equilibrium is established at OP_2 with a smaller quantity OQ_2 being sold. Whether the tax is levied upon the consumer and the demand curve lowered to D_2D_2 or upon the supplier and the supply curve raised to S_2S_2 the result will be the same. Where the elasticities of demand and supply are equal the tax will be borne equally by buyers and sellers.

from the primary producing countries was inelastic relative to the demand for them. The bargaining position of the primary producers was therefore weak. From 1945 to 1953 the position was reversed, after which the pre-war pattern tended to be resumed. By the 1970s the balance of power had again shifted. Rising industrial demand for raw materials and energy coupled with the emergence of producers' cartels, e.g. Organisation of Petroleum Exporting Countries (OPEC) now favoured the primary producers.

However, it may be observed in this connection that when trade in a commodity is world-wide its supply to a particular *national* market will be elastic, since there are alternative outlets. Equally the demand of the outside world for the products of a particular nation will be elastic when there are many alternative sources of supply. In the modern world it is therefore difficult for a single nation to shift the incidence of its import or export duties to its trading partners. The same will not be true for a number of nations acting in concert, e.g. the European Economic Community (EEC). In this case, with an immense market surrounded by a common tariff, penetration by the outsider may be dependent upon his willingness to accept the burden of EEC custom duties.

7. Incidence of expenditure taxes in perfect competition. It has been observed earlier that it frequently proves difficult to divorce an examination of tax incidence from some consideration of tax effects. This is the case when we now come to consider the probable sequence of events when a tax is imposed upon a single-use commodity supplied in conditions of perfect competition.

Normally it may be expected that a new tax will have the immediate result of raising the selling price. Demand will now be restricted as will ultimately supply. In Fig. 38, OP_1 is the price which brings into equilibrium the demand and supply curves D_1D_1 and S_1S_1. At that price quantity OQ_1 is sold. If a tax of the dimension P_2T is now imposed, a fresh equilibrium will be struck with the smaller quantity OQ_2 being sold at the higher price OP_2. The same result will be achieved whether the tax is levied on suppliers, and the supply curve raised to S_2S_2, or upon consumers, and the demand curve lowered to D_2D_2. In the case shown where demand has the same elasticity as supply, i.e. the bargaining strengths of buyers and sellers are equal, price will rise by half the amount of the tax. The incidence of the tax P_2T is shared equally by buyers and sellers, buyers paying P_1P_2 and sellers P_1T.

8. Margins of spending, saving, production and consumption. It is clear from the foregoing analysis that an expenditure tax is significant only at the margin.

(*a*) *Margins of spending and saving.* Whether one or the other contracts at the margin depends upon the incidence of tax between income groups and age groups, and whether the tax falls upon a luxury or a necessity. When the tax bears primarily upon lower income groups, upon the young, or upon luxuries, demand tends to be elastic and readjustment will take place in spending rather than saving. The opposite will be true when the tax falls primarily upon necessities and upon the elderly and the rich. Demand will then tend to be inelastic and readjustment will cause a contraction of saving rather than spending.

(*b*) *Margins of production and consumption.* Whether a tax brings about a contraction of one rather than the other depends upon the elasticity of demand for the product and the elasticity of its supply. If substitution is easy then consumption will contract and vice-versa. If the factors of production are mobile and can readily be transferred to other uses then production will contract and vice-versa.

9. Importance of margins. It is important for government to be able to predict what the consequences of expenditure taxation will be in order that it may either raise the revenue that it requires or accomplish other purposes, e.g. restrict consumption or savings. For this reason taxes levied on final products are to be preferred to those on intermediate products, since their incidence is easier to trace. It may be difficult to determine whether a tax on certain "producer" goods, e.g. petrol, is passed on. Again a tax levied at some intermediate stage of production may lead to "pyramiding", i.e. increasing the supply price to the next stage of production by more than the tax.

10. Expenditure taxes and producer and consumer surpluses. It has been shown that normally an expenditure tax may be expected to cause a contraction of both demand and supply, the extent of which is governed by their elasticities. It may consequently be objected that expenditure taxes violate Adam Smith's canon of economy since the loss of satisfaction to producers and consumers is greater than the inland revenue's gain.

(*a*) *Loss of consumer surplus.* In Fig. 42 the demand curve DD is taken as being identical with the utility curve. (This presupposes that the marginal utility of money is constant, a reasonable

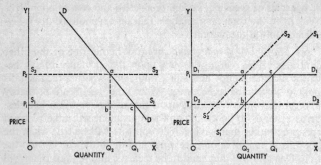

FIG. 42.—*Loss of consumer sur-*   FIG. 43.—*Loss of producer sur-*
plus   *plus*

assumption if the price change caused by the tax is a small one.)
The supply curve S_1S_1 is at constant cost. There is equilibrium
when OQ_1 is sold at price OP_1. However, on all units of consumption prior to OQ_1 the consumer enjoys a surplus satisfaction
since he would have been prepared to pay a higher price for those
units had supply for any reason been restricted. A tax P_1P_2 is
imposed and since supply is elastic the whole incidence is upon
the consumer. Price is raised to OP_2, and consumption restricted
to OQ_2. The inland revenue's gain in satisfaction is represented
by the rectangle P_1P_2ab. The total loss of satisfaction to the
consumer is shown by the larger area P_1P_2ac. There is therefore
a net loss of consumer surplus, the triangle abc, for which
government cannot compensate since its revenue is inadequate.

(b) *Loss of producer surplus*. In Fig. 43 we allow for costs not
being constant and the supply curve S_1S_1 rises from left to right.
For simplification the demand curve is taken to be wholly elastic,
which means that the full cost of a tax P_1T will be borne by the
producer. There is originally equilibrium when OQ_1 is sold at
price OP_1. However, on all units of production prior to unit OQ_1
the producer enjoys a surplus since he would have been prepared
to sell them at a price less than OP_1. After the imposition of the
tax P_1T, output is cut back to OQ_2. The gain to the inland revenue is TP_1ab, the loss to the producer the larger area TP_1cb;
i.e. there is a net loss of producer surplus shown by the triangle
abc.

If demand is completely inelastic there will be no loss of consumer surplus. Equally, if supply is completely inelastic there

will be no loss of producer surplus. In all normal cases, however, there will be *some* loss. The conclusion must therefore be that in the selection of expenditure taxes it will be desirable to impose them upon goods in inelastic demand and supply if we are to minimise the loss of surplus and cause as little dislocation as possible to the pattern of production and consumption.

11. Incidence of expenditure taxes in monopoly. In our earlier analysis of price (V, **21**) it was established that in order to maximise his profits the monopolist will restrict output to the point where marginal cost and marginal revenue equate. A tax upon his output is the equivalent of an increase in his costs. It therefore follows that if he is still to maximise profits he will restrict output further in order to secure a higher price. Closer examination reveals, however, that the detailed results of a tax upon monopoly (or upon neo-monopoly or oligopoly) will be very varied. Some situations are outlined in the paragraphs below (**13–15**).

12. Monopoly where the demand curve has a constant slope. In Fig. 44, DD is the demand (or price, PP) curve and is a straight line. This is a not unreasonable assumption, at least over a small price range. MC_1, marginal cost, is assumed to be constant. A

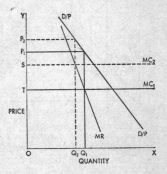

FIG. 44.—*Incidence of an expenditure tax in monopoly when the demand curve is of constant slope.* Equilibrium lies originally at the intersection of curves MC_1, and MR. The imposition of a tax, ST, raises marginal cost from MC_1 to MC_2. The intersection of MC_2 and MR determines the new output, OQ_2, and the new price, OP_2. With a demand curve of constant slope the price increase, P_1P_2 will be exactly half the amount of the tax.

tax will raise marginal cost from MC_1 to MC_2, and price from OP_1 to OP_2. The price increase will be exactly half the amount of the tax. In competitive conditions price would have been increased by the full amount of the tax, making a similar assumption of constant costs.

13. Concave demand curves. If the demand curve is concave then price will increase by an amount greater than half. If, moreover,

within the relevant range the *marginal revenue curve runs parallel*
to the demand curve, price will increase by the full amount of the
tax.

Where the *concave demand curve is of constant elasticity*, then
there will be established a constant ratio between marginal cost
and price. Marginal revenue being less than price, we discover
that in this case the marginal revenue curve slopes less steeply than
the demand curve. Price will now rise by an amount greater than
the tax.

14. Effect upon surpluses. In a monopolised industry there exists
already a *social* loss which is due to the restriction of output and
the consequent reduction of surpluses. The loss is increased when,
owing to the imposition of a tax, output is further restricted. In
this situation the taxation of competitive industries will be socially less damaging than the taxation of monopolistic industry.

In Fig. 45, OQ_1 is the output in perfect competition and OQ_2

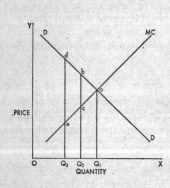

FIG. 45.—*Loss of surpluses in
monopoly.* The intersection of the
demand or price curve, DD, and
the marginal cost curve, MC, give
the competitive output OQ_1 at a
price aQ_1. Monopoly output is
assumed to be OQ_2 with a consequent raising of price to bQ_2 and
a loss of surplus bac. If a tax
which is equal to the difference
between aQ_1 and bQ_2 is imposed,
price now rises to dQ_3. This
second rise in price which is of
the same dimension as the first
results in a greater loss of surplus,
i.e. the trapezium dbce as against
the triangle bac.

the restricted output of monopoly. This produces a loss of surplus shown by the triangle bac. A tax of the same magnitude as
the difference between the competitive and monopoly prices
would have produced the same restriction of output and the same
loss of surplus. If such a tax is now imposed upon the monopoly
output, then production will be further curtailed to OQ_3 but the
loss of surplus is now much greater, i.e. the trapezium dbce as
against the triangle bac.

15. Implications for the optimum allocation of resources. Essentially the *social* cost of monopoly is the distortion which it pro-

duces in the allocation of resources. In perfect competition the factors will be deployed in such a way that marginal returns are the same in every use. In each use additional units of the factors will be employed up to the point where the value of their marginal product is equal to its cost. In monopoly, employment of the factors stops short of this point and a gap emerges between price and marginal cost. It would therefore seem desirable that measures of public finance should be directed towards closing rather than widening this gap, i.e. towards extending rather than restricting output.

INCIDENCE OF INCOME TAXES

16. Generality of income taxes. The generality of income taxes has a particular significance for the theory of incidence. By virtue of their generality it becomes impossible to shift their incidence by moving resources from taxed to untaxed uses, e.g. there is no area into which labour may move in order to escape the taxation of wages.

17. Incidence is upon the income receiver. It is generally agreed that the normal incidence of an income tax is upon the income receiver. Three arguments may be employed to support this contention:

(*a*) *Income tax is not a cost of production.* Taxes upon raw materials or local government rates may be looked upon as a cost of production and allowance made for them in price. This is not so with a tax upon the income of a business. Profits are a *realised* trading surplus or loss. They may be positive or negative and therefore it is impossible to anticipate liability to income tax. This being the case they cannot be costed and shifted to the customer.

(*b*) *The final product fetches only what the market will pay.* It is sometimes believed that income taxes are passed on in higher prices and indeed businessmen may go through the motions of doing so. In the event they must accept for their goods what the market will pay.

(*c*) *Inelasticity of the supply of resources.* The conclusive argument is that while the supply of resources to *particular* uses may be elastic, for *general* use it is highly inelastic, especially in the short run. After the imposition of a *general* income tax there is no more attractive use to which resources could be put that did not exist before the tax. Even in the long run the inelasticity of the demand for income will cause the inelasticity of the supply of resources to persist.

18. Exceptions when the supply of resources may be elastic. The preceding argument can be extended. If a tax is imposed upon wages in a particular trade it may to some extent be possible to shift its incidence. Rather than bear the tax, labour may be diverted into other trades. If the demand for that labour is inelastic the employer will prefer to accept the burden of the tax.

It may, moreover, be possible to shift the incidence of a *general* tax on wages, e.g. the employees' social insurance contributions, where there exist over-full employment and a strong, militant trade union movement. In this case, the demand for labour is inelastic whereas its supply is elastic. The incidence of the tax may therefore be shifted first to the employer and then to the consumer in higher prices.

Finally it may be argued that a monopolist who is prepared fully to exercise his power by restricting supply may, in certain circumstances noted above, be able to shift the incidence of his income tax to the consumer.

AN EQUITABLE DISTRIBUTION OF THE TAX BURDEN

19. General considerations. With statistics of income and consumption available and with a knowledge of tax incidence, it becomes possible in practical terms to ascertain the distribution of the burden of taxation. It is also possible to discuss what would be desirable if a tax system is to be equitable. Such discussion will take account of both the direct *money* burden and the direct *real* burden (*see* 1(*a*) and (*c*) above).

(*a*) The first objective of any tax system will be to minimise the total direct real burden of raising a given income. On grounds of the diminishing marginal utility of income it has been suggested that this might be achieved by the uniform taxation of all incomes above a certain level, incomes below this level being wholly exempt. This suggestion can be discounted on economic grounds since it would discourage all activity beyond what was necessary to secure the maximum untaxed income.

More reasonable is the proposition that all people in the same economic position should be taxed equally. A difficultly arises, however, in determining the extent to which people in *different* economic positions should be taxed differently.

(*b*) In considering *particular* taxes it is sometimes easier to agree what would be equitable, e.g. a tax on "windfall gains" such as a rise in land values may be deemed equitable since the gain is unplanned and unearned. It is also unexpected and therefore cannot be objected to on the economic grounds of disincentives. On the other hand it would be difficult to establish what *rate* would be equitable. Moreover, in an inflationary situation, a portion of the "gain" may be attributed to a depreciation in the value of money.

20. Three possible principles for an equitable distribution. We may now give consideration to three broad principles, each of which has been suggested as an equitable basis for the distribution of the burden of taxation.

(*a*) *Cost of service given to the individual.* This principle can be easily applied in the case of certain direct commercial services, e.g. postal services. However, it would not be possible to assess a *tax* on this basis. Services such as defence and justice financed by taxation could not be costed for the individual taxpayer in proportion to their enjoyment of those services.

(*b*) *Benefits enjoyed by individuals.* In the majority of cases this principle fails for the same reason. Since it is impossible to assess the extent of the services which individuals receive it is equally impossible to calculate the benefits which they derive from them. In certain cases this is not so; e.g. it is possible to state exactly what are the benefits enjoyed by the elderly from their pensions: they are the cost of the pensions plus the cost of their administration. It would then follow that these costs should be charged to the pensioner. If this *particular* result is not considered equitable and old age pensions are to be made an exception the difficulty now arises of establishing a *general* principle upon which exceptions are to be made.

(*c*) *Ability to pay.* This principle would seem to offer greater possibilities. It is related to the concept of the "sacrifice" to the individual of tax payments which in turn may be looked at in three different ways:

(*i*) *Equal sacrifice.* The object will be to secure equality in the distribution of the direct real burden by varying the distribution of the direct money burden.

(*ii*) *Proportional sacrifice.* The sacrifice to the individual should be proportional to the economic welfare which he enjoys from his income.

(*iii*) *Minimum sacrifice*. The total direct real burden borne by taxpayers as a whole should be minimised.

If we now assume that the relationship between income and economic welfare is the same for all taxpayers and also that an increase in income leads to a decrease in its marginal utility then the first principle (*i*) will lead to progressive taxation, the second (*ii*) to a steeper progression and the third (*iii*) to a high level of exemptions and a very high degree of progression. To give effect to the first two principles, the more rapidly the marginal utility of income declines the greater the degree of progression required in the tax system.

In the case of a *proportional tax*, its justification on the grounds of equal sacrifice depends upon a very slow decline in the marginal utility of income. Upon grounds of proportional sacrifice its justification depends upon there being *no* decline in the marginal utility of income.

A regressive tax, to be justified by the equal sacrifice principle, would require that there should be no decline in the marginal utility of income or that there should even be an increase. To satisfy the proportional sacrifice principle, marginal utility of income would have to increase, an untenable assumption.

CONCLUSION: No matter which of the three interpretations of "ability to pay" we accept we are drawn to the conclusion that an equitable distribution of the tax burden demands a degree of progression in the tax system.

PROGRESS TEST 7

1. Make a careful definition of the term "tax incidence". (**1**)

2. What are the principal advantages and disadvantages of expenditure taxes? (**2**)

3. Distinguish between specific and *ad valorem* duties. (**3**)

4. What will be the incidence of a tax upon a commodity in perfectly elastic supply and inelastic demand? Illustrate your answer. (**4**)

5. What will be the incidence of a tax upon a commodity which is supplied jointly with another? (**5**)

6. In what circumstances may a nation hope to shift the incidence of its import duties to its trading partners? (**6**)

7. Illustrate the incidence of an expenditure tax in perfect competition when the elasticities of demand and supply are equal. (7)

8. In what circumstances is the volume of savings likely to be affected by an expenditure tax? (8(a))

9. Criticise an expenditure tax on the grounds that the loss to the taxpayer is greater than the gain to the inland revenue. (10(a))

10. Illustrate the reason why it may be argued that the taxation of a monopoly causes a greater loss to the consumer than would the taxation of a competitive industry. (14)

11. Support the contention that the incidence of an income tax must inevitably be upon the income receiver. (16, 17)

12. In what exceptional circumstances will it be possible to shift the incidence of an income tax? (18)

13. State three possible principles which might serve as a basis for equitable taxation. (20)

14. Outline the argument which leads us to conclude that an equitable tax system must embody the principle of progression. (20)

CHAPTER VIII

Tax Effects

EFFECTS UPON PRODUCTION

1. The volume of production and the ability to work, save and invest. The extent to which the volume of production is affected by a tax depends upon its influence on the *ability* and the *desire* to work, to save and to invest.

(*a*) *Ability to work*. If personal efficiency is reduced then ability to work is correspondingly reduced. There are therefore strong arguments against taxes which reduce the economic welfare of the poorer element of the working community, e.g. direct taxes on low wages or indirect taxes on necessities. In practice it will be difficult to determine a level of money income below which efficiency will be impaired, particularly as this level will vary with occupation, e.g. the more strenuous and arduous forms of work will require a higher level than work of a less exacting nature.

(*b*) *Ability to save*. Savings are of two kinds:

(*i*) *Personal savings*. All personal taxation will reduce the ability to save except in the case of a tax which falls exclusively on incomes already so low that no saving is possible.

(*ii*) *Corporate savings*. Of far greater importance today than personal savings are corporate savings. They comprise the undistributed profits of the private sector and the surpluses of the public sector. Corporate savings will be less affected by taxation than personal savings since equity does not demand progression in the taxation or corporate income.

(*c*) *Ability to invest*. All taxation has the immediate effect of reducing the volume of resources available for investment in the private sector.

2. The volume of production and the desire to work, save and invest. We consider next the effect of taxation upon the *desire* to work, save and invest. It is generally assumed that *all* taxes have a disincentive effect but the problem is more complex than this simple assertion suggests. If it were suddenly possible to abolish the whole tax system, government being able to finance its expenditure from some new and extraneous source, than all incomes would be greatly increased. We might then expect people to be *less* willing to work so hard. They would probably spend more in order to raise their living standards but their margin of savings would also increase. Resources having been released for use in the private sector and consumer demand continuing to rise, it is probable that the rate of investment would also increase. We may therefore be drawn now to the broad conclusion that taxation as a whole has incentive effects in respect of our willingness to work, but disincentive effects upon our willingness to save and invest. However, this general truth will not hold good for all individuals and for every tax considered separately. The effects of a *particular* tax depend upon its character and upon the way that individual taxpayers react to it.

3. The individual taxpayer's reaction to taxation. The reaction of the individual to a particular tax depends upon the *elasticity of his demand for income,* i.e. the extent to which, in view of his personal commitments, he is willing to accept a reduction of income. It therefore follows that if demand for income is inelastic a reduction in the net income derived from work and saving will have incentive effects. The opposite will be true when the demand for income is elastic.

4. Determinants of elasticity of demand for income. We are now led to ask what are the determinants of the elasticity of demand for income. There would appear to be five relevant considerations:

(*a*) *Where personal commitments are wholly inelastic* the demand for income will be equally inelastic, especially when there exists no margin of savings to cushion the impact of an increase in taxation. This factor will therefore be of particular significance in determining the elasticity of demand for income of the lower income groups.

(*b*) *Where there exists a desire to maintain a given rate of saving* in order to achieve a given future income the demand for *present* income will be inelastic. This may be particularly relevant to the middle income groups.

(*c*) *Where the size of gross income is a status symbol* rather than a means of economic welfare the elasticity of demand for income may be zero. This will be a pertinent consideration to the upper income groups who may be motivated by a desire for greater economic power rather than increased net income. This view is reinforced by the need of top management to press for higher gross salaries regardless of the weight of taxation in order that they may pay to undermanagement salaries which yield a sufficiently attractive net income.

(*d*) *The disincentive effects of taxation are experienced on the marginal units of income*. In the case of many groups of workers output or hours of work are governed by collective agreement rather than by individual decisions to work faster or slower, longer or shorter hours. Consequently the tax which imposes a heavy penalty on an hour's over-time may have little effect on the number of hours worked.

(*e*) It has been indicated previously that *a very large part of total savings are made from corporate incomes*. These incomes may be distributed or saved but in an immediate sense savings do not have the competing alternative of consumption. Thus the flow of corporate savings will be less affected by an increase in taxation than by the desire to maintain a steady level of investment.

5. The effects of particular taxes. We may here adopt three different premises. We may assume firstly a *neutral* situation in which the elasticity of demand for income has no bearing upon the effect of the tax; secondly, the case in which the demand for income is *elastic*; and thirdly the case where it is *inelastic*.

(*a*) *A neutral tax*. The essence of a "windfall gain" is its unexpectedness. This being so, a tax upon it is likely to have very little effect upon the desire to work or save, regardless of the elasticity of demand for income. In a period of rapid economic expansion when the value of fixed assets appreciates rapidly there will be a good deal of scope for such taxes. However, when capital gains are *anticipated* the possibilities are narrowed, since a tax may have disincentive effects upon the will to work and save.

(*b*) *Elastic demand for income*. Various results will be achieved by different taxes:

(*i*) *Selective expenditure taxes*. Where only a small proportion of marginal income is spent on the taxed commodity there will be little disincentive effect and vice-versa when the taxed commodity absorbs a large part of marginal income.

(*ii*) *General income tax*. The disincentive effect of an income tax, particularly upon savings, will be greater than that of an equal yield expenditure tax. In the former case *all* income is subject to tax while in the latter case savings escape. They are only taxed when they are dis-saved.

Where the income tax is graduated, within the ranges in which it is most steeply progressive there must inevitably be a stronger disincentive effect than would be the case with a proportional tax. Equally a proportional tax will be more strongly disincentive than a regressive tax. However, while proportional and regressive taxation appear attractive on productional grounds, they will be rejected on distributional grounds.

(*iii*) *Inheritance taxes*. A graduated inheritance tax will be less disincentive to work and saving than an equal yield progressive income tax. In the latter case there is the immediate certainty of regular tax payments. In the former case, the more remote possibility that at some future date one's successor may have to bear the tax. This argument can be reinforced by examining the probable reactions of those who will inherit wealth. With a large untaxed fortune assured at some future date, they may be more inclined to relax their present efforts. A heavily graduated inheritance tax may make them more reliant upon their own work and savings.

(*c*) *Inelastic demand for income*. The preceding analysis is of course based upon the assumption that the demand for income has some measure of elasticity, If we now make the opposite assumption of a complete absence of elasticity then each of the taxes considered will have an incentive rather than disincentive effect.

6. Taxation and the pattern of production. The analysis so far has been concerned with the effects of taxation upon *incentives* and hence upon the total volume of production. Distinct from this, we may now consider the effect of taxation in *diverting resources* from one use to another.

As a starting point we may accept the general rule that the full and free operation of market forces produces the optimum allocation of resources. Preferred taxes will be those which cause the least disturbance to this pattern. We will look in the following paragraphs first to taxes of this character (*see* 7) and then make some examination of the many exceptions to the general rule (*see* 8).

7. Taxes with minimal diversionary effects. The owner of productive resources (land, labour, capital) will seek to divert them from a taxed to an untaxed use whenever the loss which he will suffer in this new use is less than the tax loss which he sustains in their present use. The extent to which this occurs will depend upon the elasticity of demand for the product of the taxed employment and the elasticity of supply of the factors to that form of production. The following are examples of particular taxes having no diversionary effects.

(a) *Taxes on windfall gains*. The unexpectedness of a windfall gain means that a tax upon it cannot be anticipated. It will therefore have no diversionary effects.

(b) *Taxes on site values*. If a tax is imposed on the site value of land without regard to the use to which the land is put there will be no diversionary effects, since the same tax is payable in *all* uses and the supply of land is wholly inelastic.

(c) *Taxes on monopoly*. Where market conditions are such as to induce no alteration of output or price, taxation will be absorbed entirely by monopoly profit. There will be no diversion of resources.

(d) *Non-differential taxes*. A tax which fell equally upon all uses to which resources could be put would have no diversionary effects. *General* taxes on income or expenditure approximate more closely to a perfect non-differential tax than do *particular* taxes on income or expenditure.

8. Taxes which achieve a desired diversion of resources. There will be many occasions when economic forces left undisturbed will establish a pattern of production which from the point of view of society seems undesirable. Taxation *may* then achieve a desirable re-allocation of resources; for example:

(a) *Taxes on products which are injurious* to health may restrict their consumption with a subsequent diversion of resources.

(b) *The restriction of domestic demand* by a general purchase tax or a selective employment tax may induce the diversion of productive resources to export trades, an important consideration for countries with balance of payment difficulties.

(c) *A tax upon monopoly* which causes the extension of supply at lower prices may result in a more productive re-allocation of resources.

(d) *Protective customs duties* may be employed by a country with chronic imbalance in its payments as a means of reducing imports and developing home industry. They may be preferred to quantitative restrictions through import licensing and other physical controls.

(*e*) *Taxation may achieve a re-allocation of resources between geographical regions* as well as between uses. Before the Second World War, the unequal burden of local taxation penalised industrial development in the distressed areas. Post-war, the introduction of the Exchequer Equalisation Grant (subsequently the Rate Support Grant) worked towards the removal of this penalty.

NOTE: The effects of taxation upon production have been here considered in isolation and without regard to the countervailing effects of public expenditure. A well-devised system of public expenditure *may* more than compensate for any restriction in production induced by taxation. Consideration will be given to this aspect of public finance in Part Four.

EFFECTS OF TAXATION ON DISTRIBUTION

9. The ideal tax system. It is readily agreed by all economists that an ideal tax system will cause the minimum check to production. It will be less universally accepted that it should reduce inequalities of income. Nevertheless, modern public finance increasingly sets out to achieve a distribution of income which maximises the economic welfare to be derived from a given volume of production. This does not necessarily imply a wholly equal distribution of income and it would in practice be impossible to define in precise terms the distribution which *would* correspond to maximum welfare. However, the disparity of incomes in most advanced economies is such that any reduction in inequality is to be considered a desirable objective.

10. Distributional effects of regressive, proportional and progressive taxes. These all tend to increase income inequalities, some more than others.

(*a*) *A regressive tax* is one whose direct *money* burden or direct real burden diminishes relative to an increase in income. Its effect is therefore to increase inequalities of income.

(*b*) *A proportional tax* leaves taxpayers in the same relative position after tax but the direct real burden is heavier upon the lower income groups, i.e. the effect is to increase income inequalities.

(*c*) *A progressive tax* which is only mildly graduated also imposes a heavier direct real burden upon the lower income groups.

On distributional grounds we are therefore led to the most steeply progressive tax which is consistent with minimal disincentive effects upon production.

11. The distributional effects of particular taxes. The examples outlined in **12–17** below include both regressive and progressive taxes.

12. A poll tax. A *per capita* tax of fixed amount would be the ideal tax from a distributional point of view *if* all gross incomes were equal. To the extent that they are unequal, a poll tax will be regressive since there will exist greater inequality after tax. Employees' social insurance contributions were of this nature when they were deducted at a flat rate.

13. Expenditure taxes. In general they are regressive but the extent of their distributional effects depends upon the type of commodity upon which they are imposed.

(*a*) *Necessities*. Particularly when the tax is *specific* and when it is imposed upon an article which is widely consumed and for which substitution is difficult, there will be a strongly regressive effect.

(*b*) *Luxuries*. These are less widely consumed and substitution is easier. Broadly, there may therefore be a progressive effect between poor and rich, particularly when it is an *ad valorem* tax, i.e. tax paid tends to be greater in the higher income groups.

14. Local rates. The British local rating system is sharply regressive in two ways:

(*a*) *Poundages*. Poundage varies from authority to authority. In general, poorer areas with heavier social commitments find it necessary to levy higher poundages, e.g. the difference between the urban area with a large slum clearance programme and the wealthy, residential, seaside resort.

(*b*) *Valuations*. The method of valuation takes no account of "ability to pay", i.e. income and commitments. There tends to be an irrational assumption that the larger the property and the "better" the neighbourhood, the greater is taxable capacity. This assumption is not borne out by present circumstances, e.g. a man may occupy a larger house and therefore pay higher rates only because he has a large family. Moreover, in many areas, retired people living on fixed incomes tend often to occupy larger houses simply because they are older and therefore cheaper to buy. A primary factor in the assessment of rateable value is the size of the house and no account is taken of the income or personal commitments of the occupant.

15. Income tax. Income tax lends itself to a greater degree of sophistication in the application of the progressive principle than any other tax. In the first instance the tax may be graduated, lower rates being charged upon the first bands of taxable income and higher rates thereafter. If desired, the rate of progression can be increased to the point where, on very large incomes, there is almost a hundred per cent penalty.

Secondly, through a system of reliefs and allowances the principle of "ability to pay" can be pressed further by exempting the lower ranges of income from taxation. However, in so far as some gross incomes are not sufficiently large for their recipients to enjoy the full advantage of their tax allowances, the distributional effects of a progressive income tax between taxpayer and non-taxpayer are not fully experienced. Moreover, there will not of course be any distributional effects between non-taxpayers with different levels of income.

16. Death duties. The transference of wealth upon death is an occasion when progressive taxation may achieve powerful distributional effects. Not only are inequalities of wealth reduced but also inequalities of the income which it generates. A death duty may be assessed in a number of different ways.

(*a*) *An inheritance tax*. Progression is accomplished by discriminating between inheritors, higher rates being charged upon larger legacies. This method fails in so far as an inheritor who receives *two* small legacies will pay less in tax than one who receives a *single* large legacy of exactly the same amount. In order to maintain progression it may then prove necessary to discriminate on the basis of the existing wealth of the various legatees.

(*b*) *Estate Duty and Capital Transfer Tax* (*CTT*). From 1893 to 1974 estate duty in Britain was assessed as a progressive tax geared to the size of the net estate passing at death and without regard to the number of inheritors, their existing wealth or the size of their legacy. Since the tax was based upon the value of the whole inheritance rather than its component parts a larger sum was paid than would have been the case with an inheritance tax. The redistributional effects between those who inherit wealth and those who do not were correspondingly greater.

The tax suffered from two weaknesses. It gave no incentive to break up large estates between a number of inheritors. Secondly, it gave every incentive for large portions of an estate to be passed on during the lifetime of the benefactor.

In 1974, a Capital Transfer Tax replaced Estate Duty and included gifts *inter-vivos*. Subject to certain exemptions and limitations all capital transfers during the lifetime of the benefactor or upon his death are subject to a progressive tax on a cumulative basis. As the sum of transfers increases so marginal increments are taxed in progressively higher tax bands.

It will be observed that this tax reduces the possibility of avoiding death duties.

17. Capital levies. A graduated tax upon wealth, either on an annual or on a once-for-all basis, will have powerful distributional effects. Like death duties it will serve to reduce not only inequalities of wealth but also inequalities of the income which wealth yields.

ADMINISTRATIVE EFFECTS

18. Economy of administration. Productional and distributional effects apart, it is important that revenue should be raised in the most efficient and economical way. In this respect the objective will be to reduce to a minimum the ratio of collection costs to revenue. It therefore follows that a higher rate of tax on a small number of items is preferable, on administrative grounds, to a lower rate on a large number.

The principle of economy militates in favour of a simple tax structure in other ways. Flat-rate taxes which do not discriminate will seem attractive. Thus a *specific* customs duty which does not distinguish between countries of origin will be preferred to an *ad valorem* duty which gives certain countries favoured treatment. A high flat-rate income tax imposed without distinction upon a small number of taxpayers will be preferred to a multi-rate system with many exemptions, imposed upon a large body of taxpayers. An income tax collected at infrequent intervals will be more economical, if less convenient to the taxpayer, than one collected regularly throughout the year.

19. Economy to the taxpayer. The cost of collection must be viewed also from the standpoint of the taxpayer. In the first place taxes must be collected at a time and in such a way that the economic activity of the taxpayer is not so disrupted as to involve him in a loss greater than his tax payment.

Secondly, in so far as part of the administrative burden is thrust upon the taxpayer himself, the tax system should be kept as simple as possible with a minimum number of easily understood forms. This is important, moreover, if the taxpayer is to enjoy all the reliefs and allowances to which he may be entitled. It has been suggested that in Britain at the present time, owing to the complexity and, to many, the incomprehensibility of tax regulations, the nation as a whole over-pays its taxes.

20. Conclusion. In assessing the overall desirability of a given system of taxes, productional, distributional and administrative effects will be balanced against each other.

PROGRESS TEST 8

1. What will be the effect of taxation upon the ability to save? (**1**(*b*))

2. In what circumstances may it be argued that taxation has incentive rather than disincentive effects? (**2**)

3. What general consideration governs the reaction of the individual taxpayer to a given tax? (**3, 4**)

4. Compare the effects of different forms of taxation upon the desire to work. (**5**)

5. Explain why taxation may be employed as a means of re-allocating productive resources. (**8**)

6. Compare the distributional effects of expenditure taxes, local rates and income taxes. (**13–15**)

7. On grounds of administrative economy what forms of taxation will be preferred? (**18**)

PART FOUR

MACROECONOMIC THEORY AND APPLICATION

CHAPTER IX

The Business Cycle

THE NATURE OF THE BUSINESS CYCLE

1. Industrial fluctuations. Variations in the level of economic activity may be observed in different time series.

(*a*) *The secular trend.* In progressive economies the long-term trend lies in an expansion of production and consumption, although the trend is not necessarily smooth and continuous. In the nineteenth and twentieth centuries the secular trend of Western countries has been one of growth.

(*b*) *Seasonal variations.* These occur within the space of one year and are to be associated primarily with the weather, e.g. holiday catering trades.

(*c*) *Erratic fluctuations.* Forces external to the economic system (e.g. earthquake, political upheaval) may cause quite erratic fluctuations.

(*d*) *Long waves.* These comprise two movements; a period in which the overall tendency is for the level of activity to rise is followed by one in which the trend is downward. Superimposed upon the long waves are business cycles proper.

(*e*) *The business or trade cycle.* This comprises a regular alternation of periods of prosperity and depression extending over a span of from three to twelve years (*see* **3** and **8**).

2. Long waves and business cycles observed historically. In the nineteenth and twentieth centuries it is possible to observe long waves within which are found a number of business cycles.

(*a*) 1822–42. *Depression.* Within this period there are two com-

109

plete business cycles but the years of depression outnumber the years of prosperity.

(*b*) 1843–73. *Prosperity*. There are here three and a half cycles but there are far more years of prosperity than of depression.

(*c*) 1874–94. *Depression*. The period contains two and a half business cycles with nearly three times as many depressed as prosperous years.

(*d*) 1895–1913. *Prosperity*. In contrast to the previous era, this was a time of great prosperity but within it are found two and a half cycles.

(*e*) 1918–39. *Depression*. This was an age of overwhelming depression but within it may be discerned two short cycles.

(*f*) 1945–66. *Prosperity*. In the post-war period to 1966 there was continuing growth and predominating prosperity. The periodicity of the "managed" business cycle increased but the recessions were much less severe, always showing some expansion of the national output however marginal. The years of depressed trade were 1952–53; 1958–59; 1962–63. Keynesian techniques for regulating the economy had *apparently* proved successful (*see* X).

(*g*) 1966–(?). *Stagflation*. After 1966 emerged the new economic phenomenon of "*stagflation*", production stagnant, unemployment rising, inflation escalating. By 1972, restrictive policies had contained the rise in the rate of inflation and improved the balance of payments. Growth however was minimal and unemployment exceeded one million. A massive stimulus was given to aggregate demand, producing an upturn in economic activity. This was quickly overtaken by resumed inflation. Restrictive policies were gradually applied and in 1976, for the first time since 1945, there was a positive fall in the level of national output.

If prosperity is viewed as a relative term one may speculate upon the possibility that 1966 marked the beginning of a long wave of depression.

3. **Phases of the business cycle.** The whole cycle falls into four parts.

(*a*) *The Upswing*. This is the phase of prosperity and expansion.

(*b*) *The Down-turn*. The point of crisis at which expansion ceases.

(*c*) *The Downswing*. A period of depression and contraction.

(*d*) *The Up-turn*. Confidence is revived prior to the next upswing.

4. Manifestations of the business cycle. There are three principal criteria which either singly or in conjunction with one another may be employed to distinguish the phases of the cycle. These are the pattern of employment (5) and the volume of production and volume of consumption (6).

5. Employment. Many economists and politicians have been inclined to accept unemployment figures as the only index of the business cycle. This can be quite misleading since unemployment may arise from a number of causes, other than the business cycle directly.

(a) *Frictional unemployment* (short-term structural unemployment). There is a constant flux in which some firms within an industry are expanding while others are contracting. There are consequently men who are unemployed for short periods.

(b) *Seasonal unemployment.* This occurs because certain occupations may only be followed at certain times of the year.

(c) *Secular unemployment* (long-term structural unemployment). Obsolescent industries will contract continuously and men will become redundant, e.g. the Lancashire cotton industry since 1918.

(d) *Cyclical unemployment.* Figures rise or fall according to the phase of the business cycle.

The hard core of unemployment in Britain in the inter-war years (1918–39) was secular, but superimposed upon it was an enormous volume of cyclical unemployment. In such a period there may therefore be an upswing in which cyclical unemployment diminishes but there remains still a high level of secular unemployment. If we add to this the inevitable numbers of seasonally and frictionally unemployed and depend upon employment figures as the sole criterion we may be drawn to erroneous conclusions.

Moreover, in a situation in which wages respond to downward pressure (commonly the case in the nineteenth century) a downswing need not necessarily be accompanied by any appreciable increase in the numbers unemployed. Work will be shared out at lower wage levels. Similarly, expansion may be brought about through increased *productivity* while the level of employment remains static or even falls.

6. Consumption and production. The two other criteria are the volume of production and the volume of consumption.

(a) *Volume of consumption.* In the case mentioned above where unemployment figures do not rise in a downswing, the consumption of goods and services will fall. This will now prove a more reliable index of the state of trade but once again it cannot be taken in isolation.

(b) *Volume of production.* A downswing may be in progress but *the volume of consumption will not fall* if a country is living off its capital. Equally, in an upswing, consumption may be falling but the *total* volume of production rising if we are *adding* to capital. In such cases production and employment will prove more accurate indices.

7. Conclusion. If all three manifestations of the business cycle point in the same direction there can be no doubt about the phase of the cycle. If they diverge then the considerations outlined above must be set against each other in order to draw an overall conclusion.

OUTLINE OF BUSINESS CYCLE THEORIES

8. Explanations of the business cycle. The business cycle is a complex phenomenon and it would be idle to pretend that it may be explained by any single cause. Nor may one claim that the same set of causes will be equally applicable to every cycle and to every country. This is acknowledged by most writers on the subject and the differences which emerge between them are largely differences of emphasis. (The bibliography (Appendix II) lists most of the writers mentioned in this chapter.)

The principal business cycle theories may be conveniently grouped under five headings (these are dealt with in the rest of this chapter).

(a) *Psychological theories.*
(b) *Monetary theories.*
(c) *Over-investment theories.*
(d) *Under-consumption theories.*
(e) *Keynesian theory.*

9. Psychological theories. Attention has been given to psychological causation by a number of writers, notably Lavington, Pigou, Taussig, and Keynes (*see also* **21**). They do not suggest that psychological factors alone account for the business cycle but that they play an important part and should be given due attention.

It is argued that the business world is affected by alternating waves of optimism and pessimism which reinforce the upswing and the downswing. In a period of expansion and rising prices investment will take place in certain areas of the economy and will be based upon sound objective considerations of the rate of interest, market potential, and other factors. There develops a feeling of optimism which is contagious. It is transmitted to other areas of the economy where investment will take place in the anticipation of a return greater than is warranted by the circumstances.

The effect is cumulative and eventually there is the realisation of *an error of optimism*. Keynes suggested that, "When disillusion comes this (false) expectation is replaced by a contrary *error of pessimism* . . .". Investment yield is now underestimated and therefore investment does not take place, although a wholly objective examination of purely economic factors would have warranted it.

In short, psychological theories stress that in attempting to forecase the future the business world is subject to certain irrational influences which distort investment decisions.

10. Monetary theories. It may be observed that cyclical fluctuations date from the development of a market economy at which point money assumed an important role. Not unnaturally monetary theories have therefore been offered in explanation (*see* 11–13).

11. Over-indebtness. The business world has become increasingly dependent upon bank advances for its working capital out of which are paid wage and material bills. The upswing of the cycle is therefore associated with an expansion of credit, the downswing with a contraction. It has been suggested that in a period of expansion bank-lending becomes too liberal, in part owing to over-optimism and in part owing to the competition which exists between banks and which induces them to lend too easily in an attempt to attract customers. A point is reached when caution prevails and credit is tightened. With finance no longer available, the boom is levelled off and the downswing set in motion.

12. Inappropriate interest rates. The theory of Knut Wicksell suggests that there is a *natural* rate of interest and a *market* rate. The former is the rate at which demand for and supply of capital are in equilibrium. The market rate charged by the banks frequently diverges from the natural rate. When it is below, the expansion of credit is excessive and when it is above the natural rate credit facilities are harmfully restricted. Only when the two rates coincide will there be stability and it is argued that such stability would only be achieved in a static economy. In a dynamic economy the two rates will inevitably be out of mesh.

The criticism of this view lies in whether variations in credit are the cause or the effect of cyclical fluctuations. Certainly expansion and contraction of credit go hand in hand with boom and slump, but the indications are that this occurs only *after* an up-turn or down-turn in business activity.

13. Sensitivity of stocks to the rate of interest. R. G. Hawtrey offers the view that the root cause of the business cycle is monetary. The level at which merchants are willing to maintain their stocks is highly sensitive to the rate of interest. A slight fall enables them to borrow more cheaply and maintain their stocks at a higher level. Similarly a rise will induce them to run down their stocks with a consequent curtailment of manufacturing production.

The difficulty with this explanation is that in the upswing when profit margins are expanding, a higher rate of interest may easily be absorbed and do little to curb the boom. In the downswing, when the business climate is bleak, a low rate of interest may do little to induce merchants to replenish stocks of which they cannot dispose.

14. Over-investment theories. The essence of all over-investment theories is the disequilibrium which occurs when capital goods industries are expanded at a more rapid rate than the consumer goods industries from which they derive. Observation supports the contention that the business cycle affects the capital goods industries more acutely than the consumer goods industries. In the upswing their output is more rapidly increased and in the downswing more severely curtailed.

The source of the problem may be traced to the upswing. The production of capital goods relative to consumer goods is increased to a level not warranted by the underlying situation. There develops a *vertical disequilibrium* in the structure of production. It is said to be vertical since the various stages of production which all contribute to the final consumer goods are no longer being developed in harmony.

Three groups of over-investment theories may be distinguished. These are discussed below (**15–17**).

15. Monetary. Hayek, Mises, Robbins and others have claimed that a vertical disequilibrium is induced by monetary causes. However, they stress that the business cycle requires more than a purely monetary explanation. It is the *real* maladjustment brought on by monetary factors which terminates the upswing. During the boom increased savings cause low interest rates which make profitable lines of investment which previously were unprofitable. There is more specialisation, mechanisation and a lengthening of the process of production. An unwarranted proportion of productive resources is being devoted to capital goods relative to consumer goods. Consequently a time arrives when it is realised that the profitability of further investment is bound to diminish and the downswing begins. Savings contract, interest rates rise and investment falls off as the attempt is now made to shorten the process of production.

16. Technological progress. Certain writers such as Cassel have minimised the role of money and stressed the importance of real changes in the field of production, e.g. inventions, new markets. These changes which come in surges offer new investment opportunities which are followed through to an extent which is not truly justifiable. A disequilibrium therefore occurs.

17. "Acceleration and magnification of derived demand." Stress has been laid upon this explanation by J. M. Clark and R. F. Harrod. The ultimate purpose of all production is consumption. The demand for capital goods is therefore *derived* from the demand for consumer goods. However, capital goods are durable and require to be renewed only every ten years, say. Simply to maintain the stock of capital at its existing level would therefore call for ten per cent of it to be replaced annually. If in one year there occurred an increase in consumer demand, then in that year there would have to be a net addition to the stock of capital equipment. Ten years later that net addition would have to be replaced, i.e. in one year out of ten there would have to be a greater output of capital goods. If in another year consumer demand fell, in that year it would be necessary to replace only a smaller amount of capital equipment and the same would be true ten years later.

In short, as the demand for capital goods is derived from the demand for consumer goods, fluctuations in the latter will be transmitted in a magnified degree to the latter. It would seem therefore that there is an inherent tendency towards vertical disequilibrium associated with fairly violent fluctuations in capital investment.

18. Under-consumption theories. Theories of under-consumption date from the English classical school of economists and many are clearly fallacious. In this century, however, scientific treatment has been given to this theme by a number of writers, in England notably J. A. Hobson (*Economics of Unemployment*, 1922). It should be stressed, however, that these theories offer an explanation of crisis and the downswing rather than an account of the whole cycle.

Two forms of the theory may be considered, deficient purchasing power (*see* **19**) and over-saving (*see* **20**).

19. Deficient purchasing power. The baldest expression of this idea is that in advanced economies there is a continuing tendency for consumer purchasing power to fall below the level necessary to absorb the whole of current production. It is argued that the value of the product does not wholly find its way into the hands of the consumer to be translated into demand. Firms will put part of the proceeds to reserve or will repay loans. Purchasing power is therefore "leaked" from the economic system and incomes fall. The remedy, it is suggested, lies in the distribution to everyone of an annual national dividend geared to the level of national production.

It would be wrong to suppose that purchasing power is lost to the economy. Every part of the value of the end product is returned to one or other of the factors as its price for having participated in production. (We have seen earlier that the value of total production must equate with national income. They are different aspects of the same thing.)

20. Over-saving. A better reasoning of under-consumption theory is to be found in its interpretation as over-saving (*cf.* J. A. Hobson). Equilibrium between production and sales is disturbed, it is said, by devoting too great a proportion of current income to savings and too little to consumption. Depression is thereby engendered. This may be caused in three ways; the kernel of the theory is to be found in (*b*) and (*c*):

(*a*) "*Pure*" *savings*. We may save without investing in capital goods. These "pure" savings therefore lie idle and the total level of demand is diminished. However, this cannot be the explanation of the point of crisis since observation shows that at this phase of the cycle investment outstrips savings and not vice-versa.

(b) *Lower demand for consumer goods.* Increased saving means that less money is spent on consumer goods.

(c) *Increased supply of consumer goods.* Savings are normally employed productively, i.e. they are invested in capital goods. The object is to increase the flow of goods for final consumption.

Simultaneously, therefore, demand declines while supply increases, reducing price and the profitability of production for the consumer. A crisis will result.

The reason for this over-saving is quite simply the maldistribution of incomes. The propensity to save of the rich is high, their propensity to consume relatively low. The poor who would consume more are not able to do so and therefore the remedy lies in a redistribution of incomes.

It is true that such a policy does increase consumer spending and also that once the downswing has begun depression is aggravated by excessive saving, *provided that* these savings do not express themselves in a demand for capital goods. However, the implication by some writers that excessive saving *and* investment are features of depression is clearly incorrect, since in the downswing it is investment which is insufficient to absorb the savings which the community is attempting to make.

KEYNESIAN EMPLOYMENT THEORY

21. A general theory. The *General Theory of Employment, Interest and Money,* by John Maynard Keynes, subsequently Lord Keynes, was published in 1936. It is this work which provided the main theoretical basis for government economic policy in Great Britain after 1945. It is a *general* theory in the sense that it is applicable both to full employment economies and to economies which are not fully employed. English classical theory could only give an account of the former. As he was writing in a time of massive unemployment, Keynes's main preoccupation lay not unnaturally with this problem. He does, however, offer an explanation of the whole business cycle and it sometimes tends to be forgotten that he had a good deal to say about full employment and the problem of inflation.

In his *General Theory* he gives due attention to the explanations of other writers and the cornerstone of his own work is in fact to be found in the under-consumption theory of J. A. Hobson (18).

However, he strikes at the heart of classical economics and its emphasis on *laissez-faire*.

22. Basis of classical theory. The basic assumption of English classical theory was that in a *laissez-faire* economy, provided market forces were in no way impeded, involuntary unemployment could not exist. Given the unrestrained interaction of supply and demand there would always emerge an equilibrium price which would guarantee that all resources were absorbed into production. If at any time labour was unemployed this was only because the wage level was too high. At a lower level unemployment would disappear. It followed therefore that any unemployment which persisted was of a voluntary nature.

A justification of this argument was offered in *Say's Law of Markets* (*see* G. Neisser, bibliography, Appendix II) which reasoned that people are willing to work and produce only in order to satisfy their desire for the produce of others. If a man increases his output his money income will be increased. The subsequent increase in his expenditure will express itself in a demand for the employment of others and will be sufficient to take from the market goods equivalent to those produced by virtue of his own employment.

The fundamental assumption is that *all* income will be spent upon either consumer goods or capital goods at a rate sufficient to maintain the full employment of all resources. In other words, the level of demand will always be consistent with full employment.

23. Effective demand, income and the level of employment. The focal point of the Keynesian analysis is the concept of *effective demand* with a low level of employment resulting when this is deficient. In simple terms, effective demand may be defined as the amount of money which is *actually* spent on the products of industry (*see* Appendix I).

Now spending generates income, while saving does not (**24**). One man's expenditure constitutes another man's income and by extension *national expenditure* will determine *national income*. They are different aspects of the same thing and must of necessity be equal. A third aspect will be the money value of the total volume of production, since the sum of what the nation pays for goods and services will be distributed in rents, wages, interest and profits to the factors which have contributed to their production. Three conclusions follow.

(a) *The level of employment is a function of national income* (*output*). If national income rises, so will employment and vice-versa.

NOTE: This fundamental Keynesian assumption was justifiable in the 1930s when heavy unemployment ensured that national income would only be increased by the use of more labour. With so much unused capacity there would have been little point in dwelling upon the possibility of increased *productivity*. In recent years, with very much higher levels of employment and with the accent consequently upon raising productivity, the assumption is perhaps less valid. One of the phenomena of recessions since the Second World War has been rising unemployment *accompanied by rising national income,* although admittedly the increase in the latter has been very small.

(b) *The level of national income will be determined by the level of effective demand.*

(c) *The production of an output of goods and services of given value generates incomes sufficient to purchase them in their entirety if we so desire.* We must do so, however, if the levels of income and employment are to be maintained.

The situation may be summarised as follows:
Total National Output=National Income=National Expenditure (Effective Demand)=Level of Employment.

24. Saving. Effective demand manifests itself in expenditure, both private and public, upon consumer and capital goods. While a part of the increased income which would accompany a higher level of employment will be spent upon consumption, a part will be saved. If the higher levels of income and employment are to be maintained, then these savings must be used for investment, i.e. the purchase of capital goods. In short, the level of effective demand and hence employment will be finally determined by the interaction of the rate of saving and the rate of investment.

A problem arises in that decisions to save and decisions to invest are taken for different motives and usually by two different sets of people. Rarely is it the case that saving is undertaken to finance specific business projects. The bulk of savings are made by individuals for personal reasons. Investment is undertaken by the entrepreneur in the anticipation of profit.

25. The propensity to save and the propensity to consume. The proportions of their incomes which people will be disposed to spend and save will in the first instance depend upon psychological factors and personal circumstances, and secondly on the level of income.

(*a*) *The paradox of thrift*. Saving may be undertaken to make provision for the future either as a matter of prudence or in order to satisfy some ambition. The decision to save will not be related to the investment needs of the entrepreneur nor will it be much influenced by the rate of interest, particularly when interest rates move through only a narrow range. It is more likely to respond to changes in the general economic climate. In the downswing of the cycle a growing sense of insecurity is likely to lead to a decrease in the propensity to consume and an increase in the propensity to save. Conversely, in the upswing greater optimism will lead us to spend more and save less. We have therefore *the paradox of thrift*, when there is too much saving in times of depression and too little in times of boom and inflation.

(*b*) *The level of income*. However, this will be the principal determinant of both the propensity to save and the propensity to consume. As incomes rise, so the *marginal* propensity to consume declines while the marginal propensity to save increases, i.e. an increase in income will be followed by a less than proportionate increase in consumption and more than a proportionate increase in saving.

It follows that in the lower income ranges the marginal propensity to consume is high, while in the higher income ranges it is the marginal propensity to save which is high. Therefore if it is desired to stimulate total effective demand and employment through increased consumption this goal may be achieved through a redistribution of incomes. Keynes recognised the legitimacy of this approach although he was not so attracted to it as to a stimulation of investment, "at a time when there is still much social advantage to be gained from increased investment".

26. The rate of investment. Investment in the Keynesian sense means specifically *the creation of fresh capital equipment* either by private firms or by public authorities. It may take the form of plant, buildings, raw materials, roads, airports, docks. It does not mean the purchase of securities on the Stock Exchange since this normally implies only the transfer of ownership of existing capital.

Investment is undertaken by entrepreneurs in the expectation of profit. This expectation will be governed by the entrepreneur's estimate of the probable yield of an asset and the rate of interest. He will only borrow money if he is confident that the yield will add to his profits at least sufficient to cover the rate of interest which he must pay. Keynes used the expression *"marginal efficiency of capital"* to describe the relationship between the *anticipated* yield of one more unit of investment and the cost of producing it.

The rate of investment is therefore controlled by the rate of interest and by the marginal efficiency of capital. It is the uncertainty attaching to the marginal efficiency of capital which Keynes believed lay at the root of the problem of unemployment. In advanced economies the tendency was for businessmen to err on the side of pessimism, i.e. to underestimate capital's marginal efficiency with a resulting chronic deficiency of effective demand owing to a shortage of investment.

It was therefore in this field that government action could be most effective. The maintenance of a level of effective demand consistent with full employment would require repeated injections of public investment.

27. The multiplier effect. Under-consumption theories in their crudest form pointed to consumption as the principal determinant of effective demand, writing down the importance of investment as being derived only from the demand for consumer goods. This is to ignore the *direct* influence of investment upon effective demand, income and employment. An investment of £100 does not bolster effective demand by that amount alone. Incomes in the capital goods industries will certainly be increased to this extent, but the *purchasing power* of the recipients is also stimulated. Assuming that they save £20, then an additional £80 will now be spent upon consumption. Income receivers in the consumer goods industries have now an extra £80. Assuming that they too save one-fifth, then their purchases of consumer goods will be increased by £64.

This multiplier effect therefore serves to stimulate effective demand by considerably more than the amount of the initial investment. It gradually loses momentum with the saving which accompanies each rise in income and its ultimate strength will be determined by the propensity to save and the propensity to consume (*see* **25**). In our example it would reach a figure of £500 Looked at from the point of view of employment, if average wages are £10, then the initial investment creates employment for

10 men. As a result of the operation of the multiplier, employment is created for 50 men.

The multiplier will of course operate in reverse. A decline in investment will be followed by a reduction in total effective demand of a far greater magnitude. This is the point of crisis when a deficiency in investment would be followed by a much more substantial decline in the propensity to consume. It is at this point that Keynes recommended government action *before the multiplier could take effect*. Effective demand should be restored either by replacing the lost unit of investment, by bolstering the propensity to consume or by both.

28. The apparent disequilibrium of saving and investment. The multiplier leads us to an explanation of the business cycle in terms of saving and investment. At first sight it would seem that fluctuations result when the two are not in equilibrium.

(*a*) *The downswing.* At the point of crisis effective demand falls below what is required to support the existing level of activity owing to-

(*i*) *A decline in investment* which is unaccompanied by an increase in consumption.

(*ii*) *A decline in consumption* which is unaccompanied by an increase in investment.

In either case it would seem that "pure" savings are made which are not absorbed into investment, i.e. there is a *deflationary gap* between savings and investment, which causes an immediate deficiency in effective demand subsequently magnified by the multiplier.

(*b*) *The upswing.* At the up-turn effective demand rises above what is required simply to maintain the current level of activity. Investment exceeds savings since either:

(*i*) *Increased investment* is unaccompanied by decreased consumption; *or*

(*ii*) *Increased consumption* is unaccompanied by decreased investment.

The resultant *inflationary gap* need not cause a steep rise in prices *provided that* there were unemployed resources which are now called into use to increase the flow of production. Once full employment has been achieved output can only be expanded through greater productivity and if an undesirable inflation is to be avoided then it will be necessary to *curb* the growth of effective demand.

We conclude that the economy may therefore be stabilised at any level of activity between depression and full employment provided that means are discovered to close the savings/investment gap.

29. Equation of savings and investment. A number of writers have adhered to the view expressed above that cyclical fluctuations are caused by a real gap between savings and investment. However, in the *General Theory*, Keynes insists that *savings and investment must always be equal*.

(*a*) *The upswing.* Given a fixed propensity to save, i.e. that people will always save the same percentage of their incomes, the entrepreneur can always call forth a volume of savings equal to his investment. The banks advance him credit with which he extends his operations. Employment and incomes are increased, making possible the accumulation of the required amount of savings. It is not therefore a situation in which investment waits upon saving but one in which saving waits upon investment.

(*b*) *The downswing.* In contradistinction, decisions to save *will not promote investment,* the volume of which is determined only by factors already considered. However, if savings *are* made without a corresponding increase in investment, then employment and income in the consumer goods industries decline to the point where savings are reduced to the volume dictated by the lower level of investment.

Once a movement has begun in either direction, the multiplier serves to magnify it. Savings and investment will always be in equilibrium but may be so at any level of employment. Stabilisation at a *particular* level can be achieved if the government stabilises the principal variable, the rate of investment (*see* **26** above).

30. A reconciliation of the two views of saving and investment. Keynes' assertion that saving and investment must always equate gave rise to a good deal of debate and a number of attempts have been made to reconcile it with the view that the cycle results from a disequilibrium of saving and investment. The Swedish school of economists (*see* X, **4**(*a*)) have offered the following explanation.

Any economic situation can be viewed from two positions.

(*a*) *The ex ante position* is the position from which one anticipates what will occur. In the expectation of a certain level of income, society makes plans for consumption, saving and investment which it believes will be sufficient to fulfil this expectation.

The plans for saving and investment, however, are made by two different groups of people. They are not co-ordinated and in the *ex ante* position it is unlikely that they will equate.

(*b*) *The ex post position* is the realised position. We are now able to observe what in fact happened. Expenditure upon consumer goods and capital goods generated a level of income just sufficient to permit a volume of saving exactly equal to the volume of investment. In other words, expenditure upon consumption supported the consumer goods industries at a certain level of activity and contributed to national income. Expenditure upon investment added the balance of national income, an amount exactly equal to what could possibly be saved.

If, therefore, *ex post* investment (which equals *ex post* saving) turns out to be less than *ex ante* saving, then there was a deflationary gap *between expectation and realisation* and the economy has moved into the downswing. Conversely, if *ex post* investment exceeds *ex ante* saving there was an inflationary gap and the economy has entered the upswing.

31. Summary of the Keynesian theory. The Keynesian theory of employment may be summarised as follows:

(*a*) *Level of income and employment.* The basic assumption is that when national income is high, employment will be high and when it is low, employment will be low.

(*b*) *Income=expenditure.* National income will be determined by the total expenditure upon consumption and investment of both the private and public sectors. Consumption and investment are in turn governed by other variables which are the ultimate determinants of national income. Their relationship may be shown in the following way.

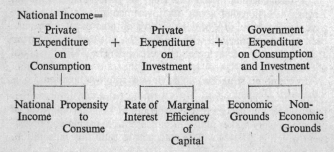

National Income=

Private Expenditure on Consumption	+	Private Expenditure on Investment	+	Government Expenditure on Consumption and Investment
National Income Propensity to Consume		Rate of Interest Marginal Efficiency of Capital		Economic Grounds Non-Economic Grounds

(*c*) *Consumption* is governed by the propensity to consume which decreases as income rises.

(*d*) *Investment* depends upon the marginal efficiency of capital and the rate of interest. The marginal efficiency of capital depends upon the anticipated yield and the cost of producing the capital.

(*e*) *Government expenditure* upon consumption and investment will be determined primarily on social and political grounds. From time to time, however, circumstances may force it to subordinate its expenditure to economic forces.

32. The instruments of control. In line with the Keynesian analysis, government may attempt to regulate the level of effective demand in three ways.

(*a*) *Direct controls*. While acceptable in times of emergency direct physical controls in normal circumstances are incompatible with the aspirations of a free society. There will be consequently a strong preference for indirect methods, viz. (*b*) and (*c*).

(*b*) *Fiscal controls*. In the *General Theory* Keynes stressed that fiscal policy would be the principal weapon.

(*c*) *Monetary policy*. The importance of monetary policy as a complementary weapon should not, however, be underestimated. Credit will be expanded or contracted in accordance with the need to stimulate or curb activity. A detailed consideration of monetary policy lies outside the scope of public finance, although it will be seen shortly that the way in which the public debt is managed is the central feature in the implementation of this policy.

PROGRESS TEST 9

1. Suggest five different types of industrial fluctuation.   (**1**)

2. Describe the phases of the business cycle.   (**3**)

3. What are the three principal indices of the level of economic activity?   (**4**)

4. Distinguish four different types of unemployment.   (**5**)

5. List the five principal groups of business cycle theories.   (**8**)

6. In what way do irrational impulses contribute to the business cycle?   (**9**)

7. Assess the importance of monetary theories as an explanation of the business cycle.   (**10–13**)

8. "Fluctuations in the capital goods industries are of far greater magnitude than those in the consumer goods industries." Explain this assertion.   (**17**)

9. What does J. A. Hobson contribute to the theory of the business cycle? (20)

10. For what reason may the theory of Lord Keynes justly be described as a "general theory"? (21)

11. Expose the weakness of the English classical theory of employment. (22)

12. Establish the relationship between effective demand, national income and the level of employment. (23, 24)

13. What are the determinants of the marginal propensity to consume and the marginal propensity to save? (25)

14. What are the determinants of the rate of private investment? (26)

15. Explain the action of "the multiplier". (27)

16. Explain the phrases "inflationary gap" and "deflationary gap". (28)

17. On what grounds does Keynes argue that the rate of saving and the rate of investment must always equate? (29)

18. How does the Swedish school of economists attempt to explain the paradox that while savings and investment must always equate the root cause of the business cycle is their disequilibrium? (30)

19. What three methods of stabilising the economy are at the government's disposal? (32)

CHAPTER X

Stabilisation Policies

THE THEORY OF FISCAL REMEDIES

1. Economic policy aims. In Part Three, we considered the distributional effects of different forms of taxation. In the search for an ideal system we have been very much concerned with social criteria. However, it should be remembered that the re-distribution of incomes will have productional effects, since the pattern of consumption and the volume of investment will be largely determined by the size of disposable incomes within different income groups.

When we turn to the *direct* effects of a system of public finance upon production we have to produce accord between the need to raise revenue and the need to ensure stability, expansion and full employment.

In advanced economies the chief concern will be at first stability, but if growth is ignored, then stagnation will result from an insufficient attention to investment. This proved to be the case in the 1930s.

On the other hand, it is not to be assumed that a fiscal system which encourages indiscriminate investment provides the solution to the problem of growth. Investment in the wrong direction can only increase the pressure of demand upon real resources and add to the burden of inflation.

2. Adaptation of fiscal policy. The maximisation of the total economic satisfactions of the community as the ultimate aim of public finance was aimed at in a crude way from the time when parliament first secured control of the revenue. Adam Smith indicated that if an economy were to prosper, it might be necessary for society to provide certain services which private enterprise would not.

3. Nineteenth century aims. Throughout the nineteenth century, the problem was tackled in a rather negative fashion. Revenue was required to pay for collective services and taxation to produce this revenue had to be devised in such a way that it did not harm private enterprise. The so-called "Treasury view" was that the public sector of the economy should be minimised.

In the nineteenth century, this view was reasonable enough since tremendous opportunities existed for private enterprise and little state action was necessary to secure a high level of activity.

Nevertheless, government had long considered it a responsibility to take action in times of distress and this had traditionally taken the form of either a transfer of incomes, i.e. public assistance, *or* public investment, i.e. public works.

In practice, such remedies could only be temporary since any expansionary tendency set in motion by public investment would soon have its "multiplier effect" neutralised by a desire to balance the budget. By making revenue equal expenditure, expansion in the public sector would soon be cancelled out by contraction in the private sector.

4. Modern thinking. Conditions in the 1930s stimulated a more positive approach to public finance.

(*a*) The first analyses were by a group of young Swedish economists, notably Gunnar Myrdal and E. Lindahl. Their contribution emphasised three essential points:

(*i*) The avoidance of fiscal measures which exacerbated the problems of depression. In the 1930s, this was very much in evidence, e.g. high taxation during a depression.

(*ii*) Investment in the public sector to stabilise or promote growth as necessary.

(*iii*) A system of public accounting which could cope with the new applications of public finance.

(*b*) It has already been noted that the first major contribution to this thinking in England was from J. M. Keynes (*see* IX, **21**). In his *Treatise on Money* (1929), he laid stress upon the ratio of savings to investment expenditure. In the downswing of the cycle, the business world preferred to increase its liquid rather than physical assets. The propensity to save was too great and the propensity to spend too little to sustain incomes and employment. A reduction in the propensity to save (and a corresponding *increase* in the propensity to spend) could be achieved primarily through a reduction in interest rates.

(*c*) In the *General Theory* there is a shift of emphasis. The level of activity and hence income is a product of effective demand. The volume of saving is governed by the level of income rather than the rate of interest. The level of effective demand is therefore the key factor and is susceptible to treatment by fiscal rather than monetary means. This being so, it has to be acknowledged that fiscal policy must stretch beyond an attempt to stabilise the economy through activity in the public sector alone. The level of effective demand throughout the *whole* economy must be controlled.

In the 1930s, public opinion was not ready to accept these revolutionary new ideas but there was a gradual increase in the understanding of the problem.

5. Developments in the forties. Beveridge's *Full Employment in a Free Society* (1942) provided the blueprint for postwar government action. In an appendix, E. Kaldor demonstrated that a greater reflationary stimulus could be expected from budget deficits rather than from activity financed by taxation.

In 1944, the White Paper, *Employment Policy*, accepted government's fiscal responsibilities in controlling the level of national economic activity although it skirted around the still controversial area of finance through budget deficits.

Keynes's *General Theory* had now been accepted as a guide for practical policy. It had also laid the foundations for the quantitative assessment of the action necessary to secure full employment, i.e. the *Estimates of National Income and Expenditure*. Any gap between the estimate of total available resources and the probable demand upon them would be filled by public policy. It is important to note, as Keynes himself pointed out, that this gap might be inflationary as well as deflationary, i.e. effective demand could as well be excessive as deficient. Just as fiscal measures might be necessary to stimulate activity in depression so equally they would be necessary to curb activity in inflation.

6. The weapons of public finance. As an instrument of control public finance has two weapons.

(*a*) On the *revenue* side, the amount and structure of taxation may be varied.

(*b*) On the *expenditure* side, the amount and direction may be varied.

These two approaches are dealt with in the next two sections (**7–15; 16–22** below).

THE REVENUE APPROACH

7. "Filling the gap." "At a level of income corresponding to full employment", says Keynes, "the gap between total income and total consumption is so great that private investment cannot fill it. If unemployment is to be avoided, total effective demand must be increased by public investment or the propensity to consume must be increased by re-distributive taxation."

The gap may therefore be filled by increased investment or increased consumption.

(*a*) *Investment*. A progressive income tax, for example, will decrease the propensity of the rich to save. Provided that the forthcoming revenue is invested (in the Keynesian sense of expenditure on producer goods), then total demand will be sustained.

(*b*) *Consumption*. It is possible to rearrange taxation in such a way that expenditure upon consumption goods is varied, e.g. a reduction of purchase tax on goods in popular demand.

8. Automatic stabilisers. It may be advantageous to adopt certain devices which take effect without the need for a public policy decision, which in itself could be taken as an acknowledgment of a weakness in the economy (which in turn could weaken business confidence). Automatic stabilisers include:

(*a*) *An unemployment insurance fund*. In times of expansion, funds are accumulated and purchasing power restrained in such a way as to exercise some braking effect upon rising prices. In recession, the funds are disbursed and this helps to sustain effective demand.

(*b*) *Capital depreciation allowances*. When tax depreciation allowances are based upon the original cost of the equipment, in times of expansion and inflation more than the *true* profit is taxed. This exercises some curb upon rising prices. In recession, with prices falling, less than true profits are taxed.

9. Disadvantages of automatic stabilisers. The stabilising effects of such automatic devices may be weak relative to those achieved by positive policy decisions. They may, however, be strengthened by varying depreciation allowances or the rates of social insurance contributions.

High initial allowances, which permit the businessman to write off a large proportion of his investment against tax within the first year, afford him some protection against subsequent variations in the price level and encourage investment.

Increased social insurance contributions during inflation serve to restrict purchasing power and restrain prices. The converse will be true if contributions are reduced in times of recession and falling prices.

10. Policy-effected stabilisers. More powerful control can be exercised when stabilising measures are the result of positive policy decisions. However, it must be recognised at the outset that purely fiscal measures are in general likely to be more successful in curbing inflation and too rapid growth than in promoting recovery. In particular, certain tax measures will be more effective in countering inflation, others in countering deflation.

11. Cost-push inflation. It has been argued that the British economy since 1945 has been subject to cost-push inflation. This is to say that in a period of expansion, rising prices and full employment, wage demands have been readily conceded. Their cost has been absorbed in a still higher level of prices which has in turn provoked more wage demands (the "wage/price spiral").

The long-term trend has been for money wages to outstrip the volume of production with further inflation now resulting from excessive demand. Ultimately a balance of payments crisis has arisen. The high British price level and the abundance of purchasing power have been attractive to foreign sellers but unattractive to buyers. For the same reasons, British manufacturers have found it easier to sell in home rather than foreign markets. Imports have increased and exports diminished and the government has been compelled to take anti-inflationary action in defence of the pound.

A period of trade recession has then followed, although it is to be noted that in contrast with earlier manifestations of the trade cycle, while unemployment has risen, so has the total volume of production, even though marginally. This indicates a continuing rise in productivity.

NOTE: It should be stressed that a wage-cost-push view of inflation is to be associated with neo-Keynesian economists who have dominated post-war economic thinking. They have advocated that inflationary pressures could be relieved, either by increasing the level of unemployment or, if this proved unacceptable, by adopting incomes policies. In as much as the

measures outlined in **13,** and **14** below aim to increase unemployment by reducing aggregate demand, their validity
depends upon the correctness of this view. Monetary economists would dispute it (*see* XIII for a full discussion of this
controversy).

12. Anti-inflationary taxation. Two approaches are possible, one
aimed at curbing consumer demand, the other at curbing investment. The effects of curbing the pressure on resources in these
ways are discussed below (**13, 14**).

13. Restricting consumption. This could take the form either of
personal taxation or of an expenditure tax.

(*a*) *Tax on income.* Some economists assert that anti-inflationary action designed to curb demand, if based upon increased
personal taxation, will accentuate the wage/price spiral. Thus the
result will be inflationary rather than deflationary. For this proposition to be true it must be assumed that an easy credit policy
permits demand to rise in step with tax liability. Clearly, therefore, restrictive taxation must be accompanied by tighter credit.

A more pressing danger lies in the possibility that the disincentive of high income taxes may reduce the volume of production,
thereby increasing inflationary pressures. The solution to this
problem may lie in a tax system which penalises expenditure (*see*
(*b*)) rather than income. The practice of exempting from taxation
life assurance and mortgage interest could be extended when
necessary to encourage other forms of saving.

(*b*) *Tax on expenditure.* An expenditure tax based upon total
annual outlay and with steeply progressive rates sufficient to
secure the equivalent of income tax revenue would, it has been
suggested, overcome disincentive effects. The principal objection
lies in the probability that such a tax would fail to satisfy the
principle of equity. There would not necessarily be a correlation
between the annual volume of personal expenditure and the individual's ability to pay. Heavy expenditure in any one year might
well be the result of emergency. If allowances were made for such
objections the tax base would be still narrower and of necessity
rates would be more steeply progressive.

However, it can be accepted that expenditure taxes (e.g. VAT,
excise duties) make useful *auxiliary* weapons since they penalise
spending without affecting saving.

14. Restricting investment. Inflation may be the result of excessive pressure of demand not only upon resources to satisfy consumer needs but also upon resources for investment. This may be the result of dramatic technological advances which cause capital to play an increasingly important part in the processes of production, in a way that has occurred, for example, in the USA since the Second World War. It may also be the result of the need to replace simultaneously large quantities of worn-out equipment.

Action may therefore be necessary to restrain the rate of investment. This may be accomplished by making depreciation allowances less favourable or by in fact placing an expenditure tax upon investment, the proceeds possibly to be disbursed at a later date when investment might require stimulation.

In principle, however, the rate of investment is likely to prove more amenable to regulation by credit policy. Hawtrey pointed out that the volume of stocks which merchants are willing to hold is very sensitive to monetary conditions. This has proved also to be the case with capital equipment, owing to the development in this field of hire-purchase. A restriction of all sources of credit will therefore serve to damp down investment.

15. Reflationary taxation. It has been noted earlier that while variations in the structure and amount of taxation may have powerful and direct anti-inflationary effects, it is unlikely, at least in the short run, to be of much value in stimulating the level of effective demand (*see* **10**).

A reduction in the standard rate of income tax is unlikely to produce any immediate increase in spending, particularly in view of the fact that relatively few tax payers earn much income upon which tax is levied at this rate. An increase in tax allowances which would increase to a greater extent the spending capacity of taxpayers in the lower income groups, perhaps by taking their incomes entirely out of the range of standard rate taxation, would prove very difficult for administrative reasons. Considerable time would have to be allowed for the revision of the tax codes.

Similarly, a reduction in expenditure taxes, if upon those goods in inelastic demand (e.g. tobacco, alcohol), would produce no more spending. The relaxation of general expenditure taxes would produce some result but it must be recognised that certain major sections of the economy are particularly sensitive to expenditure tax changes (e.g. the motor car industry). Reductions here may provide a valuable stimulus.

In general, it must be concluded that demand is more likely to respond to a relaxation of credit, particularly in the area of hire-purchase. In the application of public finance to countering depression, the principal weapon lies on the side of expenditure.

THE EXPENDITURE APPROACH

16. The special problem of regional unemployment. It has been observed already that unemployment may be classified as frictional, secular or cyclical (*see* IX, 5). The hard core of the unemployment problem of the 1930s (i.e. the problem of chronic, long-term unemployment) was secular. Certain industries which in the nineteenth century had been of major importance were contracting, e.g. cotton, steam engineering, wrought iron, shipbuilding. In accordance with the economic doctrine of comparative advantage, these industries had been concentrated in areas which afforded lowest production costs. In this respect, the chief attraction had been the steampower which a coalfield site could provide, coupled with local raw materials. The result was excessive regional specialisation. The coalfields of the North, the Midlands, Scotland and South Wales were each heavily dependent upon a single industry. When this industry contracted, there were no alternative employment opportunities.

Between the two World Wars, the industrial expansion which took place was of a different character. It was directed towards consumer rather than producer goods and the principal attraction was a large market rather than a coalfield site. Industrial growth tended to be centred upon the London area and here the burden of unemployment was much less marked than in the North. At Jarrow, for example, unemployment rose to 75% of the insured population while in the South the figure approximated to 6%.

17. Government measures. There have been various attempts to relieve the problem of unemployment over the past thirty years by means of public expenditure. These measures are outlined below.

(*a*) *Special areas* (*Development and Improvement*) *Act 1936.* The first *positive* attempt to deal with this problem was the Special Areas (Development and Improvement) Act of 1936. The parts of the country with unemployment figures above the national average were designated *Special Areas*. In some the government built trading estates, offering factories to industrialists at low rentals and with relief on rates and taxes and loans on favourable terms.

The results were not encouraging and few firms were attracted to the estates.

(b) *Distribution of Industry Act 1945.* The 1944 White Paper, *Employment Policy*, while outlining the measures the government proposed to deal with the problem of *national* unemployment, emphasised the need to plan the location of future industrial expansion if heavy concentrations of local unemployment were to be avoided. In short, in the areas which had suffered most acutely from unemployment, a deliberate policy of industrial diversification would be pursued. These recommendations were embodied in the important Distribution of Industry Act 1945. The Special Areas were re-named *Development Areas* and the government was empowered to:

(*i*) Build factories.

(*ii*) Make loans to private industrial estate companies.

(*iii*) Improve local services such as transport, housing, power.

(*iv*) Give financial assistance to firms already established in the Development Areas.

In the situation of labour scarcity after the Second World War, industry was more ready to respond to these measures and between 1945 and 1948, 52% of the country's industrial expansion took place in the Development Areas. Between 1948 and 1955, the figure was 28%.

(c) *Local Employment Acts 1960 and 1963.* These superseded the earlier legislation, aid now being concentrated upon more narrowly defined *Development Districts* (Labour Exchange areas with an unemployment figure in excess of 4.5%).

(d) *Regional planning*, 1964. In 1964 a section of the new Department of Economic Affairs was assigned to study the problem of "regional imbalance". Eight regions were designated, each with two new bodies:

(*i*) *Regional Planning Board.* Its function was to co-ordinate government activity in the regions and to draw up a plan to promote regional economic growth.

(*ii*) *Regional Economic Planning Council.* Comprised of part-time local representatives its function was to advise on the preparation and implementation of regional plans.

Although the boards and councils still exist their influence disappeared with the abolition of the DEA and a return to more traditional economic thinking.

(e) *Industrial Development Act 1966.* The Development Districts of 1960 were widened into five Development Areas: the whole of Scotland, except Edinburgh; the whole of the Northern Region; a small area around Merseyside; most of Wales; the extreme South West. In place of investment allowances the government now made *case grants* towards capital expenditure, payable at twice the national rate in these new Development Areas.

(*f*) *Special Developmental Areas, 1967.* In 1967 a number of labour exchange districts within the Development Areas and with acute unemployment problems were designated *Special Development Areas*. The list was extended in 1971.

(*g*) *Regional Employment Premiums.* An aspect of the Selective Employment Tax was its rebate to manufacturing companies operating in the Development Areas together with a SET premium of 38p and a Regional Employment Premium of £1.50 for each male employed.

Because of the persistence of the regional problem, Government undertook "the most comprehensive and extensive programme to stimulate industrial and regional regeneration ever attempted in Britain". The Industry Act 1972, provided new national and regional financial incentives to encourage investment. A new framework for *special* provision for firms in difficulty was provided. A new Industrial Development Executive was established, assisted areas extended and further retraining schemes adopted.

In April, 1975, the Accelerated Project Scheme encouraged firms to bring projects forward. The scale and form of assistance was negotiable.

18. Cyclical unemployment, public expenditure and the multiplier. The corrective effect of public expenditure depends upon the multiplier, but even without this it is highly desirable when there is under-employment. *In the private sector* activity is motivated by the prospect of profit and if this does not exist the entrepreneur is right to minimise all *variable* costs including labour. *From the public point of view* labour is a fixed cost since it must be supported and it is therefore desirable that it should produce anything rather than nothing. When we take the multiplier into account the beneficial effects of government spending are considerably enhanced.

In forestalling the downward phase of the cycle the timing of public expenditure is all-important. It is essential to sustain effective demand at the first sign that it is failing and before the multiplier can act in reverse. This is extremely difficult since there will always be an interval before public works start to bolster effective demand, for three reasons:

(a) Planning time.

(b) Plans having been completed, a considerable time may elapse before they express themselves fully in a demand for resources.

(c) The negotiation of contracts may be protracted.

Even if contingency plans are kept specifically for this purpose, they will require revision.

19. Direct action by central government. With the great expansion of the public sector since 1945 it has become easier for the government to take direct action through its own investment policies. All the nationalised industries as well as other public corporations have long-term development plans which are subject to ministerial direction. In some cases, the timing of these plans can be geared to employment policy. However, action along these lines must be carefully considered. In so far as industrial plans are subordinated to the needs of compensatory finance, so their economic viability may be endangered, e.g. the alternate speeding up and slowing down of the development programme of the electricity industry could have damaging and far-reaching effects.

20. Action through the private sector. Government may attempt to stimulate investment in the private sector, not only through tax reliefs but, as we have seen, through the positive incentive of *cash grants* (**17** (*e*) above). The experience of 1966 and 1967 would seem to indicate that the weakness of this course lies in the entrepreneur's unwillingness to invest, no matter how strong the financial inducements, if the business climate seems unfavourable and offers little prospect of profit.

21. Action through local authorities. Like public corporations, local authorities have their long-term development programmes of urban renewal, roads, schools and other public works. The speed at which these plans can be realised depends upon ministerial approval and upon the availability of finance from private sources, from the National Loans Fund and from Exchequer Grants. The government is therefore in a position to accelerate or decelerate building programmes in line with the needs of national economic policy. Action in this field can also be of value in selectively supporting activity in areas of localised unemployment when it may be necessary simultaneously to adopt national policies of an anti-inflationary nature.

22. Action through the consumer. A level of effective demand consistent with full employment may be restored not only by replacing lost units of investment but also by stimulating activity in the consumer goods industries. This may be achieved by increasing the level of income of those who are likely to spend rather than save. For example, state pensions, family allowances, sickness and other social security benefits may be increased (if desired, on a scale geared to total income).

However, the range of action in this area is limited, as will be the strength of the result. Moreover, for administrative reasons there is likely to be delay before the effects can be felt. It should also be recognised that redistributive measures which encourage consumption at the expense of saving and investment will be inimical to growth.

PROGRESS TEST 10

1. Explain the basic weakness of the action taken by government in the nineteenth century to relieve distress. (3)

2. Outline the theoretical argument which establishes fiscal policy as the principal instrument of economic control. (4, 5)

3. What two approaches may be made to close the "savings/investment gap"? (7)

4. What do you understand by the term "automatic stabilisers"? Give examples and indicate their advantages and disadvantages. (8, 9)

5. Why can it be argued that variation in the tax structure will be more effective in curbing inflation than in promoting growth? (10, 15)

6. Outline the sequence of events in Britain since 1945 which has led to recurrent sterling crisis and the application of anti-inflationary taxation. (11)

7. What forms may anti-inflationary taxation take? (12–14)

8. Making specific references to government action in this field, explain why measures of public expenditure will be of particular value in remedying the problem of secular unemployment. (16, 17)

9. Explain why "the multiplier" will considerably magnify the

effect of public expenditure in curing cyclical unemployment. **(18)**

10. For what major reason have governments since the Second World War been in a particularly strong position directly to influence the level of employment? **(19)**

11. What is the basic weakness of cash grants to private industry as an inducement to expansion? **(20)**

12. What action may government take through local authorities as a means of stimulating activity? **(21)**

CHAPTER XI

The Problem of Growth

THE BASIS FOR GROWTH

1. Growth as an objective. It is by no means a universally-held view that rapid economic growth is either morally desirable or even a condition of a higher standard of welfare. There are those who would avow that the excessive pursuit of purely materialistic objectives already distracts us too much from more important goals. The clash of ideas is illustrated by the currently fashionable paradox of advocating more rapid economic progress while simultaneously denigrating the affluence which it brings. A stage of economic development may be reached, moreover, when more leisure is to be preferred to the creation of more goods as a means to greater welfare. Upon these matters economics can shed little light and it is assumed rightly or wrongly that rising output is both morally desirable and consistent with a better and happier life.

Having made this assumption, there remains still the practical problem of making an accurate measurement of the rate of growth. The difficulties encountered in the calculation of the Gross National Product (*see* Appendix I) make comparisons and trends difficult to interpret.

2. The modern dilemma. In the 1930s, discussion of economic policy was centred upon the problem of unemployment. In the 1940s and '50s Keynesian remedies were directed primarily to securing *stability* at a high level of employment, but it was argued in the 1960s that success was achieved only at the expense of growth. "Stop-go" methods meant fiscal encouragement of expenditure and expansion for a time, only for a balance of payments crisis to prompt a reversal of economic policies.

The result was a disappointingly low growth rate, lower than almost any other European country. Of greater importance is the difficulty of meeting domestic claims for higher standards of living without inflation.

By 1960, there had emerged two distinct schools of thought on the subject of growth:

(a) On the one hand there were those who argued that faster economic expansion should not be attempted at the expense of stable prices, full employment and a sound balance of payments.

(b) On the other hand it was countered that the first step to a more rapid growth rate was to make more efficient use of our resources, particularly labour. The resulting steady increase in productivity would eliminate the need for the periodic restrictive policies which have drawn the British economy into a "high level of stagnation".

Official recognition of the importance of the second viewpoint was implied by the establishment in 1962 of the National Economic Development Council (N.E.D.C.) and by the publication in 1965 of the National Plan. Emphasis at the new Department of Economic Affairs was laid upon expansion, although the more cautious view traditionally expressed by the Treasury prevailed in 1966 when the government determined that the economy would once more have to be stabilised as a condition of successful long-term growth. The course of events from 1962–6 was repeated ten years later from 1972–6.

3. Availability of the factors of production. The rate of economic growth is dependent in the first place upon the quality and the quantity of the factors of production and their *availability at the time and place they are required* (*see* (a) and (b)).

(a) *Labour.* In this category falls labour of all kinds, skilled and unskilled, manual, clerical, managerial and entrepreneurial. Firstly, the supply of labour is governed by the size of population and its age and sex distribution. Secondly, it depends upon whether it is labour of the required kind and whether it is available in the right place. Determining considerations here will be labour's geographical and occupational mobility, which in turn will be influenced by the country's social and economic institutions and cultural background. Attitudes to work, prejudices, class barriers, educational opportunities, domestic responsibilities, ambition or lack of ambition, all have a bearing upon the quality of labour and the flexibility of its supply in response to changing demand.

(b) *Land and capital.* Conventional analysis distinguishes between these two factors, since land (natural resources) is in an ultimate sense in fixed supply while capital is in variable supply. For practical purposes it may be difficult to make a clearcut distinction. (At what point after the application of human effort do natural resources become a part of our stock of captial?) We shall therefore deal with the two factors as one, since in an immediate sense the supply of both will vary in response to the application of labour.

Before natural resources may reasonably be said to be available to production, they must first be discovered, then extracted, adapted and transported to the place where they are required. Their availability will vary in accordance with our willingness to sacrifice present for future consumption.

4. Efficient use of the factors. The rate of economic growth depends secondly on the efficiency with which the factors of production are utilised. This depends upon:

(a) Full knowledge of the possible uses to which they may be put.

(b) The organisation of the economic system and the efficiency with which it works.

5. Use of labour. For labour to be utilised with maximum efficiency it must be used fully and continuously, i.e. there must be a continuing high level of employment. There must be also a high degree of mobility, not simply in a geographical sense but, more important, between industry and industry, skill and skill and even within the same firm, *between more and less productive uses.*

Mobility may be increased by greater material incentives, but, perhaps more importantly, by the certain knowledge that change will not cause too great a dislocation of the life of the individual. It will also be aided by the avoidance of excessive specialisation. The implication here is that training, at least initially, should be broadly based.

Experience has unfortunately shown that full employment is likely to reduce the mobility of labour. In times of rising price and expanding profit margins and even in recession when it is thought to be only temporary, the employer has tended to hoard labour, particularly when it is skilled. On the side of the employee there is a natural resistance to change when he can continue to earn a comfortable living in his present occupation. This has led to the often repeated charge that British industry is overmanned and that we do not make the most efficient use of our scarcest factor, labour.

Observation also indicates quite clearly that there is a direct correlation between a labour market in which there are considerably more vacancies than men to fill them and the recurrent balance of payments crises which have made necessary action to curb demand and growth. In this situation, many economists, notably Professor Frank Paish, urged that it is essential to maintain a margin of unused productive capacity if we are to have growth without inflation. (see XIII, 12)

6. Use of land and capital. Efficiency also demands flexibility of investment in order to meet the changing demands of new technologies and new markets. Here again a major problem arises since much investment is highly specialised and long lasting. Moreover, it is likely to take place well in advance of the demand for the consumer goods which are the goal of all production. A decision to construct a power station or a steel mill in a particular location cannot easily be reversed, yet technological or market changes may invalidate the premises upon which the investment decision was first made.

It will therefore be desirable to avoid sudden and large-scale changes in both the volume and the direction of investment. Sometimes, however, this may be unavoidable. In the interest of stability it may prove necessary to restrict investment in the private or, more commonly, in the public sector. (The nationalised industries have not infrequently complained of the dangers of treating their investment programmes as an instrument of economic management.) Again, new discoveries or new markets may call for sudden increases in the volume of investment in a particular direction.

Finally, it must be emphasised that, to be efficient, investment must be highly selective. The mere creation of extra productive capacity is not in itself sufficient. It should be extra capacity of the *most* productive kind. To this end, industry must be prepared to invest extensively in research and development even though no immediate return can be guaranteed. The rate at which technology advances must ultimately be the limiting factor to the rate of growth.

TAXATION, EXPENDITURE AND THE SUPPLY OF LABOUR

7. The revenue approach. Variation of the structure and the weight of taxation will affect the supply of labour both in quantity and quality and in its allocation between competing uses.

(a) *Direct personal taxation*. The incentive or disincentive effect of income tax upon hours worked or intensity of effort is impossible to determine with any precision. When a tax is upon personal income, the only alternative to work is leisure and people may consume more of it, particularly when the rate of tax is steeply progressive. On the other hand, there is some complementarity between the demand for leisure and the demand for income since more money is required to spend upon leisure pursuits. Moreover, when personal financial obligations are inflexible, higher taxation may have an incentive rather than disincentive effect (*see* VIII, **4** (*a*)).

More predictable will be the effect of direct personal taxation upon the quality of the labour force, i.e. its composition. Deliberately or by accident, certain occupations may be discouraged or favoured, e.g.:

(*i*) A capital gains tax with no provision for an earned income allowance discriminates against organised activities in which income derives from capital gains.

(*ii*) When there is no provision for averaging, a progressive income tax discriminates against incomes which fluctuate year by year, e.g. actors, writers.

(b) *Indirect taxation*. When taxation is indirect and imposed upon a limited range of goods, people may prefer to consume more untaxed goods rather than more leisure. The taxes may be deliberately so devised that those goods which are complementary to leisure (e.g. afternoon football) are taxed heavily, while those which are substitutes for leisure are untaxed. This might include any form of consumer expenditure, e.g. a new family motor car.

If the base for an expenditure tax is widened the disincentive effect may still be less than in the case of an income tax, since although expenditure is penalised, saving is not. Whether in fact incentives are impaired or improved will depend upon the relative strength of demand for future consumption (i.e. savings) and for present leisure.

(c) *Direct business taxes*. The overall and discriminatory effects of profits taxes upon the supply of entrepreneurial effort will be similar to those of direct personal taxation upon the supply of labour. The overall effect will be indeterminate, but if the return to risk bearing and enterprise is penalised too heavily there will be an inclination to engage in less adventurous activities where returns are lower but more certain. Progressive change may therefore be inhibited.

8. Expenditure approach. Government expenditure may take two forms:

(*a*) *Personal direct transfers.* Personal incomes are varied directly through, for example, pensions, unemployment benefits or family allowances. The effect upon incentives will be similar to that of tax variations and equally uncertain. Better pensions may or may not lead to earlier retirement. Lower unemployment benefits may or may not affect the speed with which work is resumed. A more certain effect upon the supply of labour will result from direct government expenditure (*see* (*b*)).

(*b*) *Direct government expenditure on subsidies and environmental services.* Where real incomes are increased by subsidising, for example, staple foods, there is less likelihood that leisure will be substituted for consumption than might well be the case when money incomes are increased by personal transfers.

When we consider the effects of environmental services upon the supply of labour, government expenditure is seen in its most powerful role. Efficient health services affect the size of the working population and the length and efficiency of working life. Education services condition the quality of labour. Re-training facilities improve occupational mobility and hence labour's availability. Expenditure upon housing and communications improves geographical mobility.

TAXATION, EXPENDITURE AND THE SUPPLY OF CAPITAL

9. Definition. In a real sense, the *supply of capital* means the investment of resources in the satisfaction of future rather than present wants. Two separate functions (and usually two groups of people) are involved. Present consumption must be sacrificed and savings made. These savings must then be employed productively. The first function is performed both by individuals and by business companies. The second is carried out primarily by companies. Public finance can be brought to bear upon both functions.

10. Personal savings, income tax and expenditure taxes. An expenditure tax *may* be more favourable to savings than an equal yield income tax since payment is postponed until such time as expenditure in fact takes place.

EXAMPLE. A man with an income of £2,000 p.a. has the alternative of a 50% income tax or an equal yield expenditure tax at a rate of 100%. If we assume that in either case £50 is saved in year 1, that these savings are spent in year 10 and that an interest yield of 5% is spent in the intervening years, the following comparison will emerge:

	Year 1 Consumption	Tax	Saving
Income tax	£950	£1,000	£50
Expenditure tax	£975	£975	£50

	Years 2–10 Consumption	Tax	Saving
Income tax	£1,001·25	£1,001·25	Nil
Expenditure tax	£1,001·25	£1,001·25	Nil

	Year 10 Consumption	Tax	Saving
Income tax	£1,050	£1,000	−£50
Expenditure tax	£1,025	£1,025	−£50

Under income tax it is necessary initially to sacrifice £25 more in consumption than under expenditure tax in order to secure a return of 5% to the same volume of savings. In other words the return to abstinence is only 2½% net under income tax but 5% under expenditure tax (i.e. a return of £2·50 on an abstinence of £50 as against a similar return on an abstinence of only £25). In years 2–10. the relative positions will be exactly the same. In year 10, more tax is paid and less consumption enjoyed under expenditure tax. Dis-saving will therefore be discouraged.

A final conclusion on the relative merits of the two taxes can only be made when account is taken of the effect of each upon the propensity to save. If one leads to a greater volume of savings in the short term, what will be the effect upon the level of income and hence the *ability* to save in the long term? Dependent upon whether or not these savings are employed productively, total income will either rise or fall.

11. Personal savings, capital taxes and taxes on investment income.

We may next compare the effects upon the supply of savings of capital taxes and taxes on investment income.

(*a*) *Annual taxes on capital compared with taxes on investment income.* If we assume an equal yield from each form of tax, then at first sight it would seem that if the *average* return on capital is 5% then a 20% income tax or a 1% capital tax gives the same return, e.g.:

$$£100 \text{ at } 5\% \text{ yields } £5$$
$$\therefore 20\% \text{ } income \text{ tax} = £1$$
$$\text{And } 1\% \text{ } capital \text{ tax} = £1$$

However, for those who enjoy an *above-average* return on their investment, a capital tax will have less disincentive for saving than a tax upon investment income. In other words, a smaller volume of savings yields a higher return.

On the other hand, it will be equally clear that a capital tax will impinge more severely upon liquid assets and other non-income yielding capital than would an investment income tax.

We may therefore conclude that where savings are held in liquid form a capital tax is a deterrent but that the opposite will be true when savings are invested in risky ventures where the return is above average.

(*b*) *Occasional capital levies* (*e.g. estate duty*) *compared with taxes on investment income.* The relative effect upon saving of an investment income tax and an equal yield death duty proportional to the size of estate will vary with age group, e.g.:

(*i*) *For young people*—the substitution of a death duty for an investment income tax means that they are exchanging a number of small annual payments for the *possibility* of a single large one in the *distant* future.

(*ii*) *For old people*—this would be exchanging a small number of annual payments for the *certainty* of a large one in the *near* future.

Whether the net effect is to increase or reduce total savings depends upon the relative number of young and old people and upon their attitude to the interests of their heirs. It is likely, however, that the increase in saving of the young would be outweighed by the dis-saving of the old. There would therefore be a net reduction in the total volume of savings. An opposite argument is that most savings are short-term in the sense that they are destined to be spent before death. To this extent they would escape death duty but not, of course, a tax upon the income which they currently yield. Such "short-term" savings would therefore be discouraged *less* by a death duty than by an income tax.

12. Company savings. Much of the foregoing argument which concerns personal savings may be applied also to company savings. However, in the latter case three additional points may be made.

(*a*) *General effects of profits taxes.* Of profit taxes in general it may be said that in the first place they are likely to reduce the funds available for investment; secondly, they reduce the profitability of investment, and thirdly they may discriminate between different kinds of investment through varying capital expenditure and depreciation allowances.

(*b*) *Retention of profits.* Taxes may be designed to encourage the retention rather than the distribution of profits (i.e. to increase company savings). Higher rates of profits tax may be levied upon that portion which is distributed, or one rate may be charged if the profits remain in the hands of the company and another higher rate levied on the individual whose dividend income is increased.

(*c*) *Encouragement of real capital formation.* Concessions such as investment allowances and initial allowances discriminate in favour of the firm which is willing to finance expansion out of profits (i.e. in favour of increased company savings).

13. Public expenditure to encourage saving and investment. Some attention has already been given to the means by which saving and investment may be encouraged through public expenditure (*see* X, **17**).

(*a*) *Direct transfers to firms.* Cash grants may be paid to firms as a condition of further investment.

(*b*) *Grants to local government.* The Exchequer may support local authorities in the construction of roads, houses, schools, etc. To the extent that government provides an attractive and efficient economic infra-structure, so private firms may be tempted to invest.

(*c*) *Forced saving.* The government may raise taxes specifically with the object of devoting the revenue to investment in the public sector, e.g. energy, steel, transport.

EFFICIENT UTILISATION OF RESOURCES

14. Growth means change. We have considered the likely effects of different forms of taxation and expenditure upon the *availability* of productive resources. The system which will accord most with rapid growth will be that which ensures that all resources are employed as fully and continuously as will be consistent with a *smoothly* rising production curve. It has been suggested that this objective calls for a margin in excess of 2% unemployment (*see* XIII, 12).

Every measure of public finance will serve also to improve or impede the efficiency with which these resources are utilised. It has then to be recognised that the main source of growth is *change*.

(*a*) *New methods*. A growth target in excess of the rate of population increase means that output per worker has to rise faster and this calls for new working methods. Much has been achieved, e.g. the increased use of electric power tools; the substitution of welding for riveting; lightweight die casting; extruded and cast plastics; tower cranes and pre-fabrication in the building industry; supermarkets; mechanised accounting systems; diesel and electric traction on the railways. However, there remains much more to be accomplished.

(*b*) *New output*. Growth also calls for change in the production of new goods and services to meet changing tastes at home and abroad. In 1937, transport equipment, machinery and chemicals accounted for only a third of our exports of manufactures. This proportion has now risen to two-thirds. A number of industries have shown great growth potential. They include motor vehicles, electronic equipment, petro-chemicals, synthetic fibres, plastics, gas turbine engines and sheet steel. Change has also occurred in the service industries with great developments in the social services, aircraft and vehicle maintenance, communications and television. All of these changes demand new skills and a re-allocation of resources which may prove socially painful.

Public finance may assist or impede readjustment. Tax concessions and subsidies which support declining industries on social rather than economic grounds can only impair efficiency. Better that expenditure should be directed to improving factor mobility and minimising the social cost of change.

15. Labour utilisation. During the post-war period the working population has tended to expand at a rather faster rate than the total population, this phenomenon being due in part to a rise in the numbers of working age and in part to the employment of more married women. *Without* any increase in *productivity* an increase in G.N.P. would therefore be expected for this reason alone. On the other hand the working population growth rate is not nearly sufficient to give the economic growth which has been repeatedly projected. There must be increased labour productivity and financial policy can help in a number of ways (*see* **16–19** below).

16. The revenue approach. Discriminatory taxes together with a suitable structure of social insurance contributions may be used to squeeze labour out of industries in which it is not fully utilised and into industries where its productivity will be higher.

(*a*) *Social insurance contributions*. By increasing the portion of social security cost borne by the employer and diminishing that borne by the state, economy in the use of labour is encouraged. A comparison of British practice since 1945 with that of France, Germany, Belgium and Italy shows that while Continental employers have borne approximately 50% of the cost and public exchequers 20%, in the United Kingdom employers have paid only 25% while the Exchequer has contributed 50%. The implication is that in Britain labour has been relatively cheap and the employer has not paid its full price.

(*b*) *Capital taxation*. It is also true that in general the impact of taxes upon capital in Continental countries has been less severe than in the UK, e.g. the acceptance in France of *replacement* cost as the basis for capital depreciation allowances. While the total burden of taxation in the two areas may not be very different on the Continent the incidence of taxation has been such as to make capital relatively cheap and labour relatively dear. In Britain the reverse has been the case.

(*c*) *Payroll taxes*. In order to develop capital intensive rather than labour intensive industries the labour/capital cost ratio may be influenced by a payroll tax. The effects of different forms of payroll tax are described below.

(*i*) *Payroll taxes as replacements*. The structure of business taxation may be varied so that a payroll tax is a replacement and not an additional levy. The taxes replaced could be those which fall specifically upon capital rather than labour costs. Examples are profits taxes or local government rates paid by industry and which are based upon the value of buildings and *fixed capital equipment*. Clearly there would be discriminatory effects against labour intensive industries, particularly services, and in favour of capital intensive industries such as steel, chemicals and electricity. More important than this discrimination would be the widening of the gap in costs between low and high productivity methods within the *same* industry. The replacement of one by the other would therefore be hastened.

(*ii*) *Selective employment tax.* Introduced in 1966, this was a payroll tax which aimed at encouraging economy in the use of labour in the service industries in order to make more available for the expansion of manufacturing industries. The tax was levied on *all* civilian employees. In the case of those employed in manufacturing industry, not only was the tax refunded but a premium was also paid upon each employee. While such a tax *may* tend to shift labour from service to manufacturing industry it does nothing to improve the labour/capital ratio. In fact by subsidising the cost of labour in manufacturing industry the incentive to a more intensive use of capital is probably reduced. In March 1973, SET was abolished.

17. The expenditure approach. Public expenditure may be applied in a number of ways to improve both the mobility and the efficiency of labour.

(*a*) *Unemployment benefits.* The financial risk of change may be reduced by means of an adequate unemployment benefit. If social hardships are minimised, resistance to change may be weakened.

(*b*) *Housing.* Geographical mobility will be improved if adequate housing for rental is available in areas of industrial expansion.

(*c*) *Education and training.* More sophisticated production methods imply a growing need for skilled manpower, while that for semi-skilled and unskilled labour declines. Adequate public investment in education in its broadest sense and in specific industrial training is a key point for action.

In Britain there has been only a gradual improvement in secondary education and in the opportunities available for further education. Again, only in the 1960s was attention focused upon the vital need for education in scientific management. Properly co-ordinated training in industrial skills has also been lacking. This last problem has now been tackled through the establishment of *Industrial Training Boards* which raise a levy on all firms within an industry but make payments only to those with approved training programmes.

Re-training of the redundant workers of declining industries is also vital and in this respect there is a need for adequate expenditure upon *government training centres*. In the 1970s much has been done to remedy this shortcoming particularly under the auspices of the Manpower Services Commission and the Training Services Agency.

18. Other policies designed to influence the labour/capital cost ratio. There are other instruments of financial policy which can be employed to improve the labour/capital cost ratio. Of these the *pricing policies of publicly-owned industries* afford most scope. In general they have been aimed towards keeping down prices charged directly to the domestic consumer compared with those charged to industry and which affect the consumer only indirectly. For example, for many years railway passenger fares rose more slowly than those charged on industrial freight. Similar anomalies may be observed in the pricing of coal, gas and electricity where the ratio of the prices charged to the domestic as compared with the industrial user is considerably lower than on the Continent.

However, to the extent that such policies represent an artificial bias in favour of the domestic consumer, they serve to subsidise wages and keep down labour costs relative to other industrial costs. Thus the labour/capital cost ratio is adversely affected and the employer is not under sufficient pressure to substitute capital for labour.

19. Significance of wage inflation. The force of the preceding argument has in practice been diminished by the escalation of wage costs which occurred after the devaluations of 1967 and since 1972. Rising prices, partly a result of the higher costs of imports, brought a massive increase in the level of wage demands. These were frequently conceded. This dramatic change in the labour/capital cost ratio brought employers, perhaps for the first time since the war, under pressure to utilise their labour more effectively. The result has been a sharp increase in the rate of unemployment.

20. Capital utilisation. When the labour force is fully employed the only way that output can grow is through increased productivity. In the 1950s, the underlying growth in productivity was of the order of $2\frac{1}{2}\%$ p.a. compared with $1\frac{1}{2}\%$ before the Second World War. In the 1960s it moved towards 3%. However, if the growth of *output* is to average 4%, having allowed for the anticipated increase in population and on the assumption of full employment, *productivity* would have to rise by about $3\frac{1}{2}\%$ p.a.

Results can be achieved not simply by investing more but by investing in the right things.

Before budgetary measures can be applied to this end it is necessary to identify the type of investment which will be most productive.

PROGRESS TEST 11

1. To what extent do you believe "economic growth" to be the principal objective of social action. Is economics of any value in helping you to arrive at a conclusion? **(1)**

2. "The fundamental mistake in British economic policies since 1945 has been the over-zealous application of Keynesian doctrine." Would you agree with this claim? **(2)**

3. Analyse the determinants of the supply of the factors of production. **(3)**

4. What major difficulties would you expect to encounter in achieving an efficient allocation of resources? **(4–6)**

5. Do you see any inherent danger in the excessive taxation of entrepreneurial effort? **(7 (c))**

6. What forms of public expenditure are most likely to improve the supply of labour? **(8)**

7. What two functions are involved in making capital available to production? **(9)**

8. Compare the probable effect upon the supply of savings of an income tax and an equal yield expenditure tax. **(10)**

9. In what circumstances will a capital levy have a lesser disincentive effect upon savings than an income tax? **(11 (a))**

10. What measures may the goverment adopt to increase the supply of company savings? **(12)**

11. Detail the working of discriminatory taxes which may encourage a more efficient utilisation of labour. **(16)**

12. Examine critically the operation of the selective employment tax. **(16 (c))**

13. What forms of public expenditure are most likely to encourage a more efficient utilisation of labour? **(17)**

14. How may the pricing policies of public industries contribute to a more efficient deployment of labour? **(18)**

15. "Investment incentives such as cash grants, when made equally available to all industries, may encourage investment but in no way contribute to the efficient utilisation of capital." Examine this statement carefully. **(20)**

CHAPTER XII

A Keynesian View of Money

MONEY AND NATIONAL INCOME DETERMINATION

1. Introducing money to the theory of national income determination. In the preceding chapters we have examined the structure of Keynesian national income analysis and its implications for public policy. An important omission however, has been the role of money in the economy. This must now be rectified since a very significant part of Keynes's work was the attempt to show the way in which financial mechanisms and institutions made their impact upon the *real* world of output and employment.

These views are fundamental to much of his analysis and therefore to an acceptance of the validity of the public policies which they underwrite. It is in this area that there has been the greatest controversy over the past two decades. The nature of the *counter-revolution in monetary theory* will be outlined later in XIII.

2. The classical view. Following Say's law of markets (*see* IX, **22**) the English classical economists assigned to money an essentially minor role in the working of the economy. Money was simply a medium of exchange which tended to conceal what was happening in the real economy. Here the labourer might produce potatoes. When he consumed them himself he raised the demand for potatoes. The surplus which he sought to exchange for, say, clothing, raised the demand for clothing. Either way, added supply itself created added demand. It followed that there could be no such thing as over-production or unemployment.

It also followed that in the classical model money had little to do with income determination and the level of economic activity. These were determined by *real* factors. However, it had everything to do with determining the general level of prices and this central position was postulated in the quantity theory of money (*see* XIII, **3**).

3. A synthesis of real and monetary analysis. Keynes attempted to synthesise the worlds of real and monetary factors, giving to money a central role in his analysis of how the economy functioned. He did so by arguing that money was not simply a medium of exchange but that it had a unique characteristic, namely liquidity. While assets of all kinds may be converted to cash for the purchase of other goods and services, the price they realise will be uncertain and only achieved after some interval, Money, however, is a perfectly liquid asset which gives instant and general purchasing power. *As such it will be held for precautionary motives.*

4. Transactions demand and liquidity or precautionary demand for money. The basic assumptions of monetary policy as traditionally understood are as follows.

(a) *An expansion of the money supply is consistent with lower interest rates.* In this context, the interest rate may be looked upon as "the price of money" which will fall as supply is increased relative to existing demand.

(b) *Lower interest rates will encourage investment* by entrepreneurs in capital goods. Subject to the important qualification of the view (optimistic or pessimistic) that he takes of business prospects, a lower rate will expand his profit margins.

(c) *Increased investment expands national income and employment* via the operation of the multiplier (*see* IX, 27).

It would follow from this chain of reasoning that an expansionary monetary policy would lead to a growth in income, output and employment. The converse would be equally true. However, Keynesians make an important distinction between *transactions money* and liquidity or precautionary money which affects this argument.

Transactions money is required to finance the everyday business of the economy. The amount we require for this purpose will be determined by the volume of business conducted in the economy, i.e. by the national income in money terms. In assuming that an expansion of the money supply will initiate the lower interest rates which generate an expansion of the national income we have ignored the need for still further monetary growth to finance the increased volume of transactions which accompany that expansion.

Precautionary or liquidity money will be required in addition to transactions money to satisfy the general preference in the economy for liquidity. Other things being equal we shall expect that this preference will be geared to the rate of interest. When interest rates are high less money will be required for precautionary purposes and the greater part of any increase in cash balances will be devoted to the purchase of financial assets. Such purchases themselves drive down interest rates.

NOTE: If the market bids up the price of a 5% £100 bond to £200 then the yield falls to £2·50 per £100, i.e. when capital values rise interest rates fall and vice-versa.

On the other hand when interest rates are low and business prospects uncertain the economy may prefer a higher proportion of precautionary money. The opportunity cost of holding assets in liquid form rather than in financial assets has been reduced. Moreover, the risk of holding financial assets whose price may fall has been eliminated.

It follows that further expansion of the money supply when interest rates are already low will not necessarily drive them lower. The additional money will not express itself in the purchase of financial assets but will be held as cash. Since interest rates are not lowered further there is no increased incentive to productive investment and hence no increased national income.

5. "The liquidity trap." This apparent weakness of the capacity of monetary policy to cure a depression was referred to by Keynesians as "the liquidity trap". It leads to an insight into the role in the economy which they ascribe to money.

When there is a high full employment national income there will be a correspondingly high demand for transactions money. Of the existing money supply less is left to satisfy the precautionary motive. If in line with a high-activity economy interest rates are *low* some people will wish to exchange financial assets, e.g. bonds, for cash. Since the total stock of precautionary cash is limited, heavy sales will depress capital values, i.e. drive up interest rates.

At higher interest rates, investment, national income and hence the demand for transactions money are all reduced. However, a correspondingly greater proportion of the existing money stock is now available for precautionary purposes and a new equilibrium is established, albeit at a lower level of income and employment. The implication is of course that for full employment equilibrium an adequate money supply is necessary.

6. Disillusion with monetary policy, 1931. In the light of this analysis Keynesians were sceptical of the effectiveness of monetary policy as an instrument for promoting a high level of income and employment. Their viewpoint seemed to be supported by the evidence of the 1930s. In 1931, an active monetary policy was abandoned in the UK. During the following twenty years Bank Rate was held at 2%, save for a short period in 1939 when it stood at 4% and then 3%. With the whole structure of interest rates geared to this very low level, liquidity preference apparently ensured that they could not be further reduced. Moreover, even had lower interest rates been possible the entrepreneur continued to take a dismal view of the future, and would have been unlikely to increase the level of his investment. Monetary policy stood twice condemned.

It therefore seemed evident that the thrust of macroeconomic policy would depend primarily upon the more direct approach through the public finances which we have already examined. The role of monetary policy would essentially be to keep interest rates low in order to minimise the cost to Government of sustaining aggregate demand through deficit public finance, i.e. the servicing charge of an expanding national debt.

This extreme view was not abandoned until 1951 since which time governments throughout the world have been obliged by the course of events progressively to recognise the potency of monetary policy.

A GRAPHICAL PRESENTATION

7. The demand for money at a given level of national income. The transactions demand for money and the liquidity or precautionary demand are shown in Fig. 46 for a given level of national income Y_0. The transactions demand corresponds to the assumed level of money national income. To this must be added the precautionary or liquidity demand which increases as the rate of interest falls. It will be seen that the lower part of the curve is fairly flat, indicating "a liquidity trap" in which further additions to the money supply have little effect upon the rate of interest.

When the money supply is fixed at M_0 the equilibrium rate of interest will be i_0, which is to say the rate which equates the demand for money for both transactions and precautionary purposes with the available supply.

8. Demand for money at a higher level of national income. In Fig. 47 the money national income has increased to Y_1 with a

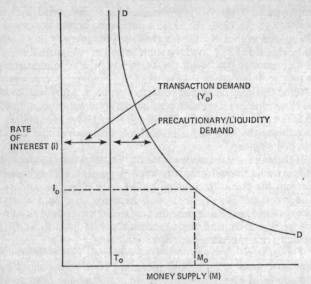

FIG. 46.—*Demand for money, national income being given.* At a given level of national income (Y_0) which corresponds to the transactions demand, the curve DD shows the total demand for money at different rates of interest. When the money stock (M_0) is fixed the only rate of interest consistent with this level of income will be i_0.

corresponding increase in the transactions demand for money to T_1. The effect is to push the whole demand curve outward to D_1D_1. Always assuming that the total money supply remains fixed at M_0, pressure is now exerted on the money remaining for precautionary purposes. If people are to be content to hold smaller amounts, then a higher interest rate must be paid in order to persuade them to surrender some of their liquidity. The equilibrium rate of interest will rise to i_1. This observation leads us to establish an important relationship. *For any given money stock the higher the national income the higher the equilibrium rate of interest will have to be.*

9. **The liquidity-money (LM) curve and investment-savings (IS) curve in equilibrium.** In Fig. 48 we observe that the LM curve characteristically slopes up from left to right. This reflects the fact that as the transactions demand for money rises with national

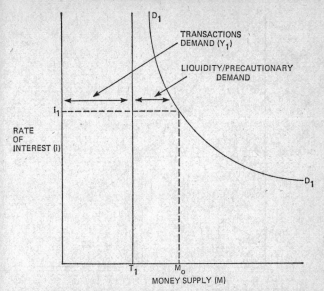

FIG. 47.—*Demand for money at a higher level of national income*. At a higher level of national income, the money stock being unchanged, the equilibrium rate of interest must rise.

income, higher rates of interest must be offered to overcome the desire to hold precautionary/liquidity money, the total money supply being given.

The IS curve typically slopes *down* from left to right. When interest rates are high investment and therefore national income will be low. As the rate of interest falls so the equilibrium level of national income increases.

Where the curves intersect we finally determine the equilibrium level of national income, Y_e and the equilibrium rate of interest, i_e. In this position investment equals savings and the amount of money which people wish to hold for both transactions and precautionary purposes exactly equals the given money stock.

10. Applications. This analysis has many applications in the illumination of economic problems. Three examples are given below.

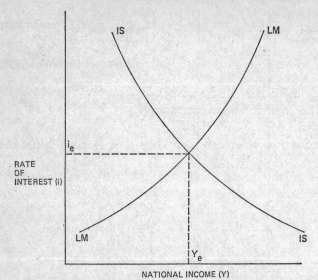

RATE
OF
INTEREST (i)

NATIONAL INCOME (Y)

FIG. 48.—*The LM and IS curves in equilibrium.* The LM curve shows
the important relationship between different levels of national income
and the equilibrium rate of interest for any given money stock. The IS
curve shows that when interest rates are high, national income will be
low. It slopes typically from left to right. The equilibrium rate of interest is i_e at which savings equal investment and the demand for money
equals the supply.

(*a*) *An increase in the money supply.* The effect here will be
upon the LM curve which will move to the right. There will be a
lower equilibrium for the rate of interest and a consequent rise
in the equilibrium level of national income.

(*b*) *An autonomous increase in the rate of investment.* The IS
curve shifts to the right raising both the equilibrium rate of interest and the equilibrium level of national income.

(*c*) *An autonomous increase in the rate of saving.* The IS curve
moves to the left lowering both the equilibrium rate of interest
and the equilibrium level of national income.

PROGRESS TEST 12

1. What importance did the classical economists attach to
money in the working of the economy? **(2)**

2. What is "a liquid asset"?   **(3)**

3. Distinguish between "transactions money" and liquidity money".   **(4)**

4. Explain the concept of "the liquidity trap".   **(5)**

5. What practical evidence led to the belief that in the 1930s monetary policy was ineffective?   **(6)**

6. Why must the equilibrium rate of interest rise with an increase in national income, the money stock being fixed?   **(8)**

7. What information does an LM curve provide?   **(9)**

8. What information does an IS curve provide?   **(9)**

9. When the money supply increases, what happens to the LM curve?   **(10(a))**

10. When the rate of saving increases, what happens to the IS curve?   **(10(c))**

CHAPTER XIII

The Monetarist Controversy

MONEY AND PRICES IN THE KEYNESIAN SYSTEM

1. The background. *So far our macroeconomic analysis has broadly followed conventional theory and practice of the past thirty years.* Unquestionably "the Keynesian revolution" in economic thinking had a tremendous impact throughout the whole of the western world and nowhere more so than in Britain. It is, however, often argued that in the development and application of this thinking many of Keynes's followers went much further and became much more inflexible than he himself would have found acceptable.

More fundamentally it tends to be overlooked that from the 1930s Keynes had his academic opponents, amongst them *Friedrich Hayek*, who consistently maintained that his analysis was essentially wrong. Such criticism was lost in post-war Britain where the "scientific" management of the economy was *apparently* delivering the goals of full employment, modest growth and fairly stable prices.

As the periodicity of the business cycle increased, with ever higher levels of unemployment in recession and steeper inflation rates in the upswing, doubts were experienced about the precision of the demand steering mechanisms. However, in Britain few were prepared to offer any serious challenge to the underlying theory.

The challenge, when it came, was from the USA in the thinking of the *monetarist school of economists*, who are usually associated with Professor Milton Friedman and the University of Chicago and whose influence has steadily increased since the 1950s.

2. The issues. The monetarists disagree fundamentally with the Keynesians in the way in which they relate money to the basic macroeconomic variables such as national income, employment and the price level.

The implications of their analysis are far reaching, going well beyond the role of monetary policy and into the broader realm of public policy as a whole. *Just as we have seen that Keynesian analysis implies the need for substantial Government supervision of the economy so monetarist conclusions imply the need for substantial Government withdrawal.*

In this controversy one basic question must be answered. We have seen in Chapter IX that in the Keynesian analysis emphasis is placed upon the factors which determine *real* national income, i.e. consumption plus investment plus Government expenditure. To this equation we have added the influence of money and the interest rate. We have not however, explained the factors which determine the size of *money* national income.

To answer this question we should need to know not simply the determinants of *real* national income (Q) but also the determinants of the general or average price level (P). Money national income would then be $P \times Q$.

The solutions of the Keynesian and the monetarists differ.

3. The quantity theory of money.

It has been observed (*see* XII, 2) that in classical theory money had little bearing upon the level of real national income but was central to the determination of prices. Traditional thinking on this matter is usually referred to as the *quantity theory of money* expressed in the formula

$$M \times V = P \times Q$$

where M is the quantity of money, V is the velocity of circulation (the number of times in a given period that the money stock changes hands), P is the general price level and Q is the *real* national income of goods and services.

For this equation to be anything more than a truism it requires further elaboration. The classical economists therefore went on to postulate firstly that Q would basically be determined by real causes such as the availability of labour and capital, the state of technology and the flexibility with which the factors of production were deployed. Velocity of circulation was largely determined by institutional arrangements such as the periodicity of wage payments, weekly or monthly, and the current state of banking practice.

With V and Q already determined it followed that what happened to P would depend upon variations in M. In short, changes in the general price level depended broadly upon changes in the quantity of money. In the 1930s this view was challenged.

4. The Keynesian challenge to quantity theory.

The criticism is

aimed essentially at the presumed stability of V. Keynes accepted that institutional factors had some influence in determining velocity. However, it will be recalled that he made a significant distinction between the transactions demand for money and the liquidity demand.

In respect of the former, quantity theory prevails. The volume of transactions money will correspond to the money national income ($P \times Q$) under a given regime of institutional arrangements. Velocity is so far accepted as stable.

On the other hand we have established that the demand for precautionary or liquidity money varies with the rate of interest. The lower the rate the higher the cash balances which people are prepared to hold. In other words *the velocity of liquidity money varies with the rate of interest*.

Since this is true for a part of the money stock, it must have relevance for the whole. In short, in Keynesian theory velocity is not simply determined by institutional factors but by the rate of interest.

It is at this point that it seems possible to break the causal connection between M and P. Assuming that interest rates are already low and that business expectations are bleak we may fall into "the liquidity trap" (*see* XII, 5).

An expansion of the money supply will not necessarily lead to a further fall in interest rates. It will simply be added to our holdings of liquidity money. In quantity theory terms the effect is that an increase in M is being offset by a decline in V which leaves $P \times Q$ unchanged.

5. Determination of the general price level in the Keynesian system.
The extreme Keynesian position is one in which money matters hardly at all in the determination of the general price level and hence the level of money national income. It should be stressed that Keynes himself did not hold this view and that he certainly had an eye to the effects upon price of monetary expansion once full employment had been achieved.

In this extreme position money wages would be established by collective bargaining between unions and management. At the same time the size of *real* national income will have determined the level of employment. The *real* wage accruing to labour will be in line with the marginal productivity of the labour force. Since we now know the level of *money* wages *and* the level of *real* wages (i.e. what the money will buy) it follows that we should have a very good idea of the general level of prices. In any case this is seen as only of passing interest.

Real national income then is determined by consumption, investment and Government spending, while prices are determined by money wages. It therefore follows that $P \times Q$ will be the size of money national income.

In this analysis, no attention at all has been paid to the influence of money itself. It is an extreme position but one towards which many post-war British economists have tended. Money has been mentioned in their analysis but since (because of the liquidity trap) it was thought to have little impact upon the level of activity in the *real* economy it was largely ignored for all practical policies.

6. A refinement of the Keynesian position. Professor Friedman has argued that the Keynesian explanation of equilibrium with unemployment depends upon rigidities in the market which impede the downward movement of wages and prices, e.g. the monopoly power of trade unions to resist pressures on money wages. Were such movements to occur then employment and output would rise.

The Keynesian response is that even assuming flexible wages and prices the analysis holds good. A fall in wages and prices will be accompanied by a fall in money national income. The quantity of money being given, less is now required for transactions purposes leaving more available for liquidity purposes. Part of this money will be used for the purchase of financial assets, driving down interest rates (*see* XII, **4**), stimulating investment and hence, via the multiplier, increasing income and employment. *However, this will only occur in the absence of the liquidity trap.* In an economy which is seriously depressed additional liquidity may simply be held as cash. Interest rates are *not* pushed lower and in any case, even with cheap money, there is no confidence to invest.

In short, just as monetary policy provides no certain path to full employment so for the Keynesians the same is true of flexible market prices.

7. "The Pigou effect." In reply to this argument (The Role of Monetary Policy, *American Economic Review*, March, 1968) Professor Friedman draws attention to the work of Professors Pigou and Haberler. They pointed out that with any systematic fall in wages and prices the value of the money supply increases in direct proportion. If the price level is halved then the purchasing power of cash balances is doubled. If the process continues there must be a point at which individuals consider themselves sufficiently wealthy to increase their consumption expenditure.

In this way, argues Friedman, changes in the *real* quantity of money (i.e. the purchasing power of money) can affect aggregate demand even if they do not affect interest rates. To the extent that this happens the liquidity trap is by-passed.

If it can then be shown that changes in the *nominal* quantity of money govern the price level and hence the purchasing power of money (i.e. the *real* quantity) then it follows that variations in the money stock have a significant bearing upon aggregate demand.

These perceptions provided a starting point for *the counter-revolution in monetary theory*.

MONEY AND PRICES IN THE MONETARIST SYSTEM

8. Determination of the general price level and money national income in the modern monetarist system. In *The Counter-Revolution in Monetary Theory* (Occasional Paper 33, Institute of Economic Affairs) Professor Friedman gives a concise version of the modern monetarist case in a number of propositions.

(*a*) *Monetary growth and nominal incomes.* There is a consistent but imprecise relationship between the rate of monetary growth and the growth of *nominal* incomes. A mass of evidence suggests a time lag of between six and nine months.

(*b*) *Monetary growth, output and prices.* The changed rate of growth of money incomes manifests itself at first in output and hardly at all in prices. On average, a *further* six to nine months elapses before any effect is observed upon prices. The sequence of events for an *increase* in the rate of monetary growth is as follows.

(*i*) In agreement with Keynesian thinking, the initial effect is a *liquidity* effect (and not an effect upon nominal incomes at all). Throughout the economy cash balances are increased relative to other assets such as bonds, equities and houses.

(*ii*) The attempt will now be made to restore the original ratio of cash to other assets. However, since one man's purchase is another man's sale and in the short run the supply of assets is fixed, the ratio for the economy as a whole remains unchanged. *But* during this process capital values are bid up, i.e. interest rates are forced down.

(*iii*) At lower interest rates encouragement is given to borrowing and spending on the production of new assets and also upon current goods and services. In this way the increased money supply is translated into spending, increased nominal incomes, employment and output.

(*iv*) Initially there is little effect upon price. In the anticipation of price stability wages and prices have been set for some time ahead. Subsequently and characteristically the prices of goods respond to an unanticipated rise in nominal demand more rapidly than prices of the factors of production, e.g. nominal wages. In other words, *real* wages paid by employers have fallen and it is this reduction, unperceived by labour which has permitted the increased level of employment.

(*c*) *The short and the long run*. In the short run, which may be as long as five to ten years, monetary changes make their biggest impact upon nominal incomes, employment and output. Over decades it is prices which are primarily affected. This happens once anticipations are adjusted to allow for the presence of inflation. Labour demands higher nominal wages to compensate for the fall in real wages. With higher costs the producer then requires higher selling prices.

9. Determination of real national income and the level of employment in the monetarist system. In the long run, "what happens to the level of output depends upon real factors: the enterprise, ingenuity and industry of the people; the extent of thrift; the structure of industry and government; the relations among nations and so on" (Friedman).

Similarly, in line with these real factors, at any one time there will be "a natural level of unemployment" governed fundamentally by the imperfections of the market. *This cannot be permanently reduced by monetary or fiscal measures to stimulate the level of aggregate demand.*

It can be seen at this point that the differences between the Keynesians and the monetarists are not superficial. As was noted earlier (*see* **2**) they have fundamental implications for the conduct of public policy.

10. Implications for fiscal policy. The measures which we have considered at some length in IX–XI are considered to be largely ineffective.

If public expenditures intended to stimulate demand are financed by taxation this results in a corresponding reduction in private sector demand, either in consumption or in savings which would have been lent to other private spenders. If the expenditures are financed by borrowing from the private sector the result is similar. Savings which would have been utilised by private borrowers are transferred to the public sector. In short there is simply a shift of resources from the private to the public sector.

"To discover any net effect on total spending, one must go to a more sophisticated level—to differences in the behaviour of the two groups of people or to effects of Government borrowing on interest rates. *There is no first order effect*" (Friedman.)

11. Implications for monetary policy. If Government spending is financed by borrowing from the banking system, then an expansion of the money supply takes place. It has been shown that the short run effect of an increase in the money supply is upon income and employment. The mainstream of monetarist thinking is, however, opposed to any attempt to "fine tune" the economy by short term adjustments of the money supply. They maintain that too little is known about the *precise* relationships between money and real magnitudes, such as the *real* rate of interest, the *real* level of national income and the rate of unemployment, for this to be feasible.

Recognising however, that a powerful relationship does exist the first objective of monetary policy will be to ensure that money itself is not a destabilising influence, e.g. an avoidance of the monetary contractions which occurred in the UK, 1925–31 and the USA, 1929–33 and which may be seen as the true cause of "the slump".

More positively, through their control of the money supply the monetary authorities are able in principle to control *nominal* magnitudes such as the exchange rate, the money national income and the price level. A stable price level is viewed as the most desirable goal since it increases business confidence by reducing risk. However, once again too little is known about the precise effect of a given change in the money supply upon prices.

In these circumstances the most realistic monetary policy would be one in which the authorities adhere to a prescribed rate of monetary growth sufficient to accomodate any real economic expansion, e.g. 3–5%. In the long run this would guarantee stable prices.

From this discussion it will be seen that the monetarists allow no role at all for discretionary policy in the area of macroeconomic stability. This, they say, follows not only from the logic of their argument but also from observation of the recurrent destabilisation and long-term structural distortion of economies where Government attempts at discretionary policies have been the order of the day.

This theme will be followed in the next section with particular reference to the UK.

IS THERE A TRADE-OFF BETWEEN INFLATION AND UNEMPLOYMENT?

12. An extension of Keynesian thinking. One of the post-war extensions of Keynesian thinking came from Professor A. W. Phillips in an essay "The Relation between Unemployment and the Rate of Change of Money Wages in the United Kingdom, 1861–1957" (*Economica*, Vol. 25, 1958). He argued that research revealed a regular inverse relationship between the level of unemployment and the rate of change of money wages. Since wages constitute a major element in total costs, if they vary so will costs and long-run prices.

The implication is that the rate of inflation may be regulated through the manipulation of the *independent variable*, unemployment. This will be achieved through orthodox adjustment of aggregate demand via the public finances. In other words inflation can be traded-off against higher levels of unemployment and vice-versa.

In the early 1960s this view was quantified with the suggestion that "full employment" should be redefined as 2·4% unemployment (in practice something like half that figure had previously been the target). It was argued that with this more realistic figure "full employment equilibrium" could be achieved without inflation.

In the late 1960s emerged the phenomenon of rising unemployment accompanied by rising prices and this situation has continued into the 1970s. Since social and political considerations precluded the possibility of deliberately raising unemployment still higher as a means of checking inflation, reliance was placed upon prices and incomes policies. These too have been largely ineffective in achieving more than a temporary slowing down of price rises.

It will be seen that the official view has remained rooted in the conviction that inflation originates essentially in wage cost push. This position the monetarists dispute, adhering to the view that "inflation is always and everywhere a monetary phenomenon".

13. The Phillips curve.

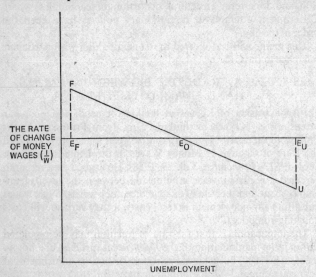

FIG. 49.—*The Phillips curve*. The curve demonstrates a supposed inverse relationship between the level of unemployment and the rate of change of money wages and hence prices.

In Fig. 49, at E_0 there exists an equilibrium with a "natural" rate of unemployment rooted in transitional, frictional and structural causes. At this point wages are stable or rising at the same rate as productivity.

At point F there is over-full employment and money wages are rising.

At point U there is more than the natural rate of unemployment and money wages are falling.

14. The monetarist criticism of Phillips.
No economic theorist has ever asserted that demand and supply were functions of the nominal (i.e. money) wage rate. In Fig. 50 *the vertical axis should refer to real wages*, since this in truth is what labour works for. This change having been made, the graph now has nothing to tell us about what is going to happen to *nominal* wages and prices.

At E_0 there is equilibrium at "natural" unemployment with no

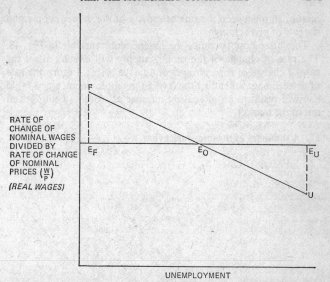

RATE OF
CHANGE OF
NOMINAL WAGES
DIVIDED BY
RATE OF CHANGE
OF NOMINAL
PRICES ($\frac{W}{P}$)

(REAL WAGES)

UNEMPLOYMENT

FIG. 50.—*The fallacy in Phillips.* Note that the vertical axis has now become W/P, money wages divided by money prices. This diagram provides no information about the relationship between unemployment and the rate of change of money wages or prices.

pressure either way on *real* wages. But that equilibrium may remain with W and P separately constant or with W and P rising at 10% or falling at 10% so long as they both change at the same rate.

15. An explanation of this error. The monetarists offer the following explanation for this error. As we have already seen, for Keynesians an increase in aggregate demand essentially made itself manifest in increased employment and output so that the price level could be taken as an institutional datum, i.e. it remained basically unaltered.

The simple way of looking at Phillips therefore is that he was assuming movements in real and nominal wages to equate. In fact he was being rather more sophisticated and assuming that anticipated changes in nominal wages would equate with anticipated changes in real wages.

16. The monetarist interpretation of the Phillips curve. The monetarists, we have established, assume there to be a direct causal relationship between the rate of growth of the money supply and the rate of price change.

The latter now becomes the independent variable in Fig. 48. The rate of change of the money supply will *directly* affect the rate of change of *money* wages and hence prices. In turn the rate of price change will affect the level of unemployment, e.g. a rapid rise will result in an increasing number of workers being priced out of the market.

17. A summary of the monetarist view.

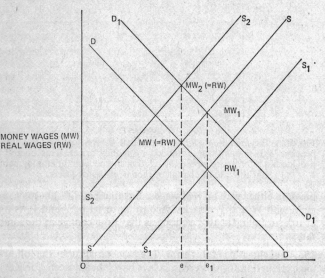

FIG. 51.—*The long-run effect of a Keynesian stimulus to aggregate demand.* Note that the horizontal axis now represents employment. An increase in monetary demand only reduces unemployment at the expense of lower real wages. When labour adjusts its selling price to a higher level of nominal wages, unemployment reverts to its original natural level.

In Fig. 51 we make the monetarist assumption that in the long run the effect of an expansion of monetary demand will be absorbed largely in higher prices rather than in an expansion of *real* national income (i.e. output) and employment. The latter depend upon appropriate changes through time in the structure of the *real* economy. For simplicity of exposition, we adopt an extreme position and assume that increased demand produces *no* increase in output.

At O_e employment with money wages (MW) equalling real wages (RW) there is equilibrium without inflation but with ee_1 unemployment. The monetarists would attribute this "natural" unemployment to imperfections in the labour markets coupled with the downward inflexibility of money wages.

If this level of unemployment is considered unacceptable then orthodox Keynesian demand management policy calls for a shift of the demand curve to the right to D_1D_1. A money wage of MW_1 establishes a fresh equilibrium in which unemployment (ee_1) has been eliminated. However, while labour was unwilling to accept a lower *money* wage in order to secure a higher level of employment it has unwittingly accepted a lower *real* wage (RW_1). (We have of course assumed no increase in output resulting from the higher level of employment, the whole impact of the extra spending being absorbed by higher money wages and prices.) In effect labour has shifted its supply curve to the right to S_1S_1.

This position can only be maintained as long as labour accepts lower real wages. In the long run expectations will adjust to inflation and higher money wages will be demanded, i.e. the supply curve will shift to the left to S_2S_2. Money wages are settled at MW_2 in order to re-establish the original real wage of RW. Unemployment is now restored to its "natural" level (ee_1), albeit at a higher level of prices.

Repetition of this manoeuvre will only reduce unemployment provided that Government successfully keeps actual inflation ahead of labour's inflationary expectations, i.e. successfully reduces real wages. In practice this means that the policy depends upon an accelerating rate of inflation.

18. A footnote. In Britain, there has remained a reluctance to depart from orthodox analysis. In 1972–3, with unemployment surpassing one million for the first time since the 1930s, a massive monetary stimulus was given to aggregate demand. There was some temporary reduction in the unemployment figure but by now inflationary expectations were firmly rooted in wage demands and unemployment rose to even higher peaks. Great emphasis was therefore placed upon the "Social Contract" as a means of artificially depressing real wages in order to avoid a worsening of the employment situation. Despite stringent wage restraint and price controls inflation continued at very high levels and it was generally accepted that for Britain at least it was no longer possible to spend a way out of recession.

The constraints upon the rate of growth of the money supply imposed by the International Monetary Fund in 1976 as a condition of a major loan to the UK subsequently lent support to the monetarist case.

PROGRESS TEST 13

1. In what respects may the Keynesian/Monetarist controversy be considered fundamental? **(2)**

2. Express the quantity theory of money as a formula. **(3)**

3. According to classical theory, how was real national income determined? **(3)**

4. Why did Keynes view the velocity of circulation as unpredictable? **(4)**

5. In what circumstances would an increase in M not lead to a rise in P? **(4)**

6. From an extreme Keynesian viewpoint, explain how prices are determined. **(5)**

7. According to Keynesian theory, why would a fall in wages and prices not necessarily restore full employment equilibrium? **(6)**

8. What do you understand by "the Pigou effect"? **(7)**

9. Trace the steps in the monetarist argument between an increase in monetary growth rate and a rise in price. **(8)**

10. Distinguish between the short- and long-run effects of an increase in the money supply. **(8(c))**

11. How useful do the monetarists consider fiscal policy as a stabilisation instrument? **(10)**

12. Do the monetarists prefer monetary policy as an instrument for steering the economy? **(11)**

13. What are the implications for orthodox stabilisation policies of accepting the validity of the Phillips curve? **(12)**

14. Explain why the Phillips curve may be considered to be invalid? **(14)**

15. How do the monetarists interpret the Phillips curve? **(16)**

16. Define "the natural" rate of unemployment. **(17)**

17. Why may prices and incomes policies be considered inappropriate to the containment of inflation? **(17, 18)**

CHAPTER XIV

The National Debt

COMPOSITION OF THE U.K. NATIONAL DEBT

1. Nature of the Debt. The Bank of England is responsible for the management of the National Debt and defines it as the amount payable in sterling shown in the *Consolidated Fund and National Loans Fund Accounts* together with stocks issued by the nationalised industries and guaranteed by H.M. Government.

In 1976, this figure stood at £54,000 million of which some £6,333 million was held by overseas residents. Since the bulk of the Debt is therefore held by U.K. residents it follows that the use of the term "national" is rather misleading. It would be more appropriate to think of it as the sum owed by citizens collectively (i.e. the government) to citizens individually, in short the Government Debt.

2. Structure. In December of each year, the Bank of England publishes a detailed analysis of the structure and distribution of the National Debt for the preceding financial year. The principal features of the 1976 analysis are shown in Tables VIII–XIII.

TABLE VIII.   CLASSIFICATION OF THE NATIONAL DEBT, MARCH 1976

Marketable debt	£ million	% of total
Funded debt	35,580	65·8
Floated debt	10,849	20·1
Non-marketable debt	7,612	14·1
Total	54,041	

Source: *Bank of England Quarterly Bulletin,* December 1976

A broad distinction can be made between that portion of the Debt which is marketable (i.e. there are highly organised markets which deal in these securities) and the portion represented by securities which cannot be bought and sold on the open market.

3. Marketable debt. There are two categories:

TABLE IX.   MATURITY OF FUNDED DEBT, MARCH 1976

Up to 5 years to maturity £13,753m.	*Over 5 years and undated* 21,827m.	*Total* 35,580m.

Source: *Bank of England Quarterly Bulletin*, December 1976

(*a*) *Funded debt.* Used in the narrowest sense the term "funded debt" applies only to those stocks for which no redemption date has been set. The most important example is $3\frac{1}{2}\%$ War Loan (1952 or after). Government borrowed on terms which permitted it *but did not oblige it* to repay at any time after 1952.

In the broader and more usual sense the phrase includes dated stocks, i.e. all other government and government-guaranteed stocks. They are of varying maturities and are publicly quoted on the Stock Exchange.

Prior to 1914 the government borrowed only against undated stock. With the subsequent increase in the scale of borrowing it became more difficult to employ this method and dated stock became the principal component of the National Debt.

(*b*) *Floating debt.* For two reasons government requires to borrow against short-term securities. In the first place it wishes to accommodate the uneven flow of tax revenue to the fairly regular flow of departmental expenditure throughout the financial year. Secondly, by regulating the availability of these liquid assets to the banking system it seeks to influence short-term interest rates and so implement its monetary policy (*see* **13**).

Short-term borrowings are made against Treasury bills which are of two types, "tap" and "tender". Tap bills represent lending by Government departments back to the Treasury. Bills payable after 91 days are offered for tender every Friday on the London Discount Market (*see* XV, **20**).

4. Non-marketable debt. There are three categories of non-marketable debt.

(*a*) *National savings.* Although there is no organised market and no redemption date is set the holder is normally able to secure repayment after giving a period of notice. Into this category fall national savings certificates, defence bonds, premium savings bonds and the contractual savings schemes of the Department for National Savings and the Trustee Savings Banks.

(b) *Certificates of tax deposit.* These certificates are instruments by which individuals, partnerships and companies can, to their own advantage, bridge the period between the earning of income and the payment of tax on it.

They are issued by the Bank of England acting on behalf of the Treasury, are non-transferable and bear tax-free interest at rates determined from time to time by the Treasury. When tax falls due the certificates are tendered to the Inland Revenue when both principal and interest are credited against tax liability.

The proceeds from the sale are paid into the National Loans Fund and upon surrender a transfer is made to the Consolidated Fund. Certificates can therefore be seen to represent loans financing the Government's borrowing requirement rather than advance payment of tax which would reduce the borrowing requirement.

(c) *Other.* Part of this category is made up of *Ways and Means Advances* by the Bank of England and the Exchange Equalisation Account to the Treasury. This is a method of very short term internal borrowing.

The remainder comprises interest free notes held by international organisations, principally the IMF, and various sterling loans from overseas governments.

5. Ownership of the National Debt, 1976. The holders of the National Debt fall into six groups.

TABLE X. OWNERSHIP OF THE NATIONAL DEBT, MARCH 1976

			Other		
Official Holdings	*Public Bodies*	*Banking Sector*	*Financial Institutions*	*Overseas Residents*	*Other*
13,634m.	54m.	5,090m.	14,063m.	6,333m.	14,867m.

Source: *Bank of England Quarterly Bulletin*, December 1976

(a) *Official holdings.* Of the 25% portion of the debt held by official institutions, just under a half was attributable to the National Debt Commissioners who administer the two funds, through which is invested money deposited in the ordinary departments of the National Savings Bank and the Trustee Savings Banks as well as the proceeds of national insurance contributions.

More than a third was held by the Issue Department of the

Bank of England as backing for the note issue. The remainder was in the hands of the Bank of England Banking Department, government departments with a temporary surplus available for investment and the Exchange Equalisation Account. In the case of the latter, when supporting operations are carried out in the foreign exchange markets, gold and hard currency reserves are used to buy up surplus sterling which is then invested in National Debt.

(b) *Public bodies.* A small and diminishing proportion of the Debt was held by local authorities and public corporations other than the Bank of England.

(c) *Banking sector.* This category includes the deposit banks, the National Giro, the accepting houses, overseas and other banks and the discount houses. Their holdings of £5,090 million were made up of £2,719 million in Treasury bills, and £2,371 million in stocks.

(d) *Other financial institutions.* Other than the banks this is the most important group of market investors.

TABLE XI.   DEBT HOLDINGS OF OTHER FINANCIAL INSTITUTIONS, MARCH 1976

Insurance Companies £6,953m.	Building Societies £2,396m.	National Savings Bank £395m.	Trustee Savings Banks £717m.	Local Authority Pension Funds £732m.	Other Public Sector Pension Funds £760m.	Private Sector Pension Funds £1,547m.	Investment and Unit Trusts £563m.

Source: *Bank of England Quarterly Bulletin,* December 1976

Apart from £346 million of Treasury bills these funds were invested in stocks, for the most part with more than 5 years to maturity.

(e) *Overseas residents.*

TABLE XII.   DEBT HOLDINGS OF OVERSEAS RESIDENTS, MARCH 1976

International Organisations 2,208m.	Central Monetary Institutions 2,478m.	Overseas Banks and Others 1,647m.

Source: *Bank of England Quarterly Bulletin,* December 1976

The figure for international organisations is explained by drawings outstanding to the IMF together with subscriptions to the IMF and the International Development Association (IDA).

The holdings of central monetary institutions reflect the investment of the official sterling reserves of overseas countries.

(*f*) *Other holders.*

TABLE XIII.   OTHER HOLDERS OF NATIONAL DEBT, MARCH 1976

Public Trustees and Non-Corporate Bodies	Private Funds and Trusts	Industrial and Commercial Companies	Other (Residual)
£270m.	10,192m.	£745m.	3,660m.

Source: *Bank of England Quarterly Bulletin*, December 1976

The figures reveal that private funds are the largest group of market investors accounting for rather less than one quarter of the total Debt. Their holdings are divided almost equally between stocks and non-marketable debt.

THE BURDEN OF THE DEBT

6. Nature of the burden. The burden of the Debt will be direct to the extent that money payments in interest and in redemption of principal deprive the debtors of goods and services which they would otherwise have enjoyed. It will be indirect to the extent that increased levels of taxation depress the level of production. Beyond this it may be pointed out that large public sector deficits which are financed by inflationary methods serve to erode the purchasing power of the consumer (*see* **22, 23**).

7. Direct burden of external debt. It has been observed that a portion of the Debt is held overseas. To the extent that payments of interest and repayment of principal impinge on the balance of payments the implication is that goods and services must be exported for which there are no corresponding imports. In the event that overseas demand for exports proves inelastic there must be a proportionate decrease in the volume of imports. Either way the standard of living of the debtor nation is affected. The burden of their loss depends upon how it is distributed throughout the community. If the debt-servicing payments derive mainly from the lower income groups then their propensity to consume will be diminished and the burden will be the greater. The opposite will be true if the payments emanate from the higher income groups whose propensity to save will be diminished.

8. Direct burden of internal debt. Table X shows that the greater part of the Dept is held internally. It follows that no increase in its size can make the country as a whole any poorer nor can any reduction make it richer. It is a matter of internal accounting. The payment of debt-servicing charges involves a transfer from taxpayer to security holder. To the extent that the debtor (the taxpayer) is worse off, the creditor (the security holder) is better off.

If the ownership of the Debt were evenly distributed throughout the community and all taxpayers made an equal contribution to the servicing charges, the burden would be nil. Every interest receipt of £1 would be exactly offset by a tax payment of £1.

There is not, of course, an even distribution of Debt ownership and servicing inevitably involves a redistribution of income from taxpayer to security holder. Although there are substantial private holdings and although indirectly a broad cross-section of the community benefits from an interest in that part of the Debt represented by national savings and the institutional investors, on balance it is likely that there is a net benefit in favour of the upper income groups whose propensity to save will be thus increased. On the other hand, there will be a corresponding reduction of the propensity to consume of taxpayers in the lower income groups. They must accept a real cut in their standard of living, a cut which represents the direct burden of internally held debt.

9. Indirect effects of Debt charges. Each year substantial sums in tax revenue must be devoted to Debt servicing. There are a number of implications.

(*a*) *Forgone alternatives*. It may be argued that in order to make interest payments more worthwhile objectives are forfeited.

(*b*) *Reduction of incentives*. If it can be proved that taxation has a disincentive effect upon willingness to work then it will be desirable to minimise the tax load. Equally it may be suggested that the incentive to work of the security holder is reduced by his unearned income receipts.

(*c*) *Demand management*. Most significantly it may be objected that the extra taxation unnecessarily depresses the level of demand and distorts its structure. Therefore the volume and composition of production will be adversely affected.

ORIGIN AND GROWTH OF THE DEBT

10. Traditional view of sound public finance. Until 1945, the first principle of sound public finance was considered to be the balanced budget. In the private sector, for any company to remain solvent its revenue in the long run must always at least equal its expenditure. It was therefore believed that the same principles should be applied to public finance. So long as the public sector remained small this was a relatively simple objective to achieve and budgets were only unbalanced in time of war. The resulting charges then placed the Revenue under severe stress since they swallowed a large proportion of total tax income in a period when it was considered obligatory to keep taxation at a minimal level. There was consequently a continuing concern to find ways of repaying the Debt in order to eliminate the taxes needed to service it.

11. The eighteenth century. The modern National Debt originated in 1694 when a group of City merchants agreed to lend the government £1,200,000. In return they received the privilege of a Royal Charter to found the Bank of England. An important relationship was in this way established between the State and what was to become the country's central bank.

There followed a period of recurrent wars which proved impossible to finance from tax revenues. In the intervals of peace, certain Chancellors, notably Walpole and Pitt, attempted to redeem the Debt through the instrument of *Sinking Funds*. Despite these efforts total borrowing expanded and by the close of the Napoleonic Wars had reached £850 million.

12. The nineteenth century. In contrast this century was one of relative calm in which military action seldom escalated above the level of a campaign. Although the Crimea and South African Wars were primarily financed by borrowing the total National Debt had, by 1914, been reduced to £707 million.

13. The twentieth-century Debt and monetary policy. To finance the First World War, the Government was obliged to borrow on an enormous scale which led to an expansion of the Debt to £8,000 million. Moreover, it was now committed to borrowing against shorter-dated securities. Hitherto, all borrowing had been against undated stocks. Dated stocks and Treasury bills now dominated the market.

During the inter-war period the management of a Debt of this size was clearly a serious responsibility. However, it did provide the Government with a powerful instrument of credit control. Since Treasury bills tended to exceed all other forms of short-term borrowing in the *money market*, careful management of their supply influenced their rate of discount which in turn influenced all other short-term interest rates. Similarly the capital market was dominated by the interest rates payable on Government long-term borrowing.

14. The twentieth-century Debt and demand management. From 1939 to 1945 the Debt trebled to £24,000 million. From that time a different approach has been made to the task of Debt management. With the acceptance of Keynesian techniques for controlling the economy it was seen that in a deflationary or stagnant situation a greater stimulus could be given to demand through public expenditure financed by borrowing, i.e. by an increase in the National Debt. Equally, when the level of demand was giving rise to inflationary pressure it would be desirable to budget for a surplus, i.e. to make a net repayment of Debt.

15. The principles of Debt management. From the preceding discussion it will be seen that the objectives of Debt management policy will be threefold:

(*a*) *To minimise the direct burden* (*see* **16–20**).

(*b*) *To budget for a surplus or a deficit in line with the current requirements of economic policy* (*see* **21–27**).

(*c*) *To manage the size and composition of the Debt in a way which accords with the required monetary policy* (*see* XV).

REDUCING THE BURDEN OF THE DEBT

16. Repudiation. It lies within the power of government to repudiate its obligations. However, it will avoid such a breach of contract which would strike at the foundations of a society based upon contractual relationships.

On wholly practical grounds repudiation would make it extremely difficult for government to borrow again.

17. Repayment. This course of action involves the consideration that over a given period, long or short, repayment of principal be added to current interest payments.

(*a*) *External debt.* To the extent that Debt is held externally, extra surpluses would have to be earned in the balance of payments. It is probable that this would necessitate policies which would be disruptive of the natural flow of international trade and which would invite retaliatory action.

(b) *Internal debt.* Repayment of this part of the Debt would accomplish an additional redistribution of wealth in favour of holders of securities at the expense of taxpayers. The size of the Debt is such that if this were attempted in the short run the taxation required would be impossible to collect and disruptive of the whole economy. If it were attempted over a longer period then the economy would be subject to the deflationary effects of repeated budget surpluses. These would be more restrictive than the expansionist effects achieved by the funds released.

Finally it must be recognised that while it is desirable to reduce the burden of servicing charges, the Debt itself is a vital instrument of economic management. This factor, together with the sheer size of the Debt therefore preclude any serious consideration of a policy of repayment.

18. Conversion. The refinancing of maturing issues of National Debt is a continuing process. If economic conditions allow it may on occasion be possible to convert Debt incurred at high interest rates to new issues made at lower rates.

In this century there have been two *major* conversions which were designed to reduce the level of interest charges. In 1932, in a period of economic depression in which low interest rates were appropriate, £2,000 million War Loan was converted from 5% to 3½% stock with an annual saving to the taxpayer of £30 million.

In the immediate post-war period, a policy of low interest rates was pursued for the purpose of facilitating reconstruction. Between 1945 and 1947 the opportunity was taken to make a number of conversions which achieved total annual savings of £38 million.

In more recent years inflationary pressures have induced much higher levels of interest rates and no conversions of this magnitude have been possible. The refinancing of maturing Debt has in fact proved more rather than less costly with the result that the servicing charge has been on a steeply rising trend. Paradoxically the burden upon the taxpayer has generally been on a falling trend due to the increasing importance of central government interest receipts.

19. Central Government interest receipts.

TABLE XIV.   CENTRAL GOVERNMENT PAYMENTS AND RECEIPTS OF
INTEREST 1961-75 (£ million)

	1961	1963	1965	1967	1969	1971	1973	1975
Debt interest payments	893	930	968	1,105	1,280	1,384	1,726	2,637
Interest and dividends from:								
Loans to local authorities	124	123	142	203	281	399	541	857
Loans to public corporations	192	246	313	414	602	736	889	1,147
Other	88	92	115	119	104	178	166	325
Interest payments *less* Interest and dividend receipts	489	469	398	369	293	71	166	290

Source: *National Income and Expenditure,* 1976

The figures in Table XI reflect the extent of central government financing of the capital account of a greatly expanded public sector. From a negligible involvement at the end of the war, outstanding government loans to local authorities and nationalised industries had risen to £26,000 million by 1976. It therefore emerges that almost one half of the existing National Debt may be viewed as *reproductive* in the sense that it is backed by income yielding tangible assets such as power stations, transport facilities and housing. This borrowing has been financed in part from current budget surpluses and in part by central government borrowing from the private sector on behalf of public corporations and local authorities.

20. The effect of inflation and devaluation on the burden of the Debt.
Inflation militates against the creditor in favour of the debtor since payment of interest at a fixed rate and repayment of principal are made in a depreciating currency. A smaller proportion of the debtor's income is required to meet his commitments.

In due course the internal depreciation of the currency will induce an external devaluation of the exchange rate. When this occurs the overseas investor is left with assets and income which are worth less in terms of his own currency.

THE NATIONAL LOANS FUND

21. Budgeting for a surplus or a deficit.
During the 1950s it became apparent that the annual budget processes did not meet the needs

of the management of public expenditure. The Budget is primarily concerned with adjusting revenue and expenditure in the short term whereas the forward planning of much expenditure placed growing emphasis upon long term projections. Control could not easily be geared to the fluctuations of annual Budgets, particularly in view of the nature of many expenditure proposals which involve only a small outlay in the first year but build up in subsequent years.

It was therefore far too simplistic to imagine that demand could be managed with any accuracy through the manipulation of Budget *current* account surpluses of deficit. The need was for a wider view and more effective control of the expenditure plans of the public sector as a whole.

22. The complication of "government expenditure below the line". The post-war expansion of the public sector involved the Exchequer in what was known in the early 1960s as "expenditure below the line" to provide long term capital to local authorities, nationalised industries and on occasion to private industry.

When local authorities were unable or unwilling to raise capital on the market they secured funds from the Exchequer through the Public Works Loans Board. Between 1956 and 1968 the nationalised industries had all their investment requirements provided by the Exchequer.

A purely *ad hoc* system developed in which current account surpluses were carried forward to the capital account ("below the line"). The investment needs of the public sector were then met and the Government was left with a *net borrowing requirement*. In short, the Chancellor borrowed from the market on behalf of the whole public sector.

The criticism has been levelled that on this broader view budgetary control was too loose and that here lay the principal source of inflation in the 1960s.

23. Current account surpluses and capital account deficits, 1961–71. Table XV shows that throughout the decade, despite the production of record current account surpluses, the central government net borrowing requirement expanded. With the exception of 1962 and until 1969, far from establishing disinflationary surpluses the central government accounts showed massive deficits.

If there was to be effective planning and control of aggregate demand it was clearly necessary to establish separate accounting

TABLE XV. CENTRAL GOVERNMENT CURRENT SURPLUSES AND PUBLIC SECTOR BORROWING REQUIREMENTS, 1961–71 (£ million)

	1961	1962	1963	1964	1965	1966
Current Surplus	369	671	240	500	880	1,229
Borrowing by:						
Central Government	233	−65	153	434	610	530
Local authorities	498	−602	636	566	561	412
Public corporations	−27	10	43	−5	17	17
	704	547	832	995	1,188	959

	1967	1968		1969	1970	1971
Current Surplus	1,043	1,732		2,914	3,723	2,841
Borrowing by:						
Central Government	1,155	757		−1,112	−678	562
Local authorities	697	587		595	527	659
Public corporations	−23	−30		41	149	151
Public sector	1,829	1,314		−476	−2	1,372

Source: *National Income and Expenditure*, 1972

procedures for the government's capital account. Moreover, whenever the central government had a borrowing requirement it was particularly important to ensure that it was financed by means which were not inflationary (*see* **24**). Finally in his estimate of the level of total effective demand upon the economy's resources and the subsequent need for compensatory action the Chancellor would have to take into full consideration the borrowing requirement of the public sector as a whole and not simply that of central government.

24. Financing of central government borrowing requirement, 1961–8. It may be argued that the absence of an appropriate method of accounting and the consequent weakness of budgetary control of public expenditure was accompanied by haphazard methods of financing the government borrowing requirement.

Had it been possible to finance the cumulative deficit of £3,807 million by "legitimate" borrowing from the market there would not necessarily have been an inflationary effect. It would simply have represented a transfer of resources from the private sector to the public sector. However, one of the problems of Debt management in the 1960s was the weakness of the gilt-edged

TABLE XVI.   FINANCING OF CENTRAL GOVERNMENT BORROWING
REQUIREMENT, 1961–8

	£ million
Cumulative deficit	3,807
Financed as follows:	
Increase in net debt to Bank of England	179
Increase in note issue	1,093
Non-marketable debt	190
Government securities	592
Treasury bills	−618
N. Ireland government debt	88
Net borrowing from overseas governments	71
IMF subscriptions	−175
Increased holdings of non-convertible currencies	2
Total overseas official financing	3,925
Loss on forward exchange dealing	−356

Source: *National Income and Expenditure,* 1972

market. Investors turned from fixed interest securities to equities
in an attempt to provide a hedge against inflation.

During this period therefore it was only possible to raise the
level of borrowing against securities by £592 million with a further
£190 million sales of non-marketable debt. The balance of the
borrowing requirement was financed by three main methods, all
of which were the equivalent of creating new money.

(a) *Increase in net indebtness to the Bank of England Banking
Department.* The additional £179 million represents an increase
in the government's short term credit.

(b) *Increase in notes in circulation.* An inflated price level increases the public's demand for notes in circulation. When the
Bank responds by printing more it must back the new issue with
increased holdings of Debt. During the period £1,093 million of
the borrowing requirement was financed in this way.

(c) *Total overseas official financing* (*net*). This comprises four
elements:

(i) Central bank assistance.
(ii) Foreign currency deposits by other monetary authorities.
(iii) Transactions with the International Monetary Fund.
(iv) Increase or decrease in the official reserves.

All receipts of foreign currency are channelled to the Exchange
Equalisation Account. When these holdings are used in opera-

tions to support the exchange rate of the £, the sterling proceeds which automatically accrue are invested in Government Debt.

During the period no less than £3,925 million of the borrowing requirement was financed by these means.

25. Debt management and public sector investment programmes. It will be concluded that the major element of the modern National Debt is attributable to the capital requirements of the public sector and that these requirements must be carefully controlled and wisely financed if public finance is to be an effective instrument of economic management.

It is clear that this conclusion was reached in 1967 when the Chancellor in his Budget statement asked: "Is it necessarily the best arrangement that so much of the borrowing requirement of the local authorities and public corporations is financed in the first instance by the Exchequer?" He then indicated that he had put in hand a review of the suitability of the existing arrangements. The product of that review was the formation on the 1st April 1968, of the National Loans Fund.

26. The National Loans Fund. What had previously been described as "below the line expenditure" was now completely separated from the government's current account. The Act which established the Fund restricted the Exchequer to the revenue and expenditure transactions of the Budget which are met from Parliamentary votes.

Subsequently all government borrowing on behalf of the public sector has been conducted through the medium of the Fund. At the close of the financial year any current account surplus is transferred to the Fund and any deficit met from it.

27. The Public Sector Borrowing Requirement and the money supply in the 1970s. It was indicated earlier (*see* 23) that in developing a properly balanced macroeconomic policy it was necessary for the Chancellor to consider the demands upon real resources

TABLE XVII.   THE PUBLIC SECTOR BORROWING REQUIREMENT,
1970–8 (£ million)

1970	1971	1972	1973	1974	1975	1976 (est.)	1977 (est.)	1978 (est.)
−17	1,373	2,040	4,181	6,364	10,482	11,200	8,700	8,600

Sources: *National Income and Expenditure, 1976; The Government's Expenditure Plans, 1977*

made by the public sector as a whole. Those demands which are not financed through central and local government taxation are of necessity financed through the *Public Sector Borrowing Requirement* (PSBR). In line with the expansion of the public sector in the 1970s this figure has continued to grow, placing considerable strains upon the financial markets.

While the National Loans Fund Accounts have presented a clearer picture and offered more effective budgetary control of public sector capital expenditure there has remained strong inflationary potential on the occasions when it has proved difficult to borrow from the gilt edged market.

In addition to the financial methods which were considered in **24** the 1970s have witnessed a huge expansion of Treasury bill finance. In 1971, Treasury bills represented only 10% of the total Debt. By 1976 this figure had doubled to 20%.

In the first instance Treasury bill finance means borrowing from the banking system with a consequential expansion of the money supply. There is however a second-round effect. When the banks acquire more Treasury bills they increase their holding of liquid assets which enables them to expand their lending activities by methods which will be examined in XV. The money supply therefore increases yet again.

To the extent that monetarist explanations of inflation (*see* XIII, 8) have been accepted the implications are threefold. Firstly, the rate of growth of the money supply must be restricted. To achieve this the PSBR must be reduced and financed by borrowing outside the banking sector. Thirdly, the rate of growth of public expenditure itself must be strictly controlled.

PROGRESS TEST 14

1. Explain why the term "Government Debt" might be considered more appropriate than "National Debt". **(1)**

2. Describe the principal features of the Debt's structure. **(2)**

3. Which securities make up the floating debt? **(3(b))**

4. What do you understand by non-marketable debt? **(4)**

5. Who are the principal "official holders" of Debt? **(5)**

6. Does an increase in the size of the Debt mean that the country as a whole is worse off? **(6–8)**

7. Why do we have a National Debt? **(10–14)**

8. Would it be feasible to consider repayment of the whole Debt? **(17)**

9. Why is the burden of the Debt diminishing?   **(20)**

10. In what respect has the government's capital account complicated the post-war task of demand management?   **(22, 23)**

11. Why may certain methods of Debt financing be considered "illegitimate"?   **(24)**

12. What is the National Loans Fund?   **(26)**

CHAPTER XV

The Management of the National Debt and Monetary Policy

RENEWED CONFIDENCE IN MONETARY POLICY

1. Fiscal policy and monetary policy. Strictly speaking monetary policy does not belong in the field of public finance. When public spending is financed by taxation or by borrowing from the private sector this is basically a fiscal matter. However, the *methods* by which the public sector finances its *borrowing requirement* have implications both for interest rates and for the money supply. It is therefore in the area of National Debt management (for which the Bank of England is responsible) that fiscal policy and monetary policy overlap.

2. Interest rates re-activated. It has been shown that for twenty years, from 1931–51, there was a general disillusion with monetary policy and interest rates were pegged at a low and stable level, (*see* XII, **6**). Friedman suggests that monetary policy was popularly viewed as "a string". "You could pull on it to stop inflation but you could not push on it to halt recession. You could lead a horse to water but you could not make him drink. Such theory by aphorism was soon replaced by Keynes's rigorous and sophisticated analysis". This analysis as we have seen confirmed that the role of monetary policy was to be secondary to direct intervention through the public finances. A policy of cheap money was therefore pursued, primarily with the objective of holding down the cost of Government borrowing but also in the hope that there *might* be some incentive to private capital investment.

By 1951, cheap money had fuelled the fires of inflation not only in Britain but in the greater part of the western world. In country after country interest rates were permitted to move up, evidencing some revival of belief in the potency of monetary policy.

Unsurprisingly, in Britain, the birthplace of "the new economics", confidence in the usefulness of monetary policy as a

191

macroeconomic weapon remained weak. It was not strengthened by the findings of the Radcliffe Committee.

3. Report of the Committee on the Working of the Monetary System (Radcliffe Report), 1959.

The Committee described the instruments of monetary control as:

(a) *The interest incentive effect*. It was argued that just as low interest rates had provided little incentive to increased investment in the 1930s, so the interest rate after 1951 proved to be only a minor deterrent to borrowing and spending. If the business world is confident of profit it will invest regardless of what it pays for its capital. In short, the economy was not thought to be as sensitive to interest rates as it may once have been.

(b) *The general liquidity effect*. While the effect of interest rates on willingness to borrow was doubtful, what was certain was that "if the money for financing the project cannot be got on any tolerable terms at all that is the end of the matter". In other words, if the economy is sufficiently illiquid then borrowing cannot take place. The Committee, in adopting this view, was not recommending that monetary policy ought to centre upon control of the money supply.

4. The traditional quantity theory of money.

The Committee pointed out that to a greater or lesser degree all exponents of the quantity theory agreed that control of the money supply was a central part of monetary policy. They held that the quantities which are relevant to the level of demand are the flow of money incomes and the quantity of money, i.e. the volume of notes and bank deposits. It therefore followed that if the central bank was willing and able to restrict the rate of growth of the money supply to the real rate of economic growth then the objectives of monetary policy could be achieved.

The Radcliffe Committee took a much broader view.

5. The money supply is only part of "general liquidity".

It is asserted that while the volume of money is important it must be seen in the perspective of the wider structure of general liquidity. The decision to spend is governed not simply by the purchaser's cash balance but firstly by his liquidity, i.e. whether he has saleable assets or can borrow against future cash receipts. The second relevant factor is the structure of the assets of the financial institutions. The extent of their liquidity governs their ability to meet the demand for loans.

It would follow from this argument that there is therefore no systematic link between the level of spending and the existing quantity of money.

6. Monetary policy and the structure of interest rates. The Radcliffe Committee concluded that monetary policy should focus upon an attempt to influence the structure of interest rates throughout the market in loanable funds. This could be accomplished by the traditional manipulation of Bank Rate supported by the open market operations which would influence capital values and hence yields (*see* **22**(*c*), **23**). Having established a pattern of interest rates potential borrowers and lenders would be drawn to a particular distribution of their assets. This liquidity structure would be consistent with easy or difficult borrowing conditions and could be varied at will through the manipulation of the interest rate structure.

However, the Committee believed that while this approach provided the only genuine basis for monetary policy it was cumbersome and would be very slow to make an impact upon the level of spending. In a crisis therefore it would be preferable to intervene directly to restrict liquidity, e.g. by control of bank advances, consumer credit and capital issues.

7. Monetary policy in the 1960s. It is clear that the Radcliffe findings influenced the direction of monetary policy during the 1960s.

In the first place, in its operations in the gilt-edged market the Bank showed that its primary concern was for its functions in respect of National Debt management. Due to the pressures of inflation the market was weak throughout the decade and the Bank frequently intervened to hold up capital values in order to restrain interest rates. In this way the cost of National Debt financing was contained. However, purchases of stock on the open market pump fresh cash into the banking system thus increasing its capacity to create credit. This is the exact opposite of the procedure called for when it is desired to restrict the growth of credit (*see* **23**). It is therefore reasonable to conclude that in common with the Radcliffe Committee the monetary authorities had little regard for the quantity of money as a determinant of the level of spending.

Secondly, it can be observed that when faced with crises which called for the restriction of effective demand the authorities came to place increasing reliance upon direct intervention. In the second half of the decade monetary policy was based almost entirely upon Treasury directives which imposed ceilings upon bank lending allied to tight control of hire-purchase spending.

8. The "new" monetary policy of 1971. In May 1971 the Bank published a paper, *Competition and Credit Control*, which declared its intention to revert to a monetary policy based upon much more flexible interest rates and upon more regard for the money supply.

The existing system of Treasury directives was unsatisfactory since loan ceilings amounted to enforced market sharing between the banks. The consequent absence of competition stultified innovation and made the banking system less responsive to the changing needs of its customers.

Moreover, since the *Radcliffe Report,* the monetary school of economists had grown in influence. The money supply had been reinstated as more than just one of a range of liquid assets and was now seen as an important indicator of the impact of monetary policy. Research also indicated that flexible interest rates have a sharper effect upon economic behaviour than had been conceded by the Radcliffe Committee.

Accordingly the Bank proposed to vary the nature of its open market operations both in gilt-edged and in money.

9. Operations in the gilt-edged market. It has been noted that during the 1960s the Bank was inhibited in its dealings in gilt-edged securities by the desire to restrain interest rates in line with the needs of National Debt financing.

In May 1971 it put into effect a policy which once more gave priority to the alignment of Debt management to the needs of monetary policy. From that time it was no longer prepared "to respond to requests to buy stock outright except in the case of stocks with one year or less to run to maturity". In other words, the Bank was no longer willing to intervene in the market by making purchases which would bolster capital values and hold down interest rates. In its open-market operations the Bank would now have a greater regard for the effect of its dealings upon monetary aggregates and interest rates would consequently be permitted to rise when necessary (*see* 23).

10. Operations in the money market. The "new" monetary policy implied no change in the basic relationship between the Bank and the discount market (*see* 20). However, it did introduce a major modification of technique. Hitherto the discount houses agreed prices between themselves not only for the weekly Treasury bill tender but also for subsequent dealings in long bills. In its day-to-day operations in bills the Bank was then willing to deal at these prices without attempting to influence them.

The new arrangements provided not only for the abandonment of the syndicated tender (i.e. the collective bid of the discount houses) but also for the Bank in its day-to-day operations in Treasury bills to deal at prices of its own choosing. As the major dealer in the market it would therefore feel at liberty to bring pressure on bill prices and hence the whole pattern of short-term interest rates (*see* **21**).

11. Two conclusions. From the preceding account of UK monetary policy certain features are apparent.

(*a*) *Moving interest rates are the criterion of traditional monetary policy*. It has been said that if monetary policy means anything it means control through flexible interest rates. With the exception of the 1930s and the 1960s this view has been accepted in the UK. It conflicts with the monetarist view that the principal criterion should be the control of the rate of growth of the money supply.

(*b*) *The money supply has been considered to be of secondary importance*. In the first half of the 1970s there is little evidence that the monetary authorities followed up their intention in 1971 to have more regard for the monetary aggregates.

In 1972, with unemployment approaching one million, an orthodox Keynesian solution was applied. Public spending increased *and the money supply was subsequently permitted to expand at a very rapid rate*. The short term result was an increase in output and a reduction in unemployment and interest rates.

This trend was quickly reversed. The impact of increased monetary demand was absorbed in escalating prices while output stagnated and unemployment rose again. *Interest rates also rose to unprecedented levels*. The monetarist explanation is that while an increased rate of growth of the money supply initially produces lower interest rates the demand for new loans shortly outstrips the increased money supply and interest rates now rise. In short, high interest rates, far from being indicative of a willingness to counter inflation are symptomatic of an inflation which is already well under way.

In 1976, there was some evidence of a willingness to accept the force of this argument. A largely successful attempt was made to fund a vast public sector borrowing requirement without borrowing from the banking system and thereby increasing the rate of monetary growth. External pressure was also applied in December 1976, when the International Monetary Fund made strict monetary control a condition of a large loan.

The conclusion must be that in Britain, by 1977, there had been a partial if reluctant acceptance that monetary policy has a larger role to play than has previously been allowed and that its implementation requires considerable attention to the rate at which the money supply is permitted to grow.

THE BANKS AND THE SUPPLY OF MONEY

12. The nature of money. It is by no means easy to provide a simple definition of what constitutes the money supply. In the broadest sense it may be said that money comprises whatever performs the functions of money. Its principal function is to serve as a *medium of exchange* and historically many commodities have been used for this purpose, from slaves, olive oil and cattle to gold and silver. In modern times commodity money was superseded by paper which in turn has been largely displaced by bank deposit money (or bank credit). These developments give rise to the conventionally accepted definition of the money supply, i.e. notes, coins and bank deposits.

Money in all its forms has always displayed one major characteristic, *universal acceptability*. Anything will serve as a medium of exchange provided that everyone is willing to accept it in payment of debt. This willingness is governed by the confidence that its value or purchasing power will not suddenly deteriorate and this confidence is in turn dependent upon some limitation upon the supply of money.

13. Limitation of the supply of paper money. The 1844 *Bank Charter Act* vested an ultimate control over the note issue in the Bank of England. It also placed the country firmly upon a gold standard. Apart from a small fiduciary issue which was backed by £11 million of direct Government Debt to the Bank (this figure having grown from the original £1,200,000 of 1694) every note issued had to be backed by gold.

In 1931 the gold standard was abandoned and in the years from 1932-9 the gold backing for the note issue was gradually transferred to the newly formed Exchange Equalisation Account. At this stage the currency was almost entirely fiduciary. Increases in the note issue were then limited by the provisions of the Currency and Banknotes Act of 1928, the general position being subsequently confirmed by another Act under the same title in 1954. These Acts stipulated that authority for the Bank to print more notes could be given by the Treasury. If, however, at the end of two years the increased circulation was to be maintained then Parliamentary approval had to be given. In practice such approval has been a formality.

It should be remembered, however, that whenever the Bank increases the note issue it requires to balance these fresh liabilities with new assets in the form of Government Debt (*see* XIV, **24**(*b*)).

14. Bank-deposit money. The final stage in the evolution of money is found in its appearance as a figure on a bank ledger which can be transferred by a number of instruments but principally by the cheque. It should be stressed that it is the deposit itself and not the cheque which is a part of the money supply.

By far the greater part of these deposits are created at the initiative of the banks themselves. This occurs on every occasion that a bank makes a loan.

When a loan is made to the public sector in the form of purchases of bonds or Treasury bills or local authority securities or in money at call to the discount houses for the purpose of financing their purchases of central and local government debt, a new bank deposit will result immediately the proceeds are spent, e.g. when a government department pays a civilian contractor's bill the cheque will increase his bank deposit.

Similarly loans to the private sector in the form of advances (overdrafts) or the purchase of commercial bills will expand deposits when the proceeds are spent.

The main point is that in neither case are notes handed over the counter. In the case of public-sector loans the banks purchase bills and bonds with cheques drawn on their Bank of England accounts. When in the private sector an overdraft facility is utilised the borrower writes a cheque on an account which now shows a debit balance. The banks are able to create credit in this way to the point where their eligible reserve assets (liquid assets) bear a minimum $12\frac{1}{2}\%$ ratio to the eligible deposit liabilities which have resulted.

EXAMPLE:
Position 1

Liabilities	*Assets*	
	Reserve	*Investments*
Deposits	*Assets*	*and Advances*
£50	£12·50	£37·50

It will be seen that in this position the banks are considerably "underlent" since their reserve assets bear a 25% relationship to their deposit liabilities. There is room for expansion for their lending activities under the heading of "investments and advances". These are the "earning assets", so called because they yield a higher rate of interest than the reserve or liquid assets.

Position 2

Liabilities	*Assets*	
	Reserve	*Investments*
Deposits	*Assets*	*and Advances*
£100	£12·50	£87·50

In the second position the banks have created for themselves £50 of fresh assets which have resulted in the expansion of deposit liabilities by a corresponding £50. They are now "fully lent" since their reserve ratio stands at the minimum permitted 12½%. These new bank deposits are money in the fullest sense, being wholly at the disposal of the depositor. They constitute by far the greater part of the total money supply.

15. Bank liquidity. It will be the desire of all banks to maximise their lending since the resulting interest payments make up the greater part of their income. On the other hand they must retain sufficient reserves in cash or other liquid assets which are easily converted to cash to meet the contingency of cash withdrawals.

In arriving at a compromise the London clearing banks voluntarily adhered to two principles, the 8% cash rule and the 28% total liquidity rule. Cash and other liquid assets were never permitted to fall below these levels. In September 1971 these rules were abandoned in favour of a single but obligatory reserve ratio of 12½%.

16. The 12½% reserve ratio. It has been observed that in May 1971 the Bank announced its intention to make monetary policy more effective. Its proposals were implemented in September of the same year. They established a uniform minimum reserve ratio of 12½% of "*eligible reserve assets*" to "*eligible deposit liabilities*" for *all* banks. Hitherto monetary policy had been aimed almost exclusively at the London clearing banks since they had always overshadowed the rest. However, the growth during the 1960s of the business of the other banks now made it desirable to subject them to the same controls.

17. Eligible liabilities. These are defined as the sterling deposit liabilities of the banking system as a whole except for those deposits made originally for a minimum two-year period. Additionally, *net* liabilities in non-sterling currencies are included.

18. Eligible reserve assets. These comprise:

(*a*) *Balances at the Bank of England.* Cash in the tills of bank branches is no longer included.

(*b*) *U.K. government Treasury bills.*

(*c*) *Money at call with the London money market.*

(*d*) *UK government stocks with one year or less to maturity.*

(*e*) *Local authority securities with an original maturity of less than six months.*

(*f*) *Commercial bills eligible for rediscount at the Bank of England up to a maximum of 2% of total eligible liabilities.*

Since credit in the form of advances and investments is built up on the base of the reserve assets it follows that if the Bank of England is able to influence the availability of these assets to the banking system it has a powerful instrument for the implementation of monetary policy. It does in fact seek to achieve this goal through its open market operations in Treasury bills and government bonds and through the Special Deposit scheme (*see* **23–25**).

19. Reserve ratio, eligible liabilities and assets of banks. The Bank of England recognises the difficulty of a suitable definition of the money supply by offering a choice of two (M1 and M3), each of which it believes to be appropriate to different purposes. The essential difference lies in the type of bank deposit which each definition includes.

On the most comprehensive definition, M3, the money supply in January 1977 amounted to £43,196 million. Table XVIII shows that bank deposits accounted for £36,144 million of the total. The biggest contribution came from the six London Clearing Banks whose eligible deposit liabilities amounted to £20,342 million. The relative importance of each type of asset with the em-

TABLE XVIII.   RESERVE RATIO, ELIGIBLE LIABILITIES AND
ASSETS OF BANKS IN THE UK, JANUARY 1977

	£ million
Eligible deposit liabilities	
Total	36,144
Of which, interest bearing liabilities	25,002
Eligible reserve assets	
Balances with the Bank of England	378
UK Government Treasury bills	1,318
Money at call	2,283
UK Government stocks with less than 1 year to maturity	508
Local authority bills	87
Commercial bills	645
Total	5,219
Reserve ratio 14.4%	

Source: *Bank of England Quarterly Bulletin,* March 1977

phasis on money at call to the London Discount Market will also
be noted.

Finally, it will be seen that with a 14·4% reserve ratio, 1·9%
above the permitted minimum, the banking system technically
had spare lending capacity.

20. The London Discount Market. The London Discount Market
comprises eleven discount houses together with a number of other
firms which have some interest in discounting operations.

The Market's function as an intermediary in the provision of
short-term finance can be seen from an examination of Table XIX.
Funds are borrowed from the banks on terms ranging from "call"
to "short notice" at a rate of interest known as "money rate".
The proceeds are then used to discount Treasury bills, *short-
dated* government stock, commercial bills, local authority securities and certificates of deposit. The various discount rates show
a profit margin over money rate. The common characteristic of
all these securities is that they represent *short-term* borrowing by
the public and private sectors, normally for periods of three
months.

Call money is repayable on demand. When this occurs or when
for other reasons the market has difficulty in finding the cash to
finance its portfolio it may have to resort to the Bank of England
where it has a unique borrowing facility enjoyed by no other

TABLE XIX.   ASSETS AND BORROWING OF THE LONDON DISCOUNT
MARKET, JANUARY 1977

Assets (Sterling)	*£ million*
UK Government Treasury bills	640
Local authority bills	62
Other public sector bills	75
Commercial bills	1,045
Sterling certificates of deposit	513
Other sterling funds lent	160
British Government stocks	439
Local authority stocks	312
Other assets	17
Total	3,263
Borrowed funds (Sterling)	
Bank of England	527
Other UK banking sector	2,361
Other United Kingdom	191
Overseas	47
Total	3,126

Source: *Bank of England Quarterly Bulletin,* March 1977

financial institution. At the Bank's Discount Office it may rediscount securities or borrow against their cover. However, it
will be reluctant to adopt this course since it must pay the Bank's
minimum lending rate (formerly known as Bank Rate) which is
substantially higher than the market's own discount rates.

THE BANK OF ENGLAND AND THE
MECHANICS OF MONETARY POLICY

21. The instruments of control. It has been emphasised that
traditional monetary policy has always centred upon the anticipated results of moving interest rates. In practice this originally
meant a variation of the key interest rate which was Bank Rate
and an attempt to make this change "effective" through open
market operations in Government Debt. By 1971, monetary
policy had evolved in a way which placed these instruments in a
new perspective and in October 1972, this was acknowledged with
the formal abolition of Bank Rate.

22. The Bank of England's minimum lending rate. Over the course of some 250 years Bank Rate developed three major functions.

(*a*) *The "prime rate"*. It was the rate to which certain other interest rates were directly linked, e.g. the overdraft and deposit rates of the banks.

(*b*) *An economic signal*. It was the means by which the Bank and subsequently the government signalled their view of how the economy was progressing. Externally, if a payments embalance was inducing a drain on the reserves it was hoped that overseas sterling holders might be persuaded to maintain their holdings by higher interest rates. Secondly, a higher Bank Rate could be taken as an indication of the Chancellor's resolve to check inflation and avoid devaluation. Foreign confidence might in this way be restored and the outflow of "hot money" halted.

Internally Bank Rate variations were taken as an indicator of further expansionary or disinflationary measures which might lie ahead.

(*c*) *The minimum lending rate to the discount houses*. A rise in Bank Rate had an immediate effect on all short-term interest rates. The discount houses could never permit their discount rates to lag too far behind in case they were obliged to satisfy their marginal borrowing requirements at the Bank. Since the Market in all loanable funds is competitive, the upward movement of short-term rates ultimately worked its way through to the capital market.

With the passage of time these functions conflicted ever more frequently. For example, if it was desired to stimulate the economy and also to check the outflow of "hot money", opposite courses of action were indicated. Consequently, for several years Bank Rate declined in importance.

In September 1971 the banks accepted the Bank of England's proposals for "*Competition and Credit Control*". Their *base rates* which provide the key to their overdraft and deposit rates are now determined separately and independently.

Economic signals are now given in speeches and directives and not in the "nod-and-wink" language of Bank Rate.

There remained the function of controlling the money market, the ultimate source of all interest rates and credit. The application in 1971 of the Bank's new method of bill dealing immediately wrote down the significance of Bank Rate (*see* 10). The Bank could now influence discount rates directly at any time without any movement of Bank Rate being necessary. Moreover, by 1972, Bank Rate as a penal rate of lending at last resort was useless, e.g. in early October 1972 the discount houses could theoretically borrow from the Bank of England at 6%, a supposedly penal rate, while the market rate for money lay a half a point *above*.

These anomalies were finally resolved with the abolition on the 9th October 1972 of the traditional Bank Rate. The "minimum lending rate" which replaced it differs in being a product rather than a cause of the interest rates prevailing in the money market. It is calculated by taking the last Treasury bill rate, adding half a percentage point and rounding up to the next quarter point. In this way it is guaranteed always to lie sufficiently above the market rate to be a real penalty to the discount houses should they be "forced into the Bank". It will be observed, moreover, that if market conditions occasion a rise in Treasury bill rate then a rise in the Bank's minimum lending rate will follow automatically.

23. Open market operations in gilt-edged securities. Conventionally, open market operations in bonds were for the purpose of making Bank Rate effective. If a rise in Bank Rate were accompanied by sales of securities to the public then the cheque payments to the Bank of England would result in a reduction of the cash balances of the clearing banks. They would make these good by recalling money from the discount houses which would now be "forced into the Bank" to borrow at the penal Bank Rate.

Secondly, if the banks were already operating close to their minimum liquidity ratio (formerly 28%) and were now forced below it by sales of gilt-edged, they would be obliged to call in advances in order to reconstitute their position. In this way credit became both scarcer and dearer.

During the 1960s it has been noted that the first purpose could not be achieved because of the Bank's commitment to intervention in support of gilt-edged prices (*see* 7). The second goal remained equally elusive since in the main the banking system was well supplied with liquid assets and was easily able to maintain liquidity ratios above the permitted minimum.

Since 1971, and subsequently confirmed by the abolition of Bank Rate, the Bank's operations in bonds can be seen in a different light. In managing the government's long-term borrowing the Bank now has a freer hand and is prepared to see interest rates rise in response to market conditions. While this implies a higher Debt servicing charge it also signifies the willingness of the authorities to allow a greater freedom to market rates of interest to serve as a mechanism for allocating available capital between the public and private sectors. This contrasts with the management of the gilt-edged market in the 1960s when, unable to attract fresh capital from the private sector, much borrowing was financed by "printing new money" with corresponding inflationary effects (*see* XIV, **24**).

24. Open market operations in treasury bills. The Bank of England's operations in Treasury bills are of monetary interest in two respects.

(*a*) *The effect on short-term interest rates.* Each Friday the Bank caters for the Exchequer's short-term borrowing needs by offering for tender an issue of Treasury bills. The bidders are the Bank itself, as agent for overseas central banks; the commercial banks, as agent for their customers; and the discount houses. By long-standing consent the latter agree to ensure that the whole amount offered for sale is absorbed, i.e. they underwrite the tender. On the assumption that the Bank has some flexibility in financing short-term borrowing from internal sources (i.e. the departments), then it may regulate the supply of bills to the market in a way which will influence interest rates. It may even force the market to borrow at the Bank's minimum lending rate by offering a greater supply of bills than it knows the market can absorb. However, it has already been pointed out that in this respect the weekly tender is of less significance than formerly since the Bank is now able to influence rates in its *day-to-day* bill dealings.

(*b*) *The effect on bank liquidity.* Government short-term debt is one of the reserve assets upon which the banking system can base the expansion of credit. It follows that one aspect of monetary policy will be the regulation of the supply of these assets. During the 1950s there was great concern to convert the vast quantities of short-term debt accumulated during the war to borrowing at longer term. Despite a number of successful funding operations the banking system remained excessively liquid. The reduction of the Treasury bill supply was more than offset by the expansion of other liquid assets.

An attempt to deal with this problem was made with the introduction in 1960 of a scheme for *Special Deposits*.

25. Special deposits. The Bank of England was empowered to call upon the clearing banks to make cash deposits (calculated as a percentage of total deposits) which could not be treated as part of their liquid assets. It was therefore hoped that the credit-creating capacity of the banks could be limited since it was expected that they would meet Special Deposit calls by the sale of bills, thus reducing their reserve assets base. It was not anticipated that cash would be raised by the alternative method of selling stocks since banks would not be prepared to suffer the capital losses consequent upon sales of this dimension.

However, it has been pointed out that during the 1960s the Bank supported the gilt-edged market. The banks were able to meet Special Deposit calls therefore from the sale of securities without undue loss and *without reducing their liquidity*. The original special deposits scheme may therefore be considered to have failed.

In its new approach to monetary policy in 1971, the Bank announced that its reliance upon much more flexible interest rates would be supported by the continuation of the Special Deposits scheme which would now be made applicable to all banks. Since the Bank was no longer prepared to support the gilt-edged market calls would now almost certainly be met by sales of reserve assets.

26. Supplementary Special Deposits ("the corset"). The modified techniques of monetary policy which were introduced in 1971 did not prove as effective as had been hoped in containing the excessive growth of bank liquidity, i.e. the build-up by the banking system of a large reserve assets base upon which to create credit.

The existing instruments were therefore augmented by a *Supplementary Special Deposits* scheme known as "the corset". Introduced in 1973, suspended in 1975, the scheme was reinstated in November, 1976.

The method differs from the previous techniques in that pressure is applied directly to the liabilities side of the balance sheet. (It will be recalled that these liabilities are "bank deposit money", the core of the money supply.) As we have seen, the other methods exert pressure upon bank assets.

The banks are required to restrain the rate of growth of their *Interest Bearing Eligible Liabilities* (IBELS), which is to say time deposits upon which they pay interest, to a specified percentage. If they choose to exceed this rate they are put under penalty by then being required to deposit with the Bank up to 50% of the excess growth at zero interest.

However, even this technique has not been completely successful since the banks may for example guide their customers away from time deposits into bigger current accounts by offering better services. Alternatively, they may guide them into "near money" such as Treasury bills or short dated local authority securities.

27. Problems of formulating an appropriate monetary policy. From the discussion in this chapter it will be apparent that a number of problems arise in formulating an appropriate monetary policy.

(*a*) *Should the criterion be interest rates or money supply?* Traditional monetary policy relies upon the manipulation of interest rates in order to influence the demand for and the supply of funds. The monetarists argue that it is impossible to peg interest rates at any level without immediately setting in train a course of events which will force them to revert to their "natural" or market level. This will be determined by the demand for loans and the availability of credit which when granted generates an expansion of "bank deposit money". It follows that control of the rate of growth of deposits, by restraining the ability of the banks to create credit will affect interest rates (*see* **26**). Even if the monetarist argument is conceded it must still be recognised that interest rates have significance beyond the domestic demand management function of monetary policy.

(*b*) *Interest rates and Debt management.* As the principal borrower on the financial markets the Government would prefer to minimise the cost to the taxpayer of servicing the National Debt, (*see* XIV, **8**).

(*c*) *Interest rates and international capital flows.* Short term deposits of foreign currency are sensitive to differentials in interest rates in the world's financial centres. To avoid sudden inflows and outflows of this "hot money" it is desirable that domestic rates should remain broadly in line with prevailing international levels.

(*d*) *Should there be a discretionary monetary policy?* If it is accepted that the money supply has a direct relationship with aggregate demand independent of interest rates the monetarists argue that the relationship is so poorly understood that no attempt should be made to "fine tune" the economy (*see* XII, **8–11**).

(*e*) *Which monetary aggregate?* Given the willingness to control monetary growth, what is to be considered an all embracing definition of the money stock? (*see* **12–19**).

(*f*) *How is effective control to be exercised?* If a suitable definition is agreed, there remain the practical difficulties of prescribing adequate control methods (*see* **21–26**).

PROGRESS TEST 15

1. Explain the nature of the "overlap" between fiscal and monetary policy.   (**1**)

2. Why might monetary policy be looked upon as "a string"? (**2**)

3. Why did the Radcliffe Committee consider the structure of interest rates of greater importance than their level?   (**3–6**)

4. What was the nature of the Bank's operations in gilt-edged securities in the 1960s?   (**7**)

5. How has the Bank operated in the gilt-edged market since 1971?   (**9**)

6. What are the two main features of current monetary policy? (**11**)

7. Outline the argument for considering the money supply as the principal criterion of monetary policy.   (**11**(*b*))

8. How is the supply of paper money limited?   (**13**)

9. Why may banknotes be considered to be a part of the National Debt expressed in an indirect way?   (**13**)

10. Explain how the banks create credit.   (**14**)

11. What do you understand by "bank liquidity"?   (**15–18**)

12. What part does the London Discount Market play in financing the National Debt?   (**20**)

13. What were the functions of Bank Rate?   (**22**)

14. How did Bank Rate come to be abandoned?   (**22**)

15. How are the Bank's operations in Treasury bills of monetary significance?   (**24**)

16. Why was the Special Deposits scheme largely unsuccessful in the 1960s?   (**25**)

PART FIVE

THE MACHINERY OF ADMINISTRATION

CHAPTER XVI

Formulation and Control of Financial Policy

THE PUBLIC EXPENDITURE SURVEY SYSTEM

1. The nature of the problem. The planning and control of public expenditure together with the subsequent verification that it has been carried out in accordance with the wishes of Parliament are aspects of the same process. It is, moreover, a process which must take account of the expenditure of other parts of the public sector such as the local authorities whose economic activities are closely linked to those of central government.

Certain features of the system may be emphasised.

(*a*) *Aggregate public sector demand.* A decision must be made on the level of total expenditure for the whole public sector.

(*b*) *Disposition of central government expenditure.* A decision must be made on the allocation of expenditure between the various services for which the central government is responsible.

(*c*) *A co-ordinating organisation.* It is clearly necessary to have an organisation which can effectively integrate decisions under the first two headings with the detailed planning and operations of the many authorities and departments concerned with the services provided under the second heading.

(*d*) *Effectiveness of expenditure.* An attempt must be made to ensure that the taxpayer receives value for money.

(*e*) *Audit of expenditure.* There must be a verification that expenditures have been made in accordance with the will of Parliament.

The subject matter of the first three headings will be dealt with in this section. The more detailed procedures of public accountability and the financial year implicit in the last two headings will be covered in the following sections.

2. The planning and control process before 1961. During the 1950s there was a growing dissatisfaction in the Treasury and the spending departments with the absence of a comprehensive expenditure framework within which individual expenditure programmes could be judged. The desirability of adopting a particular proposal was considered on its intrinsic merit. While attention was given to alternative routes to the *same* goal there existed no system for enabling priorities to be established between *different* goals.

Moreover, the enlargement of the public sector in the post-war world had made the annual budget processes increasingly unsuited to the long-range planning of many new aspects of public expenditure. The Budget is concerned essentially with establishing an equilibrium in the economy for the following year. Public expenditure on the other hand involves planning over a number of years ahead and is not easily amenable to *short-term* budgetary control. Secondly, many expenditure programmes by their nature involve a relatively small outlay at first which in subsequent years builds up. Finally, it had been traditionally argued that the difficulties a Chancellor would face in having his annual tax proposals approved by Parliament provided in themselves a check upon burgeoning expenditure. However, experience has shown that this is not so since there is no indisputable limit on the total taxation which a government may levy.

3. Report of the Select Committee on Estimates, 1957–8. In 1957–8 the Select Committee on Estimates undertook an examination of Treasury control of expenditure. Their report led to the setting up of the Committee on the Control of Public Expenditure under the chairmanship of Lord Plowden in 1959.

4. The Plowden Report. The main conclusion of the *Plowden Report*, published in July 1961, was:

"... that decisions involving substantial future expenditure should always be taken in the light of surveys of public expenditure as a whole over a period of years and in relation to the prospective resources. Public expenditure decisions whether they be in defence or education or overseas aid or agriculture or pensions or anything else should never be taken without consideration of (*a*) what the country can afford over a period of years having regard to prospective resources and (*b*) the relative importance of one kind of expenditure against another. This may appear to be self evident but in administrative (and we would hazard the opinion, in political) terms it is not easy to carry out."

The Committee went on to recommend a fresh approach to the process of decision-making based upon regular surveys which:

". . . should be made of public expenditure as a whole over a period of years ahead and in relation to prospective resources; decisions involving substantial future expenditure should be taken in the light of these surveys."

5. The implementation of the Plowden proposals. The central concept of the Plowden proposals was simple but its implementation involved technical difficulties. It was necessary to establish a system of collating, classifying and analysing information about the whole range of public expenditure in order to forecast its development over a five-year period at constant prices so that the growth of public sector demand upon productive potential could be measured. This work had to be co-ordinated with similar efforts within individual services.

The first comprehensive Public Expenditure Survey was made in 1961. At this stage the surveys were forecasts rather than instruments of policy, but from 1965 the Cabinet began to make decisions on the portion of anticipated national income to be allocated to the public sector.

6. Public expenditure White Papers. The results of these surveys were first published in White Papers in 1963 and 1966. A White Paper in January 1968 provided the detail of the post-devaluation reductions in public expenditure in 1968–9 and 1969–70. Early in 1969 a further short White Paper outlined the decisions for 1970–1 arrived at in the 1968 survey.

In April 1969 the government proposed that "there should be published towards the end of each calendar year a White Paper which will present to Parliament the result of the Government's consideration of the prospect for public expenditure". The first of the present annual series was published in December 1969 and reflected the decisions reached in the 1969 survey for each of the five years up to 1973–4.

7. Public Expenditure Surveys. There are certain important features of the annual Public Expenditure Surveys which should be noted.

(*a*) *Costings are of existing policies.* The forecasts of expenditure are based upon existing policies.

(*b*) *All public sector expenditure is included.* It follows that because the expenditure of some parts of the public sector is financed by payments from another, double counting must be eliminated in order to arrive at a valid total. For example, it would be incorrect to include Exchequer grants to local authorities as well as the local authority expenditure financed by those grants.

(*c*) *Analysis by function.* The figures are analysed by reference to the object of the expenditure, e.g. defence, health, education, social security. It is upon these comprehensive figures that the government is able to take major decisions on the size and structure of future expenditure.

(*d*) *Analysis by economic category.* The figures are also analysed by economic category, e.g. current expenditure on goods and services, gross domestic fixed capital formation, capital grants to private sector, debt interest, etc.

(*e*) *Analysis by function and economic category.* Further analysis is made of the economic categories into which expenditure on individual programmes falls.

(*f*) *Analysis by spending authority.* Figures are given for the sums attributable to central government, local authorities and public corporations.

(*g*) *A "rolling" five-year survey.* Each survey is for a period five years ahead. At the end of the first year the forecast is rolled ahead one year. In practice the Treasury maintains that in any five-year programme the third year is the earliest at which any major changes may be made without serious dislocation. Plans for the fourth and fifth years are viewed as provisional.

8. Medium-term economic assessments (MTA). Since 1961 the Public Expenditure Survey system has been linked to forecasts made each summer, normally for a five-year period. They are based on the assumption that government policy will determine the level of economic activity and take account of growth trends in population and productivity. This prediction of future growth is one of the aids to an assessment of the appropriate allocation of resources between public and private sectors and between consumption and investment. Any necessary adjustments in public sector spending programmes can then be made in good time and in an orderly way.

9. Timetable of the survey. The annual sequence of events is as follows:

December. The Treasury issues instructions on the conduct of the forthcoming survey.

End of February. The spending departments submit their preliminary estimates of expenditure to the Treasury.

March/April. Discussions of a technical nature take place between the Treasury and the spending departments in order to agree upon the correct interpretation of existing policies and upon the cost of continuing them.

May. The Treasury submits a draft report to the Public Expenditure Survey Committee.

June. The report is submitted to Ministers.

July/October. Decisions are now taken on the aggregate of public expenditure and its broad allocation to the twenty functional programmes.

10. The Public Expenditure Survey Committee. A special statistical and administrative unit has been created within the Treasury for the purpose of co-ordinating the task of preparing a report for the Committee's consideration.

The Committee is chaired by a Deputy Secretary of the Treasury and includes the Principal Finance Officers of the main spending departments. Its task is to agree a factual report which will show Ministers where present policies costed at constant prices will lead over the ensuing five years. When this development is set against the medium-term economic forecast the government can determine whether public sector demands upon productive resources should be increased, decreased or left alone. Secondly, the government is able to assess whether the development of expenditure on the various functional programmes is in accord with its own view of social, economic and political priorities.

By providing Ministers in this way with a better perspective of public expenditure as a whole it is hoped that the quality of decision-making will be improved.

11. Allocation of resources between functional programmes. While the Government will seek to impose its own scale of priorities upon expenditure on different programmes, for a number of reasons it cannot do so without reference to the impact that a *particular* expenditure will have upon the *aggregate* of public expenditure.

(*a*) *Demand intensive expenditure.* The impact upon available economic resources will be greater from some forms of expenditure than from others.

(*b*) *Inflexible expenditure.* If all existing expenditure is by nature inflexible and inescapable new expenditure arises there will be no room to accommodate it. The implication is that it is desirable to have some element of flexibility in at least some programmes.

(*c*) *Impact on the total demand for resources.* In assessing the intrinsic desirability of individual programmes consideration must be given to the impact of total public expenditure upon the rest of the economy.

It will therefore be seen that projections of individual programmes provide a realistic basis for assessing the claims which the public sector will be making on the economy. They also establish a reasonably firm foundation for the detailed planning and execution of programmes.

12. Appraisal of Public Expenditure Surveys. The weakness of the Public Expenditure Survey system in operation stems from three main causes.

(*a*) *A recurrent tendency to under-estimate future costs (see* **13**). In the years 1963–8 the percentage increase in public expenditure regularly exceeded that which had been planned. The annual increase was only brought under control in 1968–9. The reflationary policies of 1972–3 again put expenditure plans off course. It was therefore with some caution that the White Paper of December 1972 on expenditure up to 1976–7 was presented not as a forecast or blueprint but as "a very broad indicative picture based on assumptions".

(*b*) *A recurrent tendency to over-estimate economic growth.* For a successful equilibrium to be established in the economy an accurate expenditure survey must be married to an accurate assessment of growth prospects. These assessments have always tended to be too optimistic. The 1972 White Paper planned for an average annual increase of public expenditure by $2\frac{1}{2}\%$ based upon two alternative assumptions about annual growth—an optimistic one of 5% and a pessimistic one of 3·5%. However, taking five yearly averages from 1952, Britain's actual economic performance has ranged between 2·2% and 3·4%. It may therefore be objected that in the light of experience the "pessimistic" assumption is too optimistic and that even if attained in the short-run a high growth rate is unlikely to be sustained over a five-year period.

(c) *The problem of demand management.* It is reasonable to question the extent to which public expenditure plans may be expected to play their part in the regulation of aggregate demand. The theoretical solution of a "bank" of projects which can be speeded up or slowed down as the occasion demands has not been achieved in practice. Political considerations may make it difficult to adhere to a five-year plan which envisages heavy expenditure in the early years with sharp reductions in subsequent years. For example, the 1972 survey in proposing an annual average increase of 2·5% anticipated steep but "temporary" increases in the first two years (on "lame ducks", regional unemployment and subsidies to the nationalised industries), with a fall to 1·5% in the last three years. In the event, the following five years saw many more steep but "temporary" increases.

13. Technical reasons for the under-estimate of costs. Inaccuracy in the Public Expenditure Surveys may arise for a number of technical reasons.

(a) *The problem of changed expenditure classifications.* This difficulty may be illustrated by reference to the change from investment allowances to investment grants in 1966 and back to accelerated capital depreciation allowances in 1970. While the net cost to the Exchequer may be the same, for accounting purposes public expenditure was increased with the introduction of grants and decreased with their abolition. When the rate of increase of public expenditure is calculated it is therefore necessary to allow for such changes of classification.

(b) *The problems of projections at constant cost.* In estimating the effects of inflation upon costs it is possible in some public sector activities to introduce an offset for increased productivity. This is not possible with other activities such as education. It then follows that not only will the expansion of such services be a charge upon economic growth but that the maintenance of the existing level of those services at inflated prices will also have to be financed from growth in the GNP. Allowance must therefore be made for the problem that inflation itself increases the public sector share of the GNP.

(c) *The problem that central government has direct control over only a part of public sector expenditure.* For example, while the government is able to exercise a strong control over the capital expenditure of local authorities, their expenditure on current goods and services is largely autonomous. A difficulty therefore arises in making an accurate prediction of the rate of growth of this expenditure.

(d) *The problem of standardising the system of costing.* Problems have arisen because of the absence of a standard set of definitions and of standard costing techniques. Plans have been costed in different ways for different purposes and therefore with different results. Work on the standardisation of costing methods is well advanced. This will simplify the task of checking results against forecasts.

14. Programme Analysis and Review (PAR). In January 1971 the Government announced its intention to introduce a system of Programme Analysis and Review by the spending departments.

Over the past few years there have in fact been a good many detailed analyses of *particular* government activities. Consideration has been given to policy objectives, to the measurement of the inputs of resources and the outputs achieved and to alternative courses of action and their effects. The scheme for PAR now applies this approach systematically and regularly to a wide range of government programmes. It is hoped in this way to develop a more carefully selective approach to expenditure which will give the public better value for money.

It should be stressed that far from supplanting the Public Expenditure Surveys system the PAR arrangements are intended to complement and reinforce it. They should also provide Parliament and the Select Committee on Expenditure with better information and therefore closer control over government expenditure programmes.

15. The Public Expenditure Survey system and the Supply Estimates. It should now be noted that the Supply Estimates which are introduced into Parliament each year are prepared in the context of the broader decisions previously announced in the December White Paper on overall public sector expenditure.

THE FINANCIAL YEAR

16. Preliminary estimates. Effect is given to public expenditure plans in the annual Budget which covers the financial year beginning 1st April and ending 31st March. (For the purpose of income tax assessment the year begins on the 6th April and ends on 5th April.)

Preparation for the Budget begins in the February of the previous year when it has been noted that the spending departments submit their preliminary expenditure estimates to the Treasury (*see* 9). The Inland Revenue and Customs and Excise Departments submit their revenue forecasts at about the same time. During the spring and early summer revisions are made and the Treasury Accountant is able to prepare his first *Exchequer Prospects Table* which is submitted to the Budget Committee in July.

17. Treasury Budget Committee. The Committee is chaired by the Permanent Secretary to the Treasury and comprises the heads of the Public Sector and Finance divisions of the Treasury, senior Treasury economists, the chairmen of the Inland Revenue and Customs and Excise Departments and the Deputy Governor of the Bank of England. It meets continuously from July until March and at its first meeting has at its disposal the preliminary Exchequer Prospects Table and the summer National Income Forecast. (Treasury economists prepare *short-term* National Income Forecasts for the following financial year in February, June and October. They are essentially predictions of business cycle movements made on the assumption of no change in government policy.)

At this stage the Budget Committee is primarily concerned with the possible need for using the regulator during the summer.

18. The Queen's Speech. Parliament reassembles in the autumn and is opened by the Queen's Speech in which the government legislative programme is outlined and some idea given of the revenue necessary to implement it. This speech is prepared by the Cabinet together with the Address in Response. The opportunity is thereby given for debate when the Opposition may criticise and the government strengthen its case.

In line with the government's proposals the Budget Committee has by now agreed figures for public investment in capital projects such as schools, hospitals and roads. It will also have considered the need for an autumn "mini-budget" as a means of keeping the economy on course for the current financial year.

19. Firm estimates of revenue and expenditure. By early December the Treasury will have received firm estimates of expenditure from the spending departments and of revenue from the revenue departments. The Treasury Accountant is then able to revise his Exchequer Prospects Table.

The expenditure estimates will have received approval by the end of January and in February are introduced into Parliament for debate on the allocated "*supply days*".

Table XX reveals that the estimates fall into two major categories.

(*a*) *Supply Services*. These comprise the Defence Estimates and the Civil Estimates. The latter are collated in eleven *classes* cor-

TABLE XX.   SUPPLY SERVICES AND CONSOLIDATED FUND STANDING
SERVICES

Supply Services

I	Government and finance
II	Commonwealth and foreign
III	Home and justice
IV	Trade, industry and employment
V	Agriculture
VI	Environmental services
VII	Social services
VIII	Education and science
IX	Museums, galleries and the arts
X	Other public departments and common governmental services
XI	Miscellaneous
XII	Ministry of Defence

Supplementary provision (net)

Consolidated Fund Standing Services

Payment to the National Loans Fund in respect
  of the service of the National Debt
Northern Ireland share of reserved taxes, etc.
Post-war credits (including interest)
Payments to the European Communities
Other services

responding to the work of different ministries or groups of ministries. To each class there are 10–20 *votes* and under each vote a number of *subheads*. Between February and the end of July twenty-nine *supply days* are set aside for Parliamentary debate. All votes not discussed by the end of this period are passed without debate. Since supply days run on to July while the financial year has already begun on 1st April, without special provision the spending departments would be without funds after that date. However, the *Consolidated Fund Act* authorises bridging advances.

(b) *The Consolidated Fund Standing Services.* The Consolidated Fund is the central fund into which all government revenue has been paid since 1787. All expenditure is charged upon the Fund and certain *standing services* which Parliament is obliged to sanction are reviewed but agreed without much discussion by means of a *financial resolution*.

20. The Appropriation Act. Before Parliament has finished with the estimates it must authorise the release from the Consolidated Fund of the total sum needed for the supply services. In July or August an *Appropriation Act* is passed which divides up this sum and allocates it to each of the agreed votes.

21. The Budget. The expenditure estimates having received the approval of the Treasury, the Budget Committee now submits its recommendations to the Chancellor. At this point the "Budget judgment" begins to take shape and by mid-February the Chancellor is receiving advice on the size of the surplus or deficit at which he should aim. A month later a decision will have been made and most of the detail of the tax proposals firmly formulated.

The Budget speech will normally be made in April after the close of the old financial year. In it the Chancellor briefly reviews the course of the economy in the preceding twelve months but concerns himself primarily with his tax proposals for the coming year. Since the modern Budget is concerned not only with raising revenue but also with regulating the level of national expenditure these proposals will be built around an economic theme.

22. The Provisional Collection of Taxes Act. If the Chancellor were not able to give immediate effect to any tax changes which he proposed in the Budget there would inevitably be forestalments, e.g. by laying up stocks against an increase in customs duties. The *Provisional Collection of Taxes Act* gives immediate effect to a Parliamentary resolution to implement the tax proposals on a provisional basis for a period of four months. In the event that a proposed tax increase is subsequently amended then the taxpayer is of course entitled to a repayment.

23. The Finance Act. Immediately the Chancellor has made his statement the Commons votes without debate on the resolutions necessary to give provisional effect to the tax proposals. In due course the government introduces its Finance Bill which is debated at the second and third reading. It then passes to the House of Lords usually to be debated at the second reading only. At the end of July or beginning of August the bill receives the royal assent and the *Finance Act* finalises all matters pertaining to taxation.

PUBLIC ACCOUNTABILITY

24. House of Commons Standing Order No. 78. "This House will receive no petition for any sum relating to public service or proceed upon any motion for a grant or charge upon the public revenue, whether payable out of the Consolidated Fund or out of money to be provided by Parliament unless recommended from the Crown." Power to propose expenditure is therefore vested in H.M. Government alone and this rule militates in favour of a coherent and effective financial plan. It also means that responsibility for the success of the plan is placed squarely on government who will be held accountable to Parliament and the electorate.

The department of government which is concerned to see that this responsibility is effectively discharged is the Treasury of which the Prime Minister is First Lord and the Chancellor of the Exchequer the Second Lord with the special duty of advising the Cabinet on all financial matters.

25. Treasury control. Since 1861 it has been formally agreed that the estimates should include only expenditure proposals which have been sanctioned by the Treasury. When the Treasury examines the departments' expenditure intentions it does so in a commonsense way with a view to producing a balance between the various requirements in the light of what the country can currently afford and with the aim of ensuring that the best value for money is provided. The Treasury does not have an absolute veto since if the minister of a department wishes to press his case strongly enough the decision will ultimately rest with the Cabinet.

The importance of Treasury control lies chiefly in its influence over the estimates, but in other ways it exercises authority throughout the year. The preparation of estimates involves a forecast of the future but it is highly likely that government will encounter situations which had not been anticipated. The departments may therefore find it necessary to change the direction or the amount of their expenditure and it is here that the Treasury continues to exercise control in two important ways.

(a) *Virement.* A department may find that the sum that Parliament has voted is sufficient to meet its total requirements but that it wishes to transfer expenditure from one subhead to another. The Crown is allowed discretion in respect of this *virement* (transfer) which it exercises through the Treasury and *not* the spending departments.

(b) *Supplementary estimates.* In the case where a department wishes to spend *in excess of* the total sum voted to it by Parliament it must first seek the approval of the Treasury before a supplementary estimate can be submitted to Parliament. The Treasury will always be reluctant to agree to this course if the expenditure can be postponed until the following year. If this is not possible then supplementary estimates in respect of new services will be presented where possible in June or July to be voted upon and included in the summer *Appropriation Act.* In respect of existing services, supplementary estimates are not usually presented until February when there will be a clearer picture of the department's financial position.

26. Parliamentary control of the estimates. On the days allotted to Supply the Opposition is free to choose the estimates which will be debated and will do so in order most effectively to challenge ministerial policies and overall governmental economic strategy. However, the debate may range over particular services proposed in the estimates and over the administration of the departments. The House may only agree, refuse or reduce an estimate. It cannot propose increases or add conditions.

Limited Parliamentary time and the volume and technicalities of the estimates make it unlikely that the House of Commons will achieve any detailed economies. Occasionally reductions may be made but it is more likely that Members will be pressing views which, if it were permissible, would involve increased expenditure.

27. The Expenditure Committee. In 1971 the Expenditure Committee superseded the Select Committee on the Estimates which had been appointed annually since 1921. The purpose of the latter was to provide a more detailed examination of the estimates than was possible on the floor of the House. Some committees had performed a useful function in subjecting departmental administrations to external criticism, e.g. it was a Select Committee which was responsible for the criticism of Treasury control methods which led to the *Plowden Report* (*see* **3**, **4**).

With the subsequent implementation of five-year rolling plans it was thought desirable to have an Expenditure Committee with rather broader terms of reference. Its precise role is still evolving but essentially it is concerned to see that the various lines of public expenditure give the public the best value for money.

It is an inter-party committee comprising forty-nine members and sub-divided into six functional sub-committees.

(*a*) *The Public Expenditure* (*General*) *Sub-Committee.* This sub-committee is not confined to a particular area of government but is charged with the scrutiny of the central area of financial control in the light of present day techniques of resource allocation and of economic planning, programming and analysis. It believes that if it is to perform this function effectively it must have a permanent secretariat and the authority to employ whatever additional experts it may from time to time require. Parliament has yet to sanction this request.

The remaining sub-committees are concerned with scrutinising the effectiveness of selected programmes within their own fields of enquiry.

(*b*) *Defence and External Affairs Sub-Committee.*

(*c*) *Trade and Industry Sub-Committee.*

(*d*) *Education and Arts Sub-Committee.*

(*e*) *Environment and Home Office Sub-Committee.*

(*f*) *Employment and Social Services Sub-Committee.*

Not only is the Treasury held accountable for the effectiveness of public expenditure but it must also provide Parliament with proof of the technical accuracy of the public accounts. This is accomplished through a careful system of accounting and auditing (*see* **28–31**).

ACCOUNTING AND AUDITING

28. Exchequer and Audit Departments Act 1866. This Act, as amended by another of the same title in 1921, provides that each department to which supply grants have been authorised by the Appropriation Act shall prepare "accounts of appropriation" before certain dates. The departments themselves are therefore wholly responsible for spending and accounting for the money voted to them. The Treasury exercises no check on day-to-day spending but appoints an *Accounting Officer* in each department whose responsibility this now becomes.

29. Accounting Officer. The importance of this office is illustrated by the practice of appointing the permanent head of a department as the Accounting Officer. He signs the Appropriation Accounts personally and accepts full responsibility for their accuracy. Apart from safeguarding the public funds entrusted to him he must ensure that they are devoted only to the purposes designated by Parliament. In these matters he must answer to the Public Accounts Committee.

30. Appropriation Accounts. In the case of the civil accounts, departments aim to make submissions to the Comptroller and Auditor General by the end of September. The latter must forward them to the Treasury, together with his report, by mid-January and the Treasury submits accounts and reports to the House of Commons by the end of the month. For the defence estimates, a slightly longer time is allowed in each case.

Appropriation Accounts follow the form of the relevant estimates subhead by subhead, comparing the amounts granted with the actual out-turn. Notes are then made in explanation of any discrepancy.

31. Comptroller and Auditor General. The Appropriation Accounts are audited in order to verify that public money has in fact been spent in accordance with the wishes of Parliament. The audit is partial and continuous. A one hundred per cent examination of all supporting vouchers would today be a gigantic task requiring a very much greater staff. The Auditor General therefore has a degree of discretion in accepting charges to the accounts where he is satisfied that vouchers have been examined internally and certified correct. The audit continues throughout the year without waiting for a complete set of Appropriation

Accounts to be made up. This is facilitated by placing staff in the departments themselves both in London and in the provinces.

Apart from verifying the technical correctness of the accounts it is also part of the Auditor General's function to look for waste and inefficiency. When this seems sufficiently glaring he may find it necessary to report to Parliament. In this aspect of his work he receives powerful assistance from the Public Accounts Committee.

32. Public Accounts Committee. Once the Appropriation Accounts have been verified they are sent with the Auditor General's report to the Treasury who in turn submits them to the House of Commons. They are then referred to the Public Accounts Committee. House of Commons *Standing Order No. 90* provides that there should be a "Committee of Public Accounts for the examination of the accounts showing the appropriation of the sums granted by Parliament to meet the public expenditure . . .". At meetings of the Committee there are present the Auditor General, the Treasury Officers of Accounts and the Accounting Officer of the department under examination, together with any subordinates he cares to bring with him. The examination is based chiefly upon his Appropriation Accounts and the Auditor General's report. Having completed its deliberations, the Committee now publishes its reports which are considered by the Treasury and action taken as necessary.

A criticism has been levelled against the Committee that its cross-examination of civil service witnesses is sometimes imperfect. This arises because Members of Parliament serving on the Committee cannot be expected to have more than a very general knowledge of the vast range of departmental activities into which they have to enquire. On the other hand, the witnesses whom they examine are civil servants of high calibre with an expert knowledge of their particular field.

In order to redress the balance and therefore improve public accountability it has been suggested that it might be preferable to replace the existing Committee with a number of Select Committees, one for each department, which could scrutinise and investigate the complete working of a department on a continuing basis.

PROGRESS TEST 16

1. Explain the nature of the problem of controlling public expenditure. **(1)**

2. What factors led up to the Plowden enquiry? **(2)**

3. What was the substance of the Plowden recommendations? **(4)**

4. What are the main features of the annual Public Expenditure Surveys? **(7)**

5. What is the significance of the medium-term economic assessment? **(8)**

6. In what respects do the Public Expenditure Surveys display weaknesses? **(12, 13)**

7. How is the system of PAR intended to support the Public Expenditure Surveys? **(14)**

8. On what information is the first Exchequer Prospects Table based? **(16)**

9. Describe the work of the Treasury Budget Committee. **(17, 18)**

10. Distinguish between the Supply Services and the Consolidated Fund Standing Services. **(19)**

11. What is the function of the Appropriation Act? **(20)**

12. What do you understand by the "Budget judgment"? **(21)**

13. Explain the purpose of the Provisional Collection of Taxes Act. **(22)**

14. What is the significance of House of Commons *Standing Order No. 78*? **(24)**

15. Why is the Treasury so powerful? **(25)**

16. How does Parliament exercise control over the government's expenditure proposals? **(26)**

17. What are the functions of the Expenditure Committee? **(27)**

18. Who are the Accounting Officers? **(29)**

19. Explain the task of the Comptroller and Auditor General. **(31)**

20. What is the weakness of the Public Accounts Committee? **(32)**

The Concept of the National Income

1. The calculation of the national income. The national income may be regarded in two ways, as a circular flow of real things or as a circular flow of counterbalancing money values. This is illustrated in Fig. 52.

Society provides the economy, *organised into private and public sectors*, with the factors of production—land, labour and capital. The economy returns to society producer goods (i.e. capital) and consumption goods and services. In return for the use of the factors of production, the economy pays society wages, rent, interest and profits and receives a price for the volume of its output *determined at market prices*.

Two points are important:

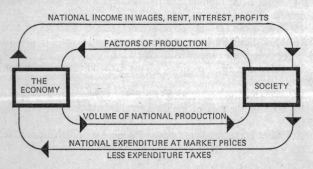

NATIONAL INCOME IN WAGES, RENT, INTEREST, PROFITS

FACTORS OF PRODUCTION

THE ECONOMY

SOCIETY

VOLUME OF NATIONAL PRODUCTION

NATIONAL EXPENDITURE AT MARKET PRICES
LESS EXPENDITURE TAXES

FIG. 52.—*The national income.* It may be seen that the concept of national income is balanced by that of national output. National income may be calculated as society's money receipts in wages, rent, interest, and profits. The level of these receipts will be determined by society's expenditure on goods and services after the deduction of expenditure taxes. It is necessary to make this deduction in order to avoid double counting since society will spend the proceeds of taxation to satisfy collective needs. National income in this sense will equate with the value of national production which in turn will be determined by the value set upon the factors which have contributed to it.

(a) The first thing which emerges from this discussion is that the terms "national income" and "volume of production" are simply different aspects of the same thing. National income may be viewed as the money value of all the goods and services produced in the public and private sectors or as the sum of money incomes generated by this activity. It may be approached in a third way as the total volume of national expenditure.

(b) There emerges secondly the point which is significant to tax analysis. National expenditure takes place at a market price which includes *expenditure taxes*. The resulting revenue will swell the volume of national expenditure when spent by government agencies. This sum of money will therefore have been spent twice but will only be distributed once in income. If national expenditure is to equate with national income, expenditure taxes must be deducted.

2. The two methods of calculation.

The White Paper on *National Income and Expenditure* takes this problem into account in estimating the national income firstly from the side of expenditure and secondly from the side of income.

(a) *Expenditure at market prices.* The attempt is made to set a value upon the total volume of production by adding all the sums spent *at market prices* in the private and public sectors. It is a subjective concept based upon the marginal utilities of different elements of the national income at given prices. The market price paid by consumers comprises factor cost (i.e. the return to the factors of production) *and* the expenditure taxes which must be paid before utilities can be enjoyed.

(b) *Factor incomes.* Employing this method, the volume of production is valued by adding the sums which have been distributed in wages, interest, rent and profits (i.e. by adding factor costs). This is an objective concept, the basis of factor valuation being the rate at which it is technically possible for each factor of production to substitute for the others at the margin. Relative factor prices are thereby established. The cost of a commodity therefore represents the fraction of the nation's resources embodied in it.

Outlay taxes represent the difference in the two methods of national income calculation. The significance of the income/expenditure tax classification may now be made clear. When statistical inquiry is made into the distribution of the national income between income groups it is necessary to determine as accurately as possible the burden of expenditure taxes borne by each group as a condition of their share in the national income.

NOTE: The two approaches employ different sources of data and not surprisingly a further discrepancy arises, this time for technical reasons. Neither the income nor the expenditure approach is deemed the more accurate and purely as a matter of convenience a residual error appears under the income calculation as a positive or negative item.

3. The national income as an instrument of economic planning. Prior to the Second World War, the only statistical inquiry into the national income was by unofficial researchers. Official estimates came later.

(a) *Unofficial research.* The first accurate assessment was by Professor Sir Arthur Bowley for the year 1911, followed by another for 1924 by Bowley and Stamp. The method employed was the income approach which has remained the most popular because of the wide coverage of information available from the inland revenue. *Studies in the National Income*, a series of estimates for the years 1924–38, was published by Bowley in 1942, again using the income method of calculation. In 1937, Mr. C. Clark's *National Income and Outlay* used both income and production methods of assessment for a series of estimates for 1924–35. These unofficial investigations were of very great interest but only sought to show a total figure for the national income and the way in which it was distributed.

(b) *Official research.* The first official estimates were produced in 1941 by two new government agencies, the Central Statistical Office and the Economic Section of the Cabinet Office. These figures were required as a means of "national housekeeping" in order to keep wartime finance on a sound base. The planning techniques developed during the war were continued in peacetime and since 1941 there has been an annual White Paper on *National Income and Expenditure* supplemented some months later by more detailed information in a Blue Book.

It should be emphasised that these figures are *estimates* but that their accuracy increases with improved statistical methods and the development of sources of information. Their purpose is much more ambitious than the pre-war unofficial estimates. They provide the statistical information necessary to government and parliament in the preparation of economic policy. For this purpose, simple totals are inadequate. A set of *accounts* is necessary just as it is to any business enterprise which is planning future development.

The government in varying the structure of public finance, on either the revenue or the expenditure side, will see the success of its policies reflected in the national income figures.

4. Problems of calculating the national income. Many practical difficulties are encountered in attempting to estimate the national income. These are outlined in paragraphs 5 to 11 below.

5. Changes in the value of money. Professor J. R. Hicks tells us that "when the national income has been converted into real terms (*when those changes which are solely due to changes in the prices at which goods are valued have been so far as possible eliminated*) it provides us with the best single measure of the nation's economic well-being or economic progress which we are likely to be able to get".

The problem of accurate comparison lies in eliminating the changes which are solely due to changes in prices. It means little to be told that the net national income in 1938 was £4,816 million and in 1965 £28,279 million if we make no allowance for the fact that there has been continuing inflation. Money incomes have increased nearly sixfold while the things that money can buy have not. The longer the period over which a comparison is made, the more inaccurate the comparison is likely to become.

An attempt is made in a number of tables in the Blue Book on *National Income and Expenditure* to overcome this difficulty with the aid of index numbers and by adjusting all figures to constant prices. A base year, currently 1970, is selected and for years on either side, due allowance is made for differences in the purchasing power of money. These practices are, however, subject to their own difficulties and inaccuracies.

NOTE: The problem of comparing two different years in which there were different price levels has its counterpart in the problem of comparing the national incomes of two different countries in which there are different price levels.

6. Incomplete information. The accuracy of the estimates made by the income method must depend upon the accuracy and completeness of the returns made to the inland revenue. There is considerable evidence to show that possibly in consequence of very high levels of taxation, many people undertake spare time work which is not declared to the inland revenue. There has also been a growth of industrial practices which lend themselves to tax evasion, e.g. in the building trade, the practice of making every labourer a sub-contractor so that he is no longer subject to P.A.Y.E. but becomes responsible for the payment of his own tax.

7. Unpaid services. Labour services for which no payment is made do not appear in the estimates. The national income will therefore appear to be smaller than it would otherwise have been.

An enormous volume of unpaid service is provided by the housewife and by the man who repairs his own car, decorates his house, or attends to his garden. If the housewife were a paid housekeeper doing the same work and the "do-it-yourself" man employed someone else, these same services would appear as positive items in the national income accounts.

NOTE: There is here found a further source of difficulty in comparing the national incomes of two countries. In underdeveloped areas of the world, there are many labour services of this nature and therefore the national income figure will appear excessively low.

8. Notional rents. A house provides the same service whether it is occupied by the owner or a tenant. In the case of the tenant, the rent he pays appears in the national accounts. It is reasonable therefore to make some estimate of what the owner-occupier would have had to pay in rent and to include this figure in the accounts. Until 1962, he was in fact assessed for tax on the notional income. There are obvious difficulties in the accurate calculation of the sort of price which market forces *might* produce.

9. Capital consumption. In the course of the year, capital equipment will have depreciated during the process of production. If a calculation is to be made of the *net* national income then there must be due allowance for depreciation. The formidable difficulties involved in making an accurate estimate have led to an increasing preference for the concept of the Gross National Product (G.N.P.), i.e. national income *without* any allowance for capital consumption. This is the concept employed in the White Paper on *National Income and Expenditure* and brings Britain into line with the practice of other countries.

10. Stock appreciation. A negative item appears in the accounts under the heading of stock appreciation. Inventory is taken of the value of physical stocks and work in progress at the beginning and end of the year. Any increase in value is likely to be in part due to inflation and therefore a compensatory deduction is made.

11. Double counting. Care must be taken that the same items are not counted twice or more, which would be the case if the value of the raw material were added to the value of the semi-finished article and that to the value of the end product.

12. Determinants of the national income. The size of a nation's income will be governed by a number of considerations. Land, labour and capital are the basic determining factors, but there are several other important and related factors to be considered (*see* 13–16).

13. The absolute and relative quantities of the factors. Clearly one will expect a larger country with a larger stock of land, labour and capital to have an absolutely larger national income. The nation's potential income will, however, be maximised only when the factors are present in ideal proportions. A labour force which is too small fully to exploit natural resources and available capital will produce a smaller income. On the other hand a country such as China has insufficient capital and land to combine ideally with its vast labour force. In a dynamic society, the relative quantity of capital will be a decisive influence on the national income.

  NOTE: It should be remembered that one factor, labour, is not only a producer but also a consumer. A country may therefore have a large national income in absolute terms but a relatively low standard of life if that income is shared amongst many people.

14. The quality of the factors. This will be a vital consideration. A country may or may not be rich in natural resources, fertile and with climatic advantages. The ability of its labour force will vary with the degree of native intelligence and with the extent of education and training. Its capital equipment may or may not be well designed, reliable and up to date. High quality factors of production in themselves are not sufficient to guarantee a high level of national income. Their wise use depends upon the presence of sufficient entrepreneurial ability.

15. Stage of technology. In a dynamic economy, the technique and the organisation of production are continuously changing. This involves both the regular improvement of the quality of the factors of production and a continuing change in the proportions in which they are combined. The key agent is capital since an improvement in its quality (e.g. an invention) will cause its substitution for the other factors and a corresponding rise in the national income.

16. Political stability. The stage of technology reached by a nation will to no small extent depend upon the prevailing political climate, e.g. Britain's rapid industrialisation and nineteenth century predominance in world trade were accomplished in a politically stable environment. Europe on the other hand was disrupted for many years by war and revolution, as was America in mid-century. Their industrialisation therefore lagged behind Great Britain's during this period.

APPENDIX II

Bibliography

Part One: The State and the National Economy

Brownlee, O. H., and Allen, E. D., *Economics of Public Finance*. Prentice-Hall International.

Buchanan, J. M., *The Public Finances*. Irwin, Homewood, Illinois.

Gill, R. T., *Economics*. Prentice-Hall International.

Hicks, U. K., *British Public Finances: their Structure and Development*, 1880–1952. Oxford University Press.

Hicks, U. K., *Public Finance* (Nisbet). Cambridge University Press.

Peacock, A. T., and Wiseman, J., *The Growth of Public Expenditure in the UK*. Oxford University Press.

Part Two: Price Analysis

Boulding, K. E., *Economic Analysis*. Hamilton.

Breit, W., and Hochman, H. M., *Readings in Microeconomics*. Holt, Rinehart and Winston.

Chamberlin, E. H., *Theory of Monopolistic Competition*. Oxford University Press.

Hanson, J. L., *A Textbook of Economics*. Macdonald and Evans.

Henderson, H., *Supply and Demand*. Cambridge University Press.

Phelps Browne, E. H., *A Course in Applied Economics*. Pitman.

Robinson, E. A. G., *Monopoly*. Cambridge University Press.

Robinson, Joan, *Economics of Imperfect Competition*. Macmillan.

Stigler, G. J., *Theory of Price*. Macmillan.

Part Three: Tax and Expenditure Analysis

Dalton, H., *Principles of Public Finance*. Routledge.

Hicks, J. R., *The Social Framework*. Oxford University Press.

Musgrave, R. A., *The Theory of Public Finance*. McGraw-Hill.

Musgrave, R. A., and Musgrave, P. B., *Public Finance in Theory and Practice*. McGraw-Hill.

Pigou, A. C., *A Study in Public Finance*. Macmillan.

Poole, K. E., *Public Finance and Economic Welfare*. Rinehart.

Prest, A. R., *Public Finance in Theory and Practice*. Weidenfeld and Nicolson.

Seligman, E. R. A., *The Shifting and Incidence of Taxation*. Columbia University Press.

Shehab, F., *Progressive Taxation*. Oxford University Press.

Official publications:

National Income and Expenditure (Annual Blue Book). H.M.S.O.

National Income; Statistics, Sources and Methods. H.M.S.O.

Part Four: Macroeconomic Theory and Application

Recommended further reading:

Beveridge, W. H., *Full Employment in a Free Society*. Allen and Unwin.

Cairncross, A. K., *Factors in Economic Development*. Allen and Unwin.

Day, A. C. L., *Economics of Money*. Oxford University Press.

Galbraith, J. K. *Economic Development*. Oxford University Press.

Haberler, G., *Prosperity and Depression*. Allen and Unwin.

Hansen, A. H., *A Guide to Keynes*. McGraw-Hill.

Hanson, J. L., *Monetary Theory and Practice*. Macdonald and Evans.

Harris, R., and Sewill, B., *British Economic Policy 1970–74, Two Views*. Institute of Economic Affairs.

Harrod, R. F., *The Trade Cycle*. Oxford University Press.

Jay, P., *Employment, Inflation and Politics*. Occasional Paper 46, Institute of Economic Affairs.

Lewis, W. Arthur, *Theory of Economic Growth*. Allen and Unwin.

Nevin, E., *The Problem of the National Debt*. University of Wales Press.

Youngston, A. J., *Possibilities of Economic Progress*. Cambridge University Press.

Official publications:

Employment Policy (1944 White Paper). H.M.S.O.

Radcliffe Report of the Committee on the Working of the Monetary System, 1959. H.M.S.O.

Authors referred to in the text:

Cassel, G. *Theory of Social Economy*. London, 1932.

Clark, J. M., *Strategic Factors in Business Cycles*. New York, 1934.

Friedman, Professor Milton, *The Counter-Revolution in Monetary Theory*. Institute of Economic Affairs, 1970.

Harrod, R. F., *The Trade Cycle*. Oxford, 1936.

Hawtrey, R. G., *Currency and Credit*. 3rd ed., London, 1928.

Hayek, F. A., *Monetary Theory and the Trade Cycle*. London, 1933.

Hayek, F. A., *Full Employment at Any Price*. Occasional Paper 45, Institute of Economic Affairs.

Hobson, J. A., *Economics of Unemployment*. London, 1922.

Keynes, J. M., *Treatise on Money*. London, 1932.

Keynes, J. M., *General Theory of Employment, Interest and Money*. London, 1936.

Lavington, J., *The Trade Cycle, an Account of the Causes Producing Rhythmical Changes in the Activity of Business*. London, 1922.

Lindahl, E., *Studies in the Theory of Money and Capital*. London, 1939.

Mises, G. von, *The Theory of Money and Credit*. London, 1934.

Neisser, G. "General Over-production. A Study of Say's Law", *Journal of Political Economy*, Vol. 42, 1934, pp. 433–65.

Pigou, A. G., *Industrial Fluctuations*. London, 1929.

Robbins, L., *The Great Depression*. London, 1934.

Wicksell, K., *Interest and Prices*. London, 1936.

Part Five: Administration

Beer, S. H., *Treasury Control*. Oxford University Press.

Lord Bridges, *Treasury Control*. Athlone Press.

Brittan, S., *The Treasury under the Tories*. 1951–1964. Penguin.

Brittain, Sir Herbert, *The British Budgetary System*. Allen and Unwin.

Chubb, B., *The Control of Public Expenditure: Financial Committees of the House of Commons*. Oxford University Press.

Hicks, J. R., *The Problem of Budgetary Reform*. Oxford University Press.

Official publications:

Appropriation Accounts (Annual). H.M.S.O.

Estimates (Annual). H.M.S.O.

Finance Accounts of the UK (Annual). H.M.S.O.

Finance Act (Annual). H.M.S.O.

Financial Statement (Annual). H.M.S.O.

Report of Commissioners of Customs and Excise (Annual). H.M.S.O.

Report of Commissioners of Inland Revenue. H.M.S.O.

Reports of Committee on Public Accounts (Annual). H.M.S.O.

Reports of Select Committee on Estimates (Annual). H.M.S.O.

Reform of the Exchequer Accounts (1963 White Paper). H.M.S.O.

Report of Colwyn Committee on National Debt and Taxation, 1927. H.M.S.O.

Preliminary Estimates of National Income and Expenditure (Annual White Paper). H.M.S.O.

Loans from the National Loans Fund (Annual White Papers). H.M.S.O.

Public Expenditure Survey (Annual White Paper). H.M.S.O.

Examination Technique

The examination candidate will profit from the following advice:

(1) Read the whole paper, *including any special instructions*, carefully and unhurriedly and make a selection of the questions to be answered.

(2) Apportion the time allowed so that the *required number* of questions are attempted. Failure to complete the paper automatically lowers the maximum possible marks which can be scored. (Remember that the first 5% for any one question is relatively easy to earn and the last 5% extremely difficult.)

(3) Before attempting a question, read it carefully and be confident that you fully understand what is required. *Then answer to the point and without irrelevancies.*

(4) Treat your answer as an argument in which you are providing the examiner with evidence of the truth of what you write. Plan this argument systematically and give it a logical progression so that you arrive at a natural conclusion. *Avoid making a series of disconnected points which don't lead anywhere.*

(5) Pay attention to the tidy presentation of your work. A carelessly composed paper immediately creates an unfavourable impression.

Examination Questions

The following specimen questions are listed in relation to specific parts of the book, but it should be appreciated that in many cases it will be necessary to draw upon material provided elsewhere in the book.

Part 1. The State and the National Economy

Part 1 is of a general and introductory nature and its contents should provide background material which is useful in many types of question. However, it is thought unlikely that examination candidates will encounter questions based exclusively on this material.

Part 2. Price Analysis

1. What is meant when it is said that a firm is in equilibrium? How does this equilibrium under perfect competition differ from that under imperfect competition? (Inter. D.M.A., D.G.A., L.G.E.B.)

2. Compare the determination of price and output by firms operating in perfectly competitive and imperfectly competitive markets. (Inter. D.M.A., D.G.A., L.G.E.B.)

3. "In the short run price is determined by demand and in the long run by the cost of production." Discuss. (Inter. D.M.A., D.G.A., L.G.E.B.)

4. Explain the difference between perfect competition and monopolistic competition. (Inter. D.M.A., D.G.A., L.G.E.B.)

5. (See also Part 1.) Show how the price mechanism regulates the production, prices and incomes of an economic system. Consider whether it is possible for a mature economy to function without prices. (Inter. D.M.A., D.G.A., L.G.E.B.)

6. Analyse the statement that perfect competition leads to the optimum allocation of resources. (Inter. D.M.A., D.G.A., L.G.E.B.)

7. Discuss the different circumstances in which a rise in the

price of an article might be followed by a rise in the quantity demanded. (Inter. D.M.A., D.G.A., L.G.E.B.)

8. Explain how the short-run supply curve of an industry is derived under conditions of perfect competition. (Inter. D.M.A., D.G.A., L.G.E.B.)

9. Is the price mechanism an equitable and efficient way of allocating economic resources? (Inter. D.M.A., D.G.A., L.G.E.B.)

10. What is the function of the price system in a mixed economy? (Inter. D.M.A., D.G.A., L.G.E.B.)

11. "Not even a monopolist can simultaneously fix price and quantity sold." Why then is monopoly said to be evil? (Inter. D.M.A., D.G.A., L.G.E.B.)

12. "The factors governing a firm's decision to continue production in the short run differ from those influencing its decision in the long run." Discuss. (Inter. D.M.A., D.G.A. L.G.E.B.)

13. Discuss the determination of prices when goods are produced in conditions of joint supply. (G.C.E.(A), J.M.B.)

14. "If we are unable to sell more cars we shall have to raise the price of our models." Comment on this statement by a motor manufacturer. (G.C.E.(A.), J.M.B.)

15. What is meant when it is said that a firm is in equilibrium? How does equilibrium under perfect competition differ from that under imperfect competition? (G.C.E.(A), J.M.B.)

16. Why is it that economists distinguish between the short period and the long period in the theory of value? (G.C.E.(A), J.M.B.)

17. What does economic theory tell us about the effect of the growth of monopoly on the level of output? (G.C.E.(A), J.M.B.)

18. Compare and contrast the way in which scarce resources are allocated (a) within a private enterprise economy and (b) within a centrally-planned economy. (G.C.E.(A), J.M.B.)

19. In a free economy, what happens to the price of beef when the price of milk goes up? (G.C.E.(A), J.M.B.)

20. "A monopolist can charge whatever price he likes." Discuss. (G.C.E.(A), J.M.B.)

21. Discuss with examples the concept of elasticity of demand. (H.N.C., L.C.C.C.)

22. Discuss the principles on which prices are determined under conditions of imperfect competition, indicating the senses in which there might be "spoiling of the market". (H.N.C., L.C.C.C.)

Part 3. Tax and Expenditure Analysis

23. Define the national income. What determines its size? (Inter. D.M.A., D.G.A., L.G.E.B.)

24. Could the real national income be increased by increasing the nation's stock of money. If so, how would the effect come about? (Inter. D.M.A., D.G.A., L.G.E.B.)

25. If progressive taxation is held to be more equitable than other forms of taxation, why does the state levy any regressive taxes at all?

26. "The effect of a tax on a commodity might seem at first sight to be an advance in price to the consumer. But an advance in price will send the price down again. Therefore it is not certain after all that the tax will really raise the price" (H. D. Henderson). Explain this statement. (Inter. D.M.A., D.G.A., L.G.E.B.)

27. Explain why the national income per head of the population is much higher in the USA than in India. (Inter. D.M.A., D.G.A., L.G.E.B.)

28. What kinds of information would be needed to show that the British people are, on the average, materially better off in 1966 than they were in 1956? (Inter. D.M.A., D.G.A., L.G.E.B.)

29. Explain what is meant by the national income and distinguish between (a) money national income; (b) real national income. What determines the size of the national income? (Inter. D.M.A., D.G.A., L.G.E.B.)

30. Explain and illustrate how the economic activities of spending, producing and saving are connected in national income accounting. (Inter. D.M.A., D.G.A., L.G.E.B.)

31. "The less taxation there is, the better." Discuss. (Inter. D.M.A., D.G.A., L.G.E.B.)

32. Why should luxuries and semi-luxuries be regarded as especially suitable objects of taxation compared with other consumers' goods? (G.C.E.(A), J.M.B.)

33. What is the national income? Does the provision of houses, roads and hospitals add to the national income? (G.C.E.(A), J.M.B.)

34. Would you include the following in a definition of the national income: (a) a wife's housekeeping money; (b) the earnings of a daily help; (c) family allowances; (d) an M.P.'s salary; (e) the prize money on premium bonds? Give reasons for your answer in each case. (G.C.E.(A), J.M.B.)

35. What are the economic effects of highly progressive taxation? (G.C.E.(A), J.M.B.)

36. Define as carefully as you can the meaning of "tax incidence". (B.Sc.(Econ.), Part 2, London External)

37. Discuss critically the arguments usually presented concerning the superiority of direct taxes over indirect taxes. (B.Sc.(Econ.), Part 2, London External)

38. Analyse the effects on the aggregate supply of work of a progressive income tax. (B.Sc.(Econ.), Part 2, London External)

39. Are there reasons why large families should pay less income tax than small families with the same gross income? (B.Sc.(Econ.), Part 2, London External)

40. Analyse the possible effects of the UK capital gains tax on (a) the propensity to save; (b) the market price of land. (B.Sc.(Econ.), Part 2, London External)

41. "The important outstanding problems of equity in the British tax system concern the distribution of personal wealth rather than income." Discuss with reference both to principle and to the practical difficulties of tax reform. (B.Sc.(Econ.), Part 2, London External)

42. "Flat rate national insurance contributions are inequitable and inefficient." Discuss. (B.Sc.(Econ.), Part 2, London External)

Part 4. Macroeconomic Theory and Application

43. What are the consequences of a budget deficit in a period of heavy unemployment? (Inter. D.M.A., D.G.A., L.G.E.B.)

44. The major task of a modern central bank is the management of the National Debt. Explain this conclusion of the Radcliffe Committee. (Inter. D.M.A., D.G.A., L.G.E.B.)

45. Explain what an economist means by "investment". What are the main determinants of private investment? (Inter. D.M.A., D.G.A., L.G.E.B.)

46. What is meant by a credit squeeze and what are its effects? (Inter. D.M.A., D.G.A., L.G.E.B.)

47. Examine the importance of an increase in the mobility of labour in the present economic circumstances in Britain. (Inter. D.M.A., D.G.A., L.G.E.B.)

48. Discuss the role of one of the following in industrial fluctuations: (a) innovations; (b) structural maladjustments; (c) money. (Inter. D.M.A., D.G.A., L.G.E.B.)

49. Explain why a Chancellor of the Exchequer may deliberately plan to have an unbalanced budget. (Inter. D.M.A., D.G.A., L.G.E.B.)

50. Define the National Debt. To what extent is it a burden on the economy of the United Kingdom? (Inter. D.M.A., D.G.A., L.G.E.B.)

51. Discuss the view that the Chancellor of the Exchequer should budget for a surplus in a boom and a deficit in a depression. (Inter. D.M.A., D.G.A., L.G.E.B.)

52. When and why would a public authority prefer taxation to borrowing and borrowing to taxation? (G.C.E.(A), J.M.B.)

53. Discuss the view that inflation is the price we have to pay for full employment. (G.C.E.(A), J.M.B.)

54. How and why has the government intervened in the location of industry since World War II? (G.C.E.(A), J.M.B.)

55. How did Keynes define *savings* and *investment*? Will an increase in savings by one individual necessarily lead to an increase in investment in the economy? (G.C.E.(A), J.M.B.)

56. Define the National Debt. How has it come into existence? What is its composition? Does it represent a burden to the community? (G.C.E.(A), J.M.B.)

57. What monetary measures have been used by the authorities to control the British economy since 1951? (G.C.E.(A), J.M.B.)

58. "Monetary measures cannot alone be relied upon to keep in nice balance an economy subject to major strains from both without and within" (*Radcliffe Report*). Explain and comment on this statement. (H.N.D., L.C.C.C.)

59. What changes in economic theory flowed from Keynes's work which resulted in the acceptance by the government of responsibility for the level of employment? (H.N.D., L.C.C.C.)

60. Why did the government impose a temporary import surcharge in November, 1964, in preference to taking the various alternative measures which might have been employed to deal with a too high level of imports? (H.N.D., L.C.C.C.)

61. Is an increase in overall effective demand an appropriate remedy for all types of unemployment? (H.N.D., L.C.C.C.)

62. "A successful regional development programme would make it easier to achieve a national growth programme." What policies are seen as necessary to achieve such development? (H.N.D., L.C.C.C.)

63. The role of the government is to maintain the level of full

employment and from this the level of investment. Explain clearly how this stabilisation action would be applied. (H.N.D., L.C.C.C.)

64. What is meant by "mobility of labour"? Why is it important and how might mobility be increased? (H.N.C., L.C.C.C.)

65. Discuss the budget as an instrument of economic control, indicating in what ways it might be regarded as preferable to the use of monetary measures. (H.N.C., L.C.C.C.)

66. "The problem of post-war Britain has been over-full employment, not unemployment. The policy of regional aid has therefore meant misallocation of resources." Comment on this statement in the light of the distribution of industry policy in this country since 1930 and its application on Merseyside. (H.N.C., L.C.C.C.)

67. The government is faced with an inflationary situation at home which has produced an unusually high balance of payments deficit. Produce a policy which might reduce the size of the problem. (H.N.C., L.C.C.C.)

68. What is the case for restoring the tax differentiation between distributed and undistributed company profits in the UK? (B.Sc.(Econ.), Part 2, London External)

69. How can the need for annual estimates of government revenue and expenditure be reconciled with the requirements of development plans covering (say) five-year periods? (B.Sc. (Econ.), Part 2, London External)

70. Discuss the case for a payroll tax differentiated according to regions in the United Kingdom. (B.Sc.(Econ.), Part 2, London External)

71. "Effective stabilisation policy depends on accurate short-term forecasting." Explain and discuss. (B.Sc.(Econ.), Part 2, London External)

72. Discuss in terms of the available evidence the effectiveness of the UK budget as an instrument of stabilisation policy since 1945. (B.Sc.(Econ.), Part 2, London External)

73. Analyse the effects of current UK tax policy with respect to the so-called regional problem. (B.Sc.(Econ.), Part 2, London External)

74. Discuss the influence of short-term stabilisation policies on long-term growth. (B.Sc.(Econ.), Part 2, London External)

75. Discuss market failure as a reason for government intervention in the economy. (B.Sc.(Econ.), Part 2, London External)

76. What measures would you recommend to improve the built-in stability of the UK economy? (B.Sc.(Econ.), Part 2, London External)

Part 5. The Machinery of Administration

77. Outline the main sources of government income and assess their relative importance. (Inter. D.M.A., D.G.A., L.G.E.B.)

78. Describe the main categories of government expenditure in the United Kingdom. What forces have determined the size of each category? (Inter. D.M.A., D.G.A., L.G.E.B.)

79. Describe and comment on the main features of the British system of taxation of personal incomes. (Inter. D.M.A., D.G.A., L.G.E.B.)

80. What are the merits and de-merits of the system under which local authorities receive various types of grant from the central government? (Inter. D.M.A., D.G.A., L.G.E.B.)

81. "Rates are a form of property tax and should be abolished." Discuss. (Inter. D.M.A., D.G.A., L.G.E.B.)

82. Outline the main sources of public revenue, central and local, in this country. Give some idea of the relative amounts contributed by each of these sources. (G.C.E.(A), J.M.B.)

Index

Absolute monarchy, 2
Accelerated Project Scheme, 136
Accounting Officer, 223
Accounting Prices, 18
Ad valorem taxes, 84, 104
Advertising, 43, 69, 70
Aggregate demand, 10, 33, 157, 166, 167, 173, 191, 195, 206
Allocation function, 27–29, 33
Appropriation Accounts, 223
Appropriation Acts, 214, 219, 221
Appropriation of supplies, 3
Automatic stabilisers, 130
Average cost, 59, 60
Average revenue, 65

Balance of payments, 102, 131, 140–1
Bank Charter Act 1844, 196
Bank of England, 3, 177, 194, 196–7, 201–7
Bank rate, 157, 193, 202–3
Benefit principle, 28
Bentham, Jeremy, 5
Beveridge, William, 129
Bills discounted, 200
Board of Commissioners, 7
Board of Education, 7
Board of Trade, 5
Board of Treasury, *see* Treasury
Boards of Guardians, 6, 7
Boards of Health, 6
Bowley, Professor Sir Arthur, 228
Branding, 69
British Leyland, 9
Budget, 210, 217, 219
Budget judgment, 219
Business cycle theories, 112–125

Cabinet Office, Economic Section of the, 228
Capital depreciation allowances, 130, 133, 148
Capital expenditure allowances, 148
Capital gains, 100
Capital gains taxes, 144, 146–7
Capital goods, 114, 115, 117–119
Capital levies, 106, 147
Capital, marginal efficiency of, 121, 125
Capital market, 182
Capital taxation, 150
Capital Transfer Tax, 105
Cash grants, 136, 148
Central government trading, 8
Central Statistical Office, 228
Chadwick, Edwin, 6
Cheap money policy, 183
Clearing banks, 189, 190, 198–200
"Collateral aids", 5, 6
Collective wants, 29
Combination Laws 1799, 1800, 4, 5
Command economy, 16, 17
Committee on the Control of Public Expenditure, 210
Competition and Credit Control (Bank paper), 193, 194, 202
Competitive market, 21
Composite demand schedules, 39
Composite supply schedules, 40, 41
Comptroller and Auditor General 223, 224
Consolidated Fund, 218, 219
Consolidated Fund Acts, 219

Consolidated Fund and National Loans Fund Accounts, 175
Consolidated Fund Standing Services, 219
Consumer goods, 114, 115, 117, 118, 138
Consumer's surplus, 57, 76
Consumption margin, 56, 57, 89
Consumption, volume of, 112
Conversions, 183
"Corset", 205, 206
Cost-push inflation, 131
Counter Revolution in Monetary Theory (occasional paper), 154, 166
Currency and Banknotes Act 1928, 1954, 197
Craft gilds, 1
Customs duties, 3, 4, 5, 87, 102, 103
Cyclical unemployment, 111, 136

Dated stocks, 176
Death duties, 105, 147
Defence bonds, 176
Defence estimates, 218
Deflationary gap, 122
Demand
  changes in conditions of, 42–48
  competing, 47
  composite, 48
  curves and schedules, 39–42
  derived, 48
  effective, 118, 119
  elasticity of, 48–51, 84,–86, 99–101
  joint, 47
demand and supply, 37–54, 84–87, 117, 118
  equation of, 31, 42
Department of Economic Affairs, 141
depreciation, 230
Devaluation, 184
Development Areas, 134, 135
Development Districts, 135
Diminishing utility, 56

Discount houses, 200–204
Discount market, 194, 200, 201
Discounting, 80, 81
Dis-saving, 101, 147
Distressed areas, 103
Distribution of Industry Act 1945, 135
Double counting, 231
Downswing, 110, 112, 113, 120, 122, 124
Down-turn, 110, 114
"Dumping", 67

Education, 151
Education Act 1870, 5
Education, Board of, 7
Elasticity, 48–53
Eligible deposit liabilities, 199, 200
Eligible reserve assets, 199, 200
Employment, pattern of, 111
Employment Policy (White Paper), 9, 129, 135
Environmental services, 5, 6
Equilibrium, 62, 63
Equilibrium price, 20, 42
Equi-marginal utility, 57
Estate duty, 105, 147
Estimates of National Income and Expenditure, 129
ex ante position, 123, 134
Exchange Equalisation Account, 178
Exchequer and Audit Department Act 1866, 223
Exchequer Prospects Table, 218, 219
Excise duties, 3, 4, 5, 132
Exhaustive expenditure, 29
Expenditure Committee, 222
Expenditure taxes, 83–93, 100, 104, 132–4, 146, 226
ex poste position, 124

Factor costs, 227
Factor incomes, 227
Factor prices, 227

Factors of production, 12, 62, 141–3, 226, 231
Factory system, 4
Family allowances, 138, 145
Final benefits, 79
Finance Act, 220
Financial year, 217–220
Floating debt, 176
Foreign banks, 178
Free trade, 4, 7
Friedman, Milton, 162, 165–8
Full employment, 118, 122
Full Employment in a Free Society, 129
Funded debt, 175, 176

General Board of Health, 6
General Theory of Employment, Interest and Money, 117, 123, 128
Gladstone, William Ewart, 5, 7
Gold standard, 196
Government training centres, 152

Haberler, Professor Gottfried, 165
Harcourt, Sir William, 8
Hawtrey, R. G., 114, 133
Hayek, Professor Friedrich, 162
Herbert, 9
Hicks, Professor J. R.
Highways Boards, 6
Hire-purchase, 134
Hobson, J. A., 116, 117
House of Commons Standing Order No. 78, 220
House of Commons Standing Order No. 90, 224
Housing, 151
Huskisson, 5

Imperfect competition, 22, 68–71
Imperfect equilibrium, 63
Imperfect market,
Import licensing controls, 103

Incentives, 17
Income tax, 4, 8, 93, 94, 100, 101, 105, 130, 132, 133
Index numbers, 229
Industrial competition, 21, 63
Industrial Development Act 1966, 135
Industrial Development Executive, 136
Industrial Training Boards, 151
Industry Act 1972, 136
Industry Act 1975, 9
Inflation, 10, 117, 120, 126, 127, 169–74, 186, 187, 229
Inflationary gap, 122, 124, 129
Inheritance taxes, 101, 105
Initial allowances, 148
Inland revenue, 90
Insurance companies, 178
Intangibles, 77, 79, 82
Interest Bearing Eligible Liabilities, 205
Interest rates, 113, 114, 120, 125, 155–60, 164, 166, 168
Intermediate benefits, 79
International Development Association, 178
Investment, 98, 115, 116, 119, 120–125, 132, 133, 143
Investment-savings curve, 158–160
Investment trusts, 178

Keynes, John Maynard, 9, 112, 113, 117–125, 129, 130

Labour supply, 143–145
laissez-faire, 3, 5, 19, 23
laissez-fasser, 5
Land tax, 3
Lange, Oskar, 18
Law of Disminishing Utility, 56
Liquid assets, 147, 197, 198
Liquidity money, 158–160, 164
Liquidity trap, 156, 165, 166
Lloyd George, David, 8
Local authorities, 137, 138

Local Employment Acts 1960, 1963, 135
Local Government Board, 7

Macroeconomics, 14
Manorial courts, 1
Manpower Services Commission, 152
Margin, theory of, 55
Margin of consumption, 56–57, 89
Margin of transference, 57
Marginal benefit, 73, 74, 76
Marginal cost, 59–62, 67, 73, 74, 92
Marginal income, 100
Marginal productivity, 164
Marginal rate of substitution, 58
Marginal revenue, 61, 65, 66
Marginal utility, 55–57
Margins, 89
Market competition, 21, 62
Market economy, 4, 19–24, 29, 30
Market prices, 226
Market socialism, 18, 19
Marketing Boards, 8
Marshall, Alfred, 58
Marx, Karl, 38
Medium term economic assessment, 212, 213
Mercantilism, 2
Merchant gilds, 1
Microeconomics, 14
Mill, John Stuart, 5
"Mini-budget", 218
Minimum lending rate, 201–204
Ministry of Education, 7
Ministry of Health, 7
Mixed economy, 12, 24
Monetarist controversy, 32, 132
Monetarist school of economists, 162
Monetary policy, 156, 157, 168, 169, 201–207
Money at call and short notice, 199, 200
Money market, 182, 202

Monopoly, 38, 63–67, 91–93, 102
Multiplier, 121–123, 128, 136, 155
Municipal trading, 8

Nation state, 1
National Debt, 3, 4, 175–189
National Debt Commissioners, 177
National Economic Development Council, 141
National expenditure, 118, 226
National income, 118, 119, 226–232
National income forecasts, 217
National Income and Expenditure (Blue Book), 228, 229
National Income and Expenditure (White Paper), 228
National Income and Outlay, 228
National Insurance Act 1911, 7
National Loans Fund, 177, 184–189
National Plan, 141
National Savings, 176, 177
National Savings Bank, 177
National savings certificates, 176
Nationalised industries, 8, 9, 137
"Natural unemployment", 170, 171, 173
Neutral taxes, 100
Non-differential taxes, 102

Old Age Pensions Act 1908, 7
Oligopoly, 68, 69, 91
Open market operations, 204
Opportunity cost, 76, 156
Overheads, 59
Over-saving, 116, 117

P.A.Y.E., 230
Payroll taxes, 150
Peel, Sir Robert, 5
Pensions, 95, 138, 145
Perfect competition, 20, 21, 29, 61, 62, 88, 92, 93
Perfect equilibrium, 63
Perfect market, 21

Phillips curve, 170
Phillips, professor A. W., 169
Pigou, Professor, A. G., 165
Pitt, William, 4, 181
Plowden Report, 210, 211, 222
Policy effected stabilisers, 131
Politics, 14, 15
Political market, 27, 28, 73, 79, 82
Poll tax, 104
Poor Law (Amendment) Act 1834, 5, 7
Poor Law Commissioners, 6
Poor relief, 5, 7
Postal services, 8, 95
Poundages, 104
Precautionary money, 155, 157, 158
Premium bonds, 176
Price cutting, 68
Price discrimination, 67
Price mechanism, 19, 20, 23
Pricing policies, 152
Private goods, 25, 27
Private sector, 76, 124, 136, 226
Private wage, 10, 24
Production margin, 89
Production possibility curve, 12 14
Production possibility schedule, 13
Production volume of, 112
Profits taxes, 148
Programme Analysis and Review, 216
Progressive taxes, 9, 34, 96, 98, 103, 104, 105
Propensity to consume, 119, 120, 122, 125, 128
Propensity to save, 119, 120, 121, 128
Proportional taxation, 95, 96
Proportionality, principle of, 8, 103
Provisional Collection of Taxes Act 1913, 219, 220
Public accounting, 128
Public Accounts Committee, 224

Public corporations, 28, 137, 178
Public enterprise, 28
Public Expenditure Surveys, 211–216
Public Expenditure Survey Committee, 213
Public Expenditure (White Papers), 211, 214
Public Health Act 1876, 6
Public sector, 9, 28, 29, 33, 76, 79, 81, 124, 128, 137, 148, 226
Public Sector Borrowing Requirement, 188, 189
Public Works Loan Board, 185
Purchase tax, 102, 130, 132
Purchasing power, 116
Pyramiding, 89

Quantity theory of money, 154, 163, 192
Queen's Speech, 217

Radcliffe Report, 192–194
Regional Economic Councils, 135
Regional Employment Premiums, 136
Regional Planning Boards, 135
Regional unemployment, 134–136
Regressive taxation, 96, 103
Reserve ratio, 199, 200
Retailing, 70, 71
Revolution of 1688–1699, 2, 3
Rolls Royce, 9

Saving, 98, 115, 116, 119, 120, 122–124, 145–148
Saving margin, 89
Savings banks, 176, 178
Say's Law of Markets, 118
Schools Boards, 6
Scientific socialists, 38
Seasonal unemployment, 111
Secular unemployment, 111
Securities, 120
Select Committee on Estimates, 210, 222

Selective employment tax, 102, 151
Sickness benefits, 138
Sinking Fund, 4, 181
Site values, 102
Smith, Adam, 19, 29, 37, 89, 127
Social contract, 173, 174
Social goods, 25, 27, 34, 77, 79
Social insurance contributions, 150
Social wage, 10, 24
Special Areas, 134, 135
Special Areas (Development and Improvement) Act 1936, 134
Special deposits, 204, 205
Specific taxes, 84
Spending margin, 89
Stabilisation function, 31–33
Stagflation, 110
Stock appreciation, 230, 231
Stock Exchange, 120
"stop-go" policies, 140
Studies in the National Income, 228
Supplementary special deposits, 205, 206
Supplementary estimates, 221
Supply,
    changes in conditions of, 45–47
    competitive, 48
    curves and schedules, 40, 41
    elasticity of, 52, 53, 85–93, 102
    joint, 48
Supply estimates, 216, 217
Supply services, 218, 219
Supply votes, 218, 219
Swedish school of economists, 123
Syndicated tender, 195

Tangibles, 77, 78, 82
Tax effects, 88, 98–107
Tax incidence, 83–96
Thrift, paradox of, 120
Total cost, 60

Total revenue, 65
Total utility, 57
Trade cycle, 24
Trading estates, 134
Training Services Agency, 152
Transactions money, 155–158
Transfer expenditure, 29
Treasury, 141, 177, 210, 220, 221
Treasury bills, 176, 178, 182, 187, 195, 197, 199, 201, 204
Treasury Budget Committee, 217, 219
"Treasury view", 128
"Treatise on Money", 128
Trustee Savings Bank, 178
Tudors, 2

Unemployment,
    cyclical, 111, 136, 137
    frictional, 111
    regional, 134–136
    seasonal, 111
    secular, 111
Unemployment benefits, 145, 151
Upswing, 110, 112–114, 120, 123
Up-turn, 110, 114
Utilitarianism, 5

Valuations, 104
Value
    cost of production theory of, 38
    labour theory of, 37, 38
    paradox of, 37
Velocity of circulation, 163
virement, 221

"wage/price" spiral, 131
Walpole, Sir Robert, 4, 181
War Loan, 176
Ways and Means Advances, 177
Wealth of Nations, 19
Wicksell, Knut, 113
"windfall" gains, 95, 100, 102

Details of some other Macdonald & Evans
publications on related subjects can be found
on the following pages.

For a full list of titles and prices write for the
FREE Macdonald & Evans Business Studies
catalogue and/or complete M & E Handbook
list, available from Department BP1,
Macdonald & Evans Ltd., Estover Road,
Plymouth PL6 7PZ

Applied Economics
E. SEDDON & J. D. S. APPLETON
This HANDBOOK is intended for a very wide range of students, from those taking G.C.E. "A" Level to those preparing for papers in Applied Economics in the examinations of academic and professional bodies. It analyses the main problems which confront the British economy today and tests the validity of theoretical solutions to these problems against the results that have been achieved.
Illustrated

Auditing
LESLIE R. HOWARD
The text of this HANDBOOK covers the subject of auditing to the final examination level of the accountancy bodies, but the book will be of equal assistance to intermediate students. The latest edition includes the most recent relevant data from the various accounting bodies and the International Accounting Standards Committee.

British Political History 1784—1939
S. T. MILLER
This HANDBOOK has been produced for all those who are beginning a study of nineteenth century British and British Imperial history leading to the G.C.E. "O" and "A" Level examinations and their equivalents. Covering most of the developments in government up to the Second World War, it will also be of value to students of British Government and Politics in both schools and colleges.

British Tax Law
MERVYN LEWIS

For law and accountancy students of taxation and for professional practitioners, this book states the main principles of tax law in relation to the major direct taxes and explains them in considerable depth, illustrating the practical application of various statutory rules with numerous examples of a computational nature.

Business Communications
R. T. CHAPPELL & W. L. READ

This introduction to communication studies in business has in mind especially those with responsibility for supervision in an increasingly complex economic system, and is concerned with all the main points of using written and spoken English in the business world. The latest edition has been revised to take account of new concepts such as management by objectives.
Illustrated

Business Mathematics
L. W. T. STAFFORD

This HANDBOOK is designed for the business student taking the examinations of the professional bodies, universities and technical colleges, which increasingly require a knowledge of mathematics. Also for those already in business who feel they have an insufficient grasp of the newer mathematical techniques and their applications in the fields of finance, operational research and mathematical statistics.
Illustrated

Business Organisation
RONALD R. PITFIELD

This HANDBOOK has been prepared as an aid to those studying for various examinations in the business field, and will be of particular use to those working for H.N.D. or H.N.C. in Business Studies or similar professional examinations. The first part of the book provides a survey of the framework within which a business operates. The second and major part deals with the organisational features and management practices relevant to business.

Illustrated

Commerce
L. GARTSIDE

The aim of this comprehensive work is to give a guide to all the important elements in the modern commercial scene in the United Kingdom. Valuable illustrations of documentary procedures are included and the legal background to all areas of business life is discussed.

Illustrated

Economics for Professional Studies
HENRY TOCH

This HANDBOOK draws on the author's experience over fifteen years of teaching economics to professional students, and uses topical situations and examples to illustrate a detailed survey of economic theory and practice.

Illustrated

General Principles of English Law
P. W. D. REDMOND

Originally designed for those preparing for intermediate professional examinations, this HANDBOOK has also proved itself immensely popular with "A" Level and university students. The latest edition includes the facts of appropriate recent cases and several important new topics.

Geography for Business Studies
H. ROBINSON
This book caters primarily for students studying geography for the O.N.C. and O.N.D. examinations and the various papers in economic and commercial geography set by many professional bodies. Sixth-form students will also find it a comprehensive introduction to the subject.
Illustrated

An Introduction to Applied Economics
J. L. HANSON
This book is primarily intended for students taking a course in applied economics for the H.N.C./D. in Business Studies or Management Studies. It covers such topics as economic growth and the standard of living, the population problem, the European Community, the balance of payments and international monetary relations.
Illustrated

Labour Economics
J. D. S. APPLETON
This HANDBOOK is intended for students studying economics for "A" Level, professional, Higher National and degree examinations in which the papers invariably contain questions on labour economics for which the relevant information can seldom be found in one publication. The text analyses the structure of labour markets generally, examining many specific topics in detail.
Illustrated

The Law of Meetings
SIR SEBAG SHAW & E. DENNIS SMITH

This book provides a comprehensive survey of the rules, legal and conventional, which regulate the constitution and conduct of meetings. The latest edition incorporates many relevant statutes, and takes particular account of the law relating to offences against public order.

Local Government
MICHAEL P. BARBER

This HANDBOOK, designed for students preparing for examinations in local government administration, also provides the local government officer with an overall historical and structural picture to supplement his practical knowledge of his own work. The latest edition incorporates a concise summary of the Local Government Act 1972 and the subsequent restructuring of local government.

Managerial Economics
J. R. DAVIES & S. HUGHES

Specifically written for those studying for D.M.S., this HANDBOOK will also assist those taking H.N.C./D. and first- and second-year degree students of Business Studies. All the economic theory used is shown to be relevant in practice and coverage of the main decision areas of management includes choice of corporate form, demand analysis, cost analysis, pricing decisions and investment analysis.
Illustrated

Model Business Letters
L. GARTSIDE

Over 500 specimen letters, indexed for quick reference, deal with almost any business situation likely to arise, with a commentary outlining the commercial and legal relationships each one creates. Other features are the glossaries of terms and classified lists of expressions useful when composing letters. The latest edition incorporates some additions to the explanatory text providing more detailed information on certain types of transactions.

Modern Economic History
EDMUND SEDDON

A clear outline of British economic and social history for G.C.E., professional and university students, this HANDBOOK traces the development of technology since the point of industrial "take-off" around 1760, and the parallel development of agricultural methods. The latest edition contains extended information on the post-1945 period.

An Outline of Monetary Theory
J. L. HANSON

This HANDBOOK traces the development of the British monetary system from the origin of commercial banks to the present day. Part One considers the early use of money and growth of banking institutions; Part Two international monetary relations, the gold standard and its alternatives; Part Three money as a dynamic force in world economics; and Part Four current monetary problems.

Principles of Accounts
E. F. CASTLE & N. P. OWENS
This HANDBOOK is a useful aid to those who, about to begin a study of accounts, need a grounding in the basic principles of the subject. Students taking company secretarial or other professional courses will find it particularly valuable. In the latest edition the scope of the text has been enlarged to deal with the effect of V.A.T. on accounting methods.

Public Administration
MICHAEL P. BARBER
Of value to all Local Government and Public Administration students, this HANDBOOK provides a comprehensive guide to the structure of British public administration, the theories on which it is based and the problems currently facing local and central government administrators. A detailed comparative study of European and Amercian administration shows clearly the strengths and weaknesses of the British system.

Staff Management
P. W. BETTS
This book is intended to illustrate how the effective use of staff management can improve a company's efficiency. It is also hoped that it will help dispel many erroneous impressions that some employers have of staff management. The emphasis throughout the book is on the practical aspects of the subject, and liberal use is made of case studies and examples.
Illustrated